AF594674

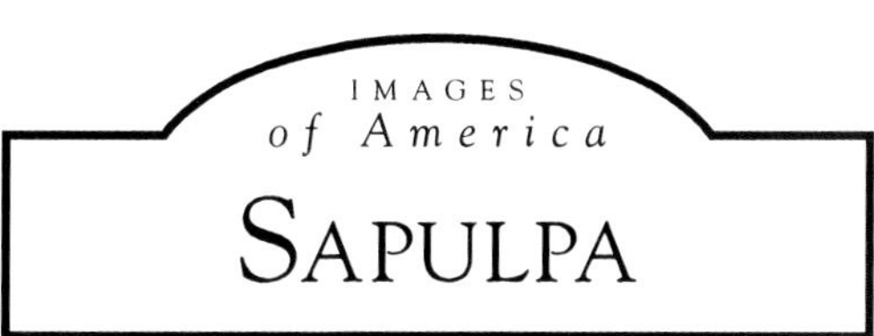
IMAGES
of America
SAPULPA

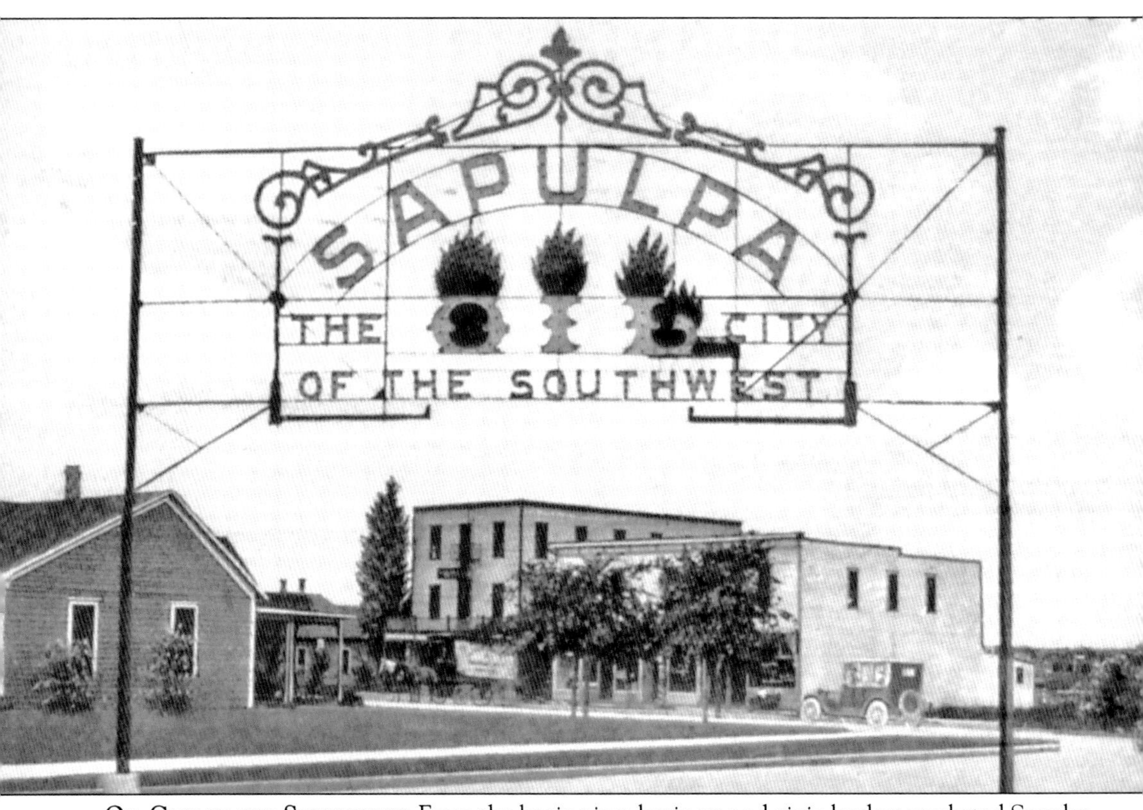

Oil City of the Southwest. From the beginning, business and civic leaders marketed Sapulpa using various slogans. They touted resources of water, lumber, clay, crops, and natural gas. The railroad extended its tracks into Indian Territory, and Sapulpa became a "railroad town." There were buildings to erect, infrastructure to construct, generators to install, and overhead lines to power the electric trolley system. All of these were promoted and photographed, but it was the discovery of oil on the Ida Glenn Indian allotment and its aftermath that caused this huge lighted sign to be erected over Hobson Street near the train depot to proclaim "Sapulpa, Oil City of the Southwest." (Courtesy of the Sapulpa Historical Society.)

On the Cover: Welcoming Committee. Tourists from all over the world come to Sapulpa to see iconic remnants of famous Route 66, but there also was a time when locals gathered at the Frisco Depot to greet special visitors. These youngsters, on the hood of a new Pontiac in 1948, wait for a train carrying "some important person." They enjoy soda pop (probably bottled locally) from bottles made at Liberty Glass and perhaps pastries from a local bakery while sporting school clothes and shoes bought from downtown stores, all the while wondering what the future holds as their parents decide who to vote for in the upcoming presidential election between Harry S. Truman and the train's passenger, Thomas Dewey. (Courtesy of Sapulpa Historical Society.)

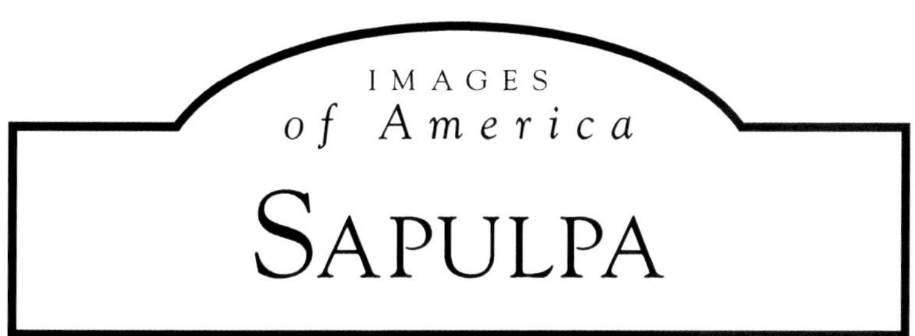

Donald L. Diehl
for the Sapulpa Historical Society

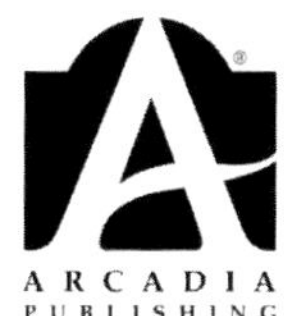

ISBN 978-1-4671-2559-8

Published by Arcadia Publishing
Charleston, South Carolina

Printed in the United States of America

Library of Congress Control Number: 2016954828

For all general information, please contact Arcadia Publishing:
Telephone 843-853-2070
Fax 843-853-0044
E-mail sales@arcadiapublishing.com
For customer service and orders:
Toll-Free 1-888-313-2665

Visit us on the Internet at www.arcadiapublishing.com

Dedicated to the pioneers who built the roads and rails before us; established schools, churches, and institutions; and those who have kept pioneer spirit and love of history alive. Dedicatory gratitude also to past writers of history like Virginia Lane, Jim Hubbard, Virginia Wolfe, Pete Egan, and Clyde McMasters; a host of newspaper reporters and photographers like Jack Doudican; and to Pauline P. Jackson for her 1956 thesis on the history of Sapulpa while a student at Tulsa University.

Contents

ACKNOWLEDGMENTS

The cliché "no man is an island" is an appropriate description when it comes to giving credit for a work like this, which involved searching through thousands of photographs that span a hundred years in order to glean a good representation for a pictorial history of Sapulpa, Oklahoma, and then producing an equal number of captions to identify for viewers what they are looking at and why the image is significant. It occurs to this author that the period of time covered from the 1890s, when Sapulpa developed as a town in Indian Territory, parallels the development of photography itself. As it turns out, there were a lot of black-and-white photographs taken during the period, albeit the quality lagged some in the early years. What is offered here is a sampling. Had space allowed, there are so many more images that could have been included—magnificent old photographs of church buildings, events, pageants, parks, picnics, athletic contests, clubs, clinics, and hospitals—many of which are displayed at the museum. I am grateful to director Mike Jeffries and his helpmate (and wife) Christy. They are two of the busiest people I know devoted to the preservation of Sapulpa's history and presenting it to locals and visitors in an interesting and relevant way. The Jeffrieses and a small army of volunteers oversee an ever-expanding collection of artifacts and articles that keep us in touch with our past and those who journeyed here before us. Christy also was one of the half-dozen members agreeing to work as a focal group collecting pictures and information for this book, searching literally thousands of documents and images, many still in negative form. Other extreme devotees to Sapulpa history met nearly every week for months, including Darwin "Chief" Eaton, Pete Egan, David Main, Cookie Jobe, and Russell Crosby (who joined the group later), along with his daughter Brean Fowler, to scan many of the hard-to-find photographs. And of course, thanks also go to my Arcadia editor Liz Gurley for her guidance and for keeping the project on target with quality photographs and details to meet the expectations of local enthusiasts as well as those around the world who enjoy Images of America.

All images are courtesy of Sapulpa Historical Society Museum unless otherwise noted.

INTRODUCTION

It was not that long ago in the scheme of things—a little more than a century—when the town of Sapulpa, Indian Territory, was born. The story begins with a settler—actually an Indian—in the Arkansas River basin between Rock and Pole Cat Creeks. The area abounded with fish, migratory waterfowl, deer, wild turkey, and small animals. It was full of woods, grasses, and diverse soil types. Although east of the Cross Timbers, which were too thick for roaming buffalo, the area was a favorite of Osage and other Plains Indian hunting parties. French and European fur trappers once had a presence here, as did the Spanish. President Jefferson had sent explorers here after his Louisiana Purchase. As Jefferson planned (at least partially but never everlastingly so), this would be "Land of the Red Man," also known as Oklahoma. Andrew Jackson may have been the facilitator of the Indian removal, but Jefferson was its architect.

Enter a young Muscogee (Creek) Indian making some geographical and lifestyle changes. To him, this seemed an ideal spot to start a new life and family, establish a farm or ranch, and open a trading post. It is from the name that he would come to be called in English, and his trading post, that the town of Sapulpa is named. His Mvskoke, or at least his busk (dance) name, is believed to have been Aha-lark-Yahola. By the time the town of Sapulpa was incorporated, he was well known as Chief Sapulpa.

According to a history paper completed as a thesis by graduate student Pauline P. Jackson at Tulsa University in 1956, Sapulpa "came alone" to Indian Territory's Creek Nation after Chief Sapulpa's and the other four "civilized tribes" were relocated from the Southeastern United States. Another president, our first, George Washington, is credited with using the term "civilized" to define those tribes who had adopted attributes of the colonists, such as Christianity, centralized governments, literacy, market participation, written constitutions, and plantation slavery practices. The Muscogee (Creek) are said to be the first civilized tribe.

At any rate, by the Treaty of 1826, tribes were required to relocate to lands assigned to their nation. In what became known as the Trail of Tears, the Creek, Cherokee, Choctaw, Chickasaw and Seminole people were escorted west by the US Army in 1836 and 1837.

Meanwhile, the young "wild Indian" who would become known as Sapulpa had been accused of stealing stock from white settlers in Alabama and was on the run in Florida. The conflict over hunting and grazing lands with the whites was intense. Sapulpa was from Oschee Town. His father's name was Omija, but his mother's name is unknown. He was an orphan at three years of age and was reared by two paternal uncles.

There are conflicting dates ascribed to both Sapulpa's birth and when he actually arrived in Indian Territory. Birthdates range from 1804 to 1824. The 1824 date is based on his entrance into the Confederate army during the American Civil War. He reportedly gave his age as 40. The 1824 date, however, does not fit the rest of the narrative. It is likely that since the most acceptable age for fighting men was 18 to 40, someone simply decided 40 was a good age to record. At the time of his death in 1887, Sapulpa's son James said his father was at least 75. The 1824 date also would have made him a 12-year-old when his tribe arrived at Fort Gibson. A birthdate between 1804 and 1814 is more likely if we understand the conflicts between European settlers and Native Americans as well as tribal upheavals in Sapulpa's homeland following the Red Stick Rebellion and the Creeks' own civil war.

Sapulpa was probably somewhere between 25 and 35 years old when he took his second and maybe third wife (having multiple wives were a common Muscogee practice), built a home in Indian Territory, did blacksmithing, and set up a general store (trading post) in his home.

One historian suggests that "Indian instincts" also showed Sapulpa specific reasons for stopping here. The area, including the eventual town site, is like the bottom of a huge saucer, with low hills making the rim. He reasoned that the surrounding hills would keep the place safe from tornados. They did, according to the article, "Oklahoma, Land of the Red Man," until the 1940s, when one struck the southwest corner of town, and again in May 1960, when one hit North Heights Hill, which is actually on the rim of the saucer.

Sometime around 1850, Sapulpa opened a store in connection with a blacksmith shop at his home. He sold coffee, sugar, tobacco, dry goods, flour, spices, and other articles he reportedly hauled in by team and packhorses from Fort Smith.

When the Civil War broke out, Sapulpa is said to have loaned $1,000 in gold to the Confederate cause. He joined the Creek Regiment of the Confederate army and rose to the rank of first lieutenant. Family history has it that he stayed in the army until after the Battle of Elk Creek near Checotah, where he was wounded. His discharge states that Sus-Pul-Ber, born in the old Creek Nation in the state of Alabama, was 40, stood five feet eight inches, was of dark complexion, had black eyes and black hair, and was a farmer by occupation. He enlisted on April 1, 1863, and was discharged on July 1, 1864. After his discharge, Sapulpa moved his home a half-mile up the hill from its former location. The first home and blacksmith shop had been burned during the Civil War. He was back in business with a larger trading post and shop in the early 1870s near the cattle trail that cut across from the Chisholm to Eastern Kansas. This time, according to accounts, he bought and hauled his merchandise from Coffeyville, Kansas. Each summer, the Osages came to camp south of the present Sapulpa courthouse lawn. They would stay for two weeks or more to trade corn, sweet potatoes, peas, beans, peanuts, bacon, and hogs. Later, Sapulpa confined himself mostly to ranching.

Railroaders, seeking routes to expand tracks into Indian Territory, met and conversed with Sapulpa in the mid-1880s and gave him the name "Chief." The spelling of "Sapulpa" may have come at that time, when a railroad representative wrote down what he heard pronounced. An account written by a family member, however, said that when children were born in the old Creek Nation in Alabama, they were given Biblical names, and Chief had been named Sepulcher after the burial place of Christ hewn out of rock.

Sapulpa reportedly was married three times. His first wife was Tenofe. They had no children. His second wife, Na-Kitty, bore him seven children: James, Hannah, John, Sarah, Lucy, and two whose names are unknown. By his third wife, Cho-pok-sa (English name Mary) he had Moses, Yarna, Samuel, William, Rhoda, Rebecca, and Nicey, according to various records. Some of the children died at birth or died young. After joining the Methodist Church, Sapulpa dismissed Mary but continued to provide for her.

In 1886, Chief Sapulpa made one of the first—if not the first—train trips into what would be called Sapulpa Station, about where Farmers' Feed is today on North Main Street. He died the next year. His headstone can be seen in the Sapulpa Family Cemetery, maintained by the Nancy Green Chapter, Daughters of the American Revolution in the 1000 block of South Division Street.

Coming with the Creek tribe during the removal were the Euchee bands who had joined the Muscogee Confederacy. Although not recognized federally as a tribe, the Euchee of Sapulpa have maintained their own distinctions as far as tradition and language is concerned. Together with the Creek, their influence and input played major roles in early education, organizing the town and looking out for the welfare of tribal members. Some of the early white settlers and town founders, like John Egan, were made honorary tribal members and consulted with tribal councils.

Increased presence of white settlers in Indian Territory prompted the US government to establish the Dawes Act in 1887, the year of Chief Sapulpa's death. That divided the lands of individual tribes into allotments for individual families, encouraging farming and private land ownership among Native Americans but expropriating land to the federal government. It also would impact licensing of whites and blacks doing business on Indian lands, including land use and oil leases.

On the eve of becoming a town, Sapulpa had only a few business establishments, and the population was probably no more than 200 to 300 people, writes longtime resident Clyde McMasters in his history of the First Presbyterian Church. But with the coming of the train in 1886 and new laws and agreements with the Creek, "new residents were arriving daily." A census put the population at 400 when the town was incorporated in early 1898. Life had been typically "wild west frontier." Indian Territory had become a sanctuary for gangs of outlaws seeking refuge from the surrounding states of Texas, Arkansas, Kansas, and Missouri, where law enforcement was fairly efficient. The principal law officers in the territory were tribal police known as "Lighthorsemen," who had little if any authority over white men. There was a scattering of US marshals sent into the territory by "Hanging Judge" Isaac Parker of Fort Smith, Arkansas, but not having a white man's court made extradition difficult. Consequently, well-known gangs of outlaws like the Daltons, the Cook gang with Cherokee Bill, the Frenches and James brothers, Cole and Bill Younger, Henry and Belle Starr, and Ned Christi came through Sapulpa on numerous occasions. The coming of statehood would also establish law and order, courts, and lockups.

After Oklahoma became a state, each county held an election to determine the location of the county seat. Native American resident male and freedmen (former black slaves who had become tribal members) were citizens of the new state with voting rights. Sapulpa competed with Bristow for the location of the seat of Creek County. After seven years of contested elections and court suits, the question was settled by the Oklahoma Supreme Court on August 1, 1913. Sapulpa was ruled the winner, but it may have been the fight with Bristow over the county seat that caused Sapulpa to lose focus on the economic opportunities with its new oilfield and important railroad. Soon after the oil discovery and rapid growth of the Glenn Pool, neighboring Tulsa began to capture the oil interests as well as the title of "Oil City" that was supposed to be Sapulpa's. The Frisco division point and roundhouse moved to west Tulsa in 1927.

Sapulpa seems to have done okay, however. The new Creek County Courthouse was completed in 1914, replacing an earlier structure built in 1902, before statehood. Hotels, a hospital, a library, school and church buildings, multi-storied brick structures downtown, and nice homes were going up. There were theaters and brick and glass plants. Route 66 would soon be on the drawing board to come right through downtown, bringing travelers and tourists to buy gas and fill up motels.

Before oil, gas, glass, and brick, the area around Sapulpa mainly produced walnut trees, livestock, and cotton. The biggest cotton compress in the state operated here in the 1920s until it was destroyed by fire. In 1898, the Sapulpa Pressed Brick was established, followed in a few years by the Sapulpa Brick Company, beginning the clay products industry. The founding of Premium Glass Company in 1911 marked Sapulpa's entry to glass manufacturing. Premium was absorbed into Liberty Glass Company in 1918. Sapulpa's first "gusher" was not oil but the discovery of natural gas. In huge headlines, the town's dominant newspaper, the *Sapulpa Light*, reported the find. The press, along with emerging community leaders, called for immediate installation of gas lines. Those seeping oil springs long used by the Indians for medicine and various purposes now provided a lubricant for wagon wheels. Of course, horses and wagons were the power source and main mode of transportation for the Indian farmers as well as their black and white intruders. After the railroad extended its tracks into Indian Territory to Sapulpa Station, the railroad town became a key shipping point for all kinds of things—livestock, lumber, cotton, and other crops as well as passengers. The St. Louis–Frisco terminal and roundhouse employed a sizable workforce. The coming Fred Harvey House would need its "Harvey Girls." New glass plants had plenty of natural gas to fuel their furnaces, as did Sapulpa's first brick companies. The other needed materials, such as sand and clay, were nearby. That combination also attracted what would become world-famous Frankoma Pottery.

The founding years of Sapulpa's rapid growth can be attributed to such railroad activities and to the exploitation of natural resources, including oil that still reverberates—and then came Route 66. There have been booms, busts, upsides, and downturns. Here are some of the images of those times, places, people, and events.

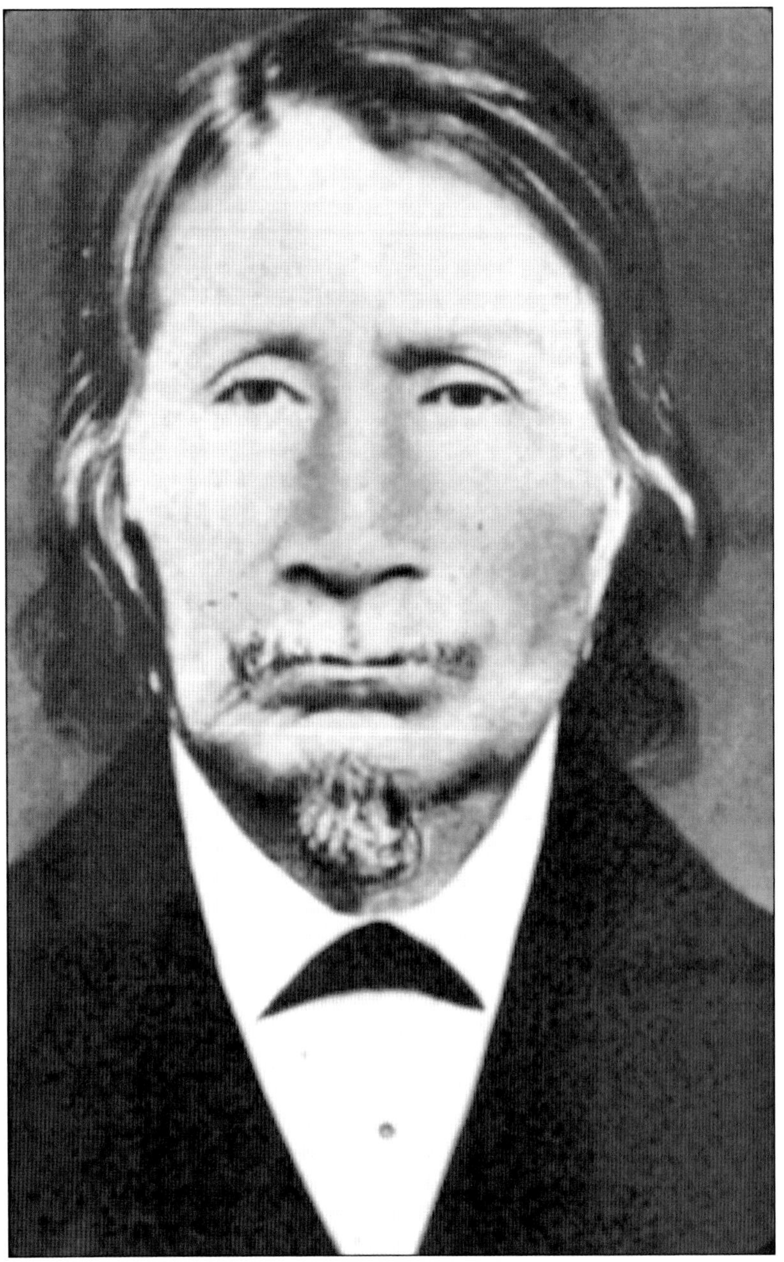

Chief, but not a Chief. What would become "Chief" Sapulpa's first name may have been given him as a mock by railroaders. And the name "Sapulpa" may have come from the Bible. The Creek was not an Indian chief, although he became an important tribal leader. His name and life are key reasons why there is a Sapulpa, Oklahoma. He was born between 1804 and 1824 and died on March 17, 1887.

One

Settling Sapulpa
Indians, Pioneers, Cowboys, and Wildcatters

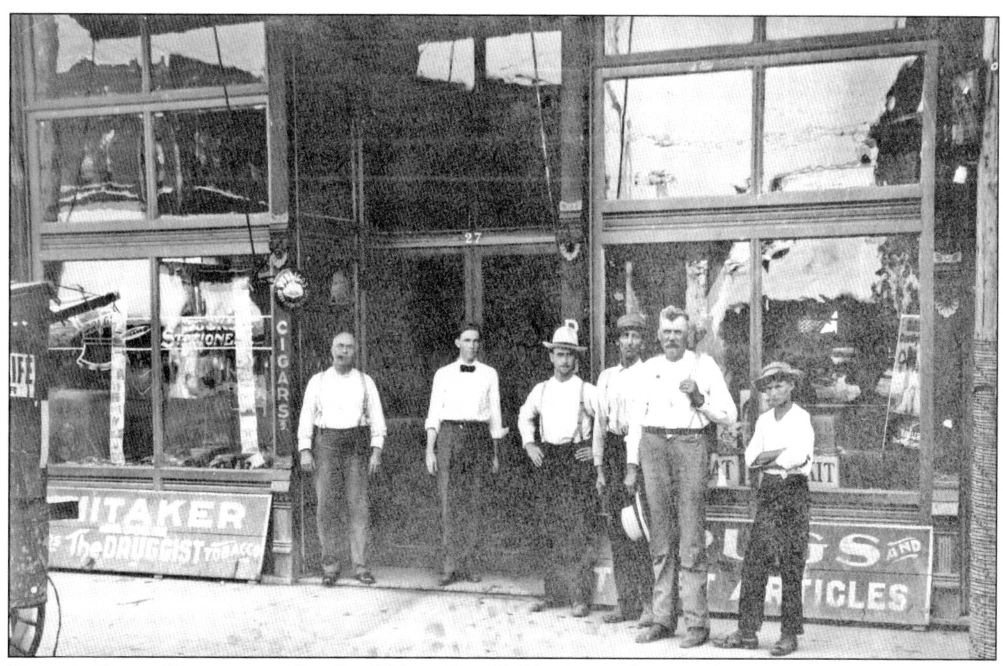

Town's First Druggist. Charles Whittaker (left), shown here at his store at 27 North Main Street in early 1900s, is credited with opening Sapulpa's first drugstore, which was probably initially in his home in 1895. Other stores at that time included J.C. Menifee's store, the Ripley Hotel, Smith's Livery Barn and Hotel, and H.C. Hall's and John Egan's stores.

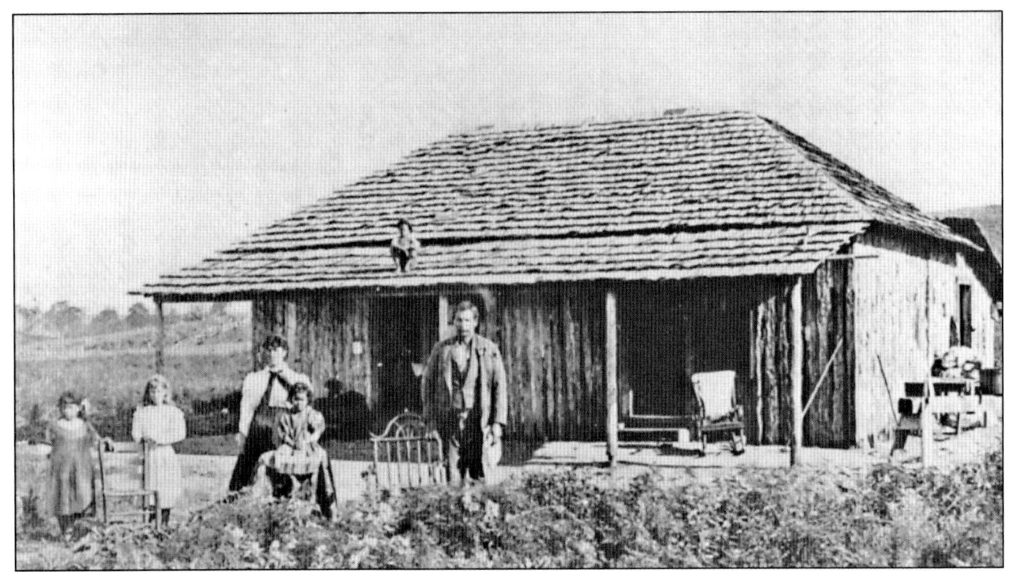

First Structure, 1895. The Antone Stockade, believed to be the first structure built in what would be incorporated as Sapulpa, served as family home as well as a waystation for travelers. The siding of the house was vertical, resembling a stockade, thus the name. C.D. Antone, by his own claims, was a Mohican Indian who spoke English.

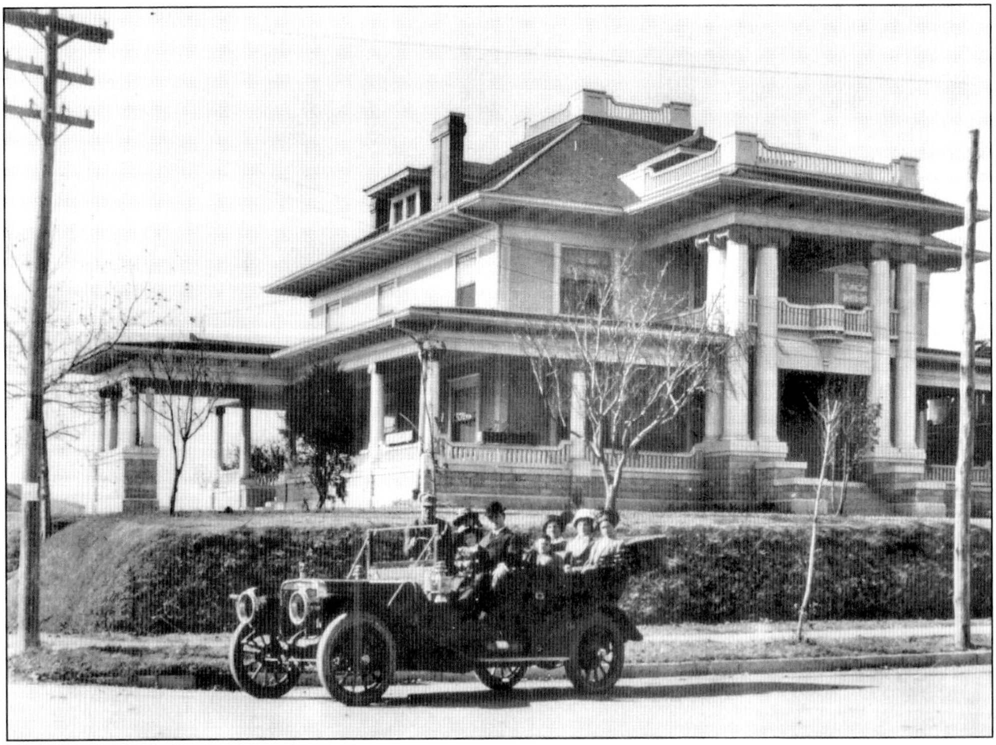

Man about Town. Bates Burnett came to Sapulpa to install the town's electric streetcar system. He also built the St. James Hotel downtown and the Burnett Mansion at 320 South Main Street. Burnett brought one of the first classy automobiles to town, shown in this 1915 photograph in front of the home, taking a spin around town with his family.

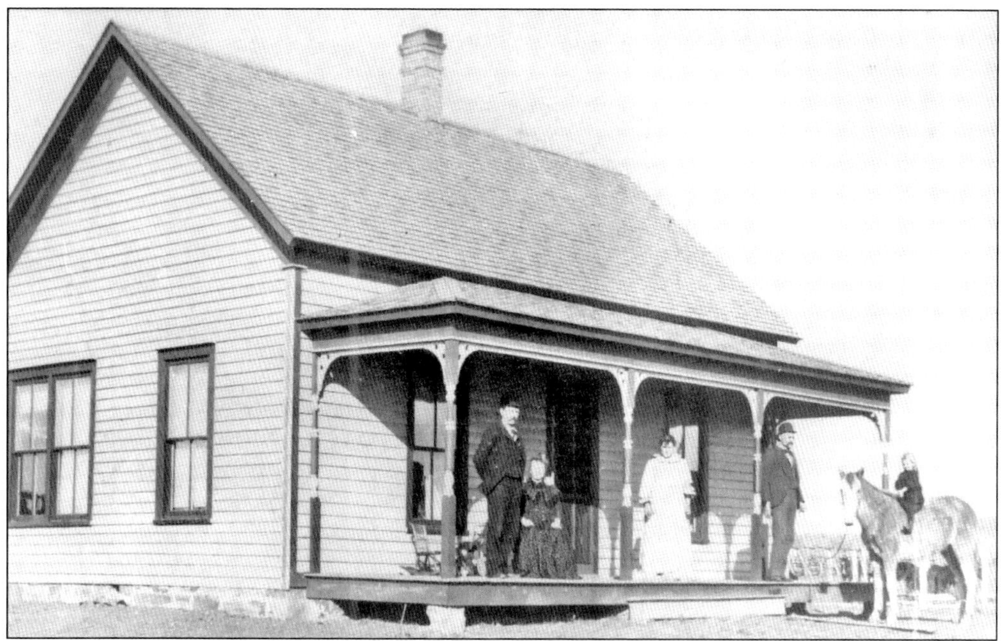

First Founder's Home. John F. Egan, shown at far left at home (about Mound Street and Hobson Avenue) was granted license to do business in Indian Territory and came to the area in 1892. The others, from left to right, are Matilda Egan, Mabel Gilbert, and Dr. Sterling McAllister, with Lucile Egan on Buck, the horse of famous outlaw Cherokee Bill.

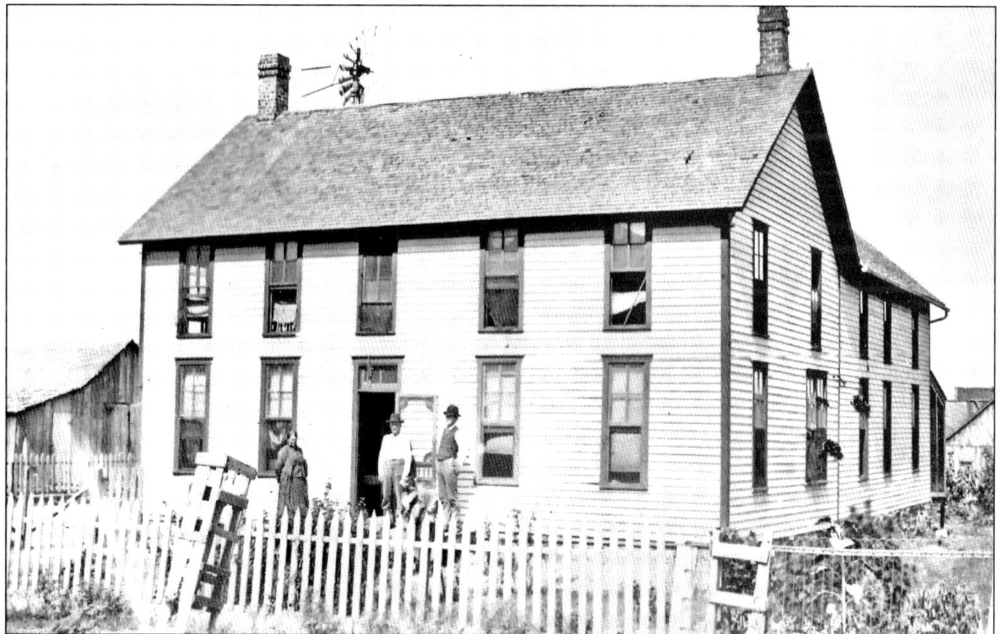

Oldest Existing Building. In 1889, W.A. "Dad" Smith, a Civil War veteran, built Sapulpa's first hotel, livery barn, and blacksmith shop. Sapulpa's first school was held in the livery barn's office in 1894. Cassie Medders was the first teacher; she had completed the fourth grade. The hotel was moved in 1906 to the northeast corner of Poplar Street and Hobson Avenue and is a residence today.

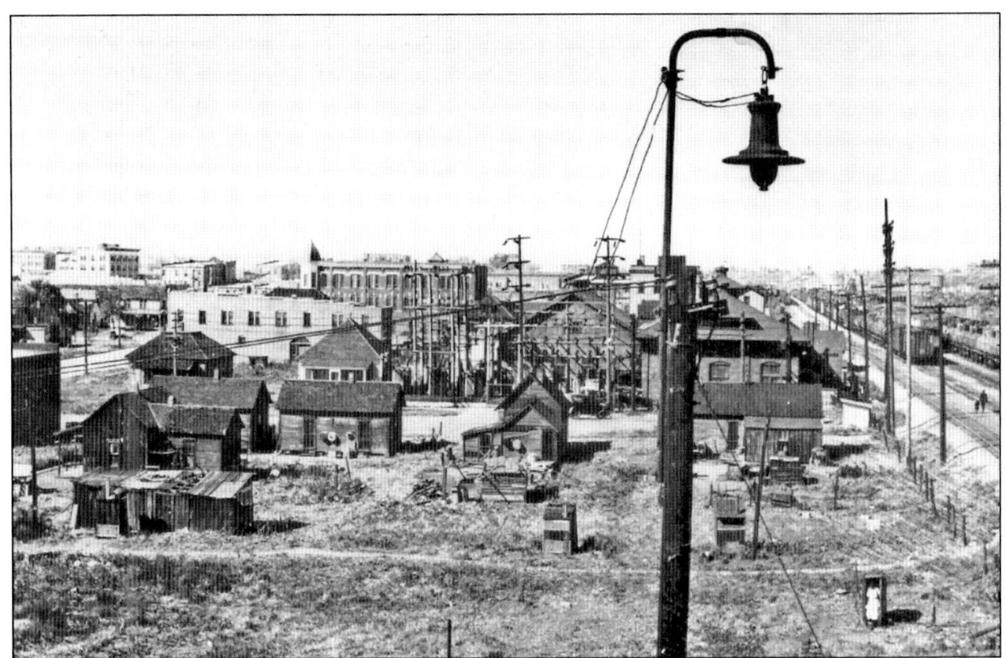

Looking out the Back Door. This c. 1920s photograph, taken from the Frisco overpass looking west toward downtown and the Oklahoma Gas and Electric plant, shows some residences before the days of more modern conveniences. Note the outside toilets and the washtubs hanging on the backside of the houses.

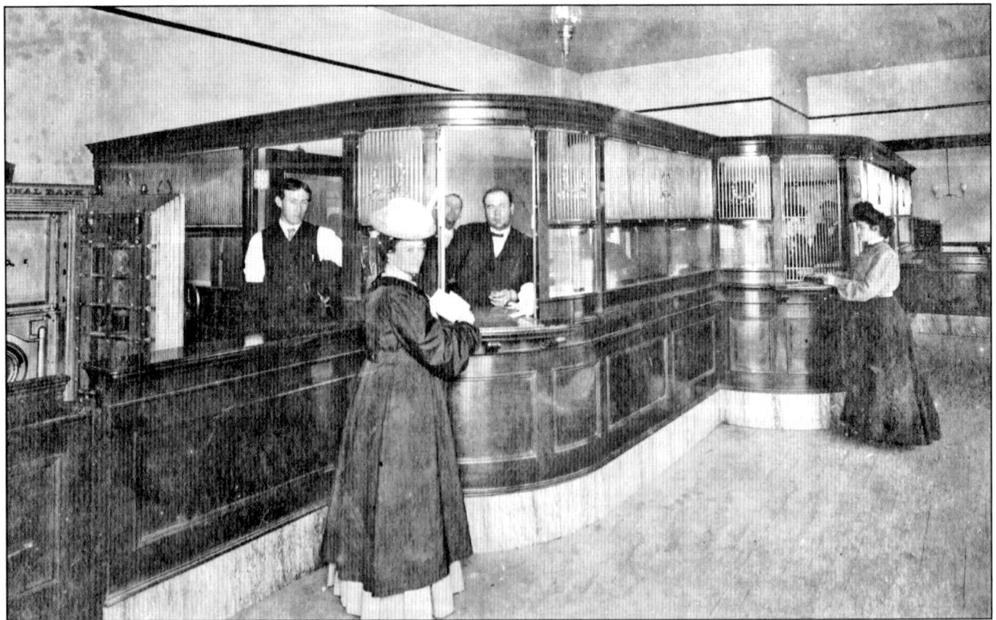

Banking Transactions. Customer Monte Shipman conducts business at First State Bank in 1907. First State would later occupy the First National Bank building at 2 South Main Street. It had been rebuilt in 1922 at a cost of $80,000 after the first building was destroyed by fire. First National filed for bankruptcy before it could occupy the building. The American National Bank (now American Heritage Bank) purchased the building in 1930 and has occupied it ever since.

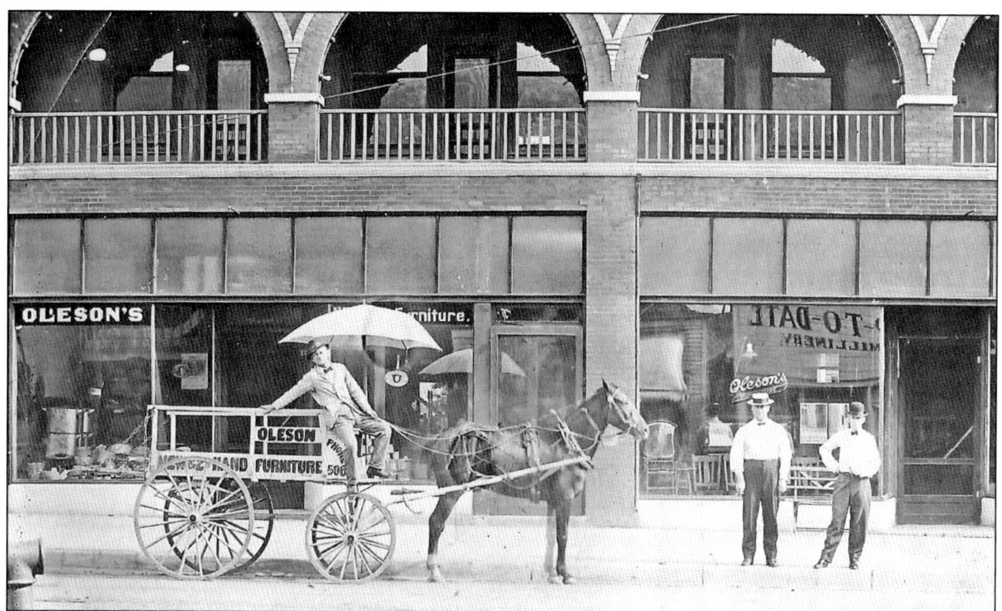

Furniture Needs Met. True enough, some settlers brought their furniture with them via wagon, but as new homes went up, new furniture was needed. Oleson's met the need and set a trend for years to come. Local history is full of furniture names like Davis-Rule, Gilliam, Wells, Tyler, and LaFever. Oleson, shown here in the 400 block of East Dewey Avenue with two associates, delivered. Watchorn Apartments are seen in background.

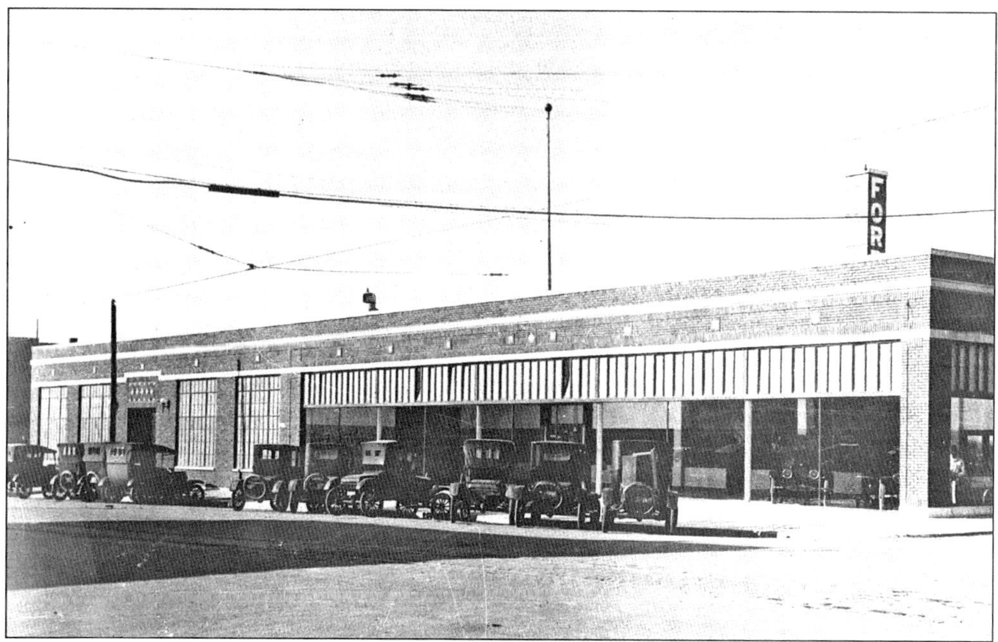

The Model T Impact. The popularity of the Model T is revealed in this 1920s photograph, taken when Ford moved its dealership and assembly plant a couple of blocks south to 100 South Main Street. This same building would later house Chrysler, Dodge, and Chevrolet dealerships before becoming Sooner Tire Company, which was acquired by Cecil and Son Discount Tire in 2015.

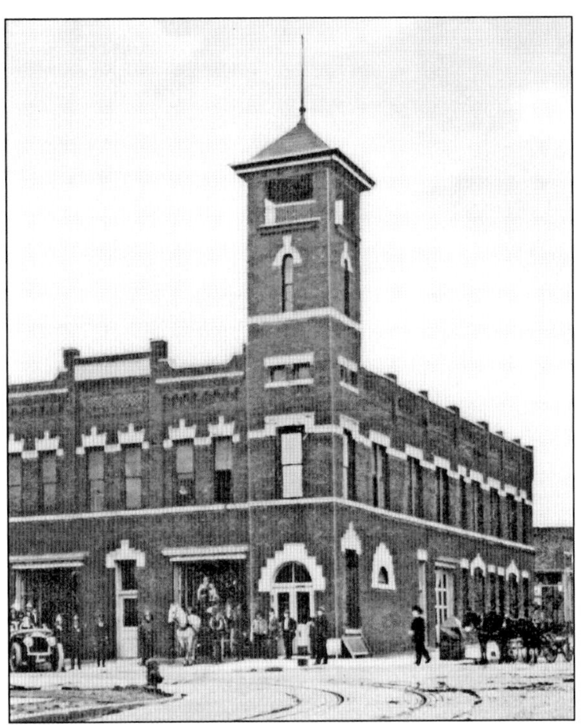

Sapulpa's Old City Hall. One of the town's early city halls featured an impressive corner tower at the corner of Hobson and Park Streets. City offices and police and fire departments were here. The tower served as a place to hang and dry the fire hoses. Today, Creek County Ambulance operates from this same location.

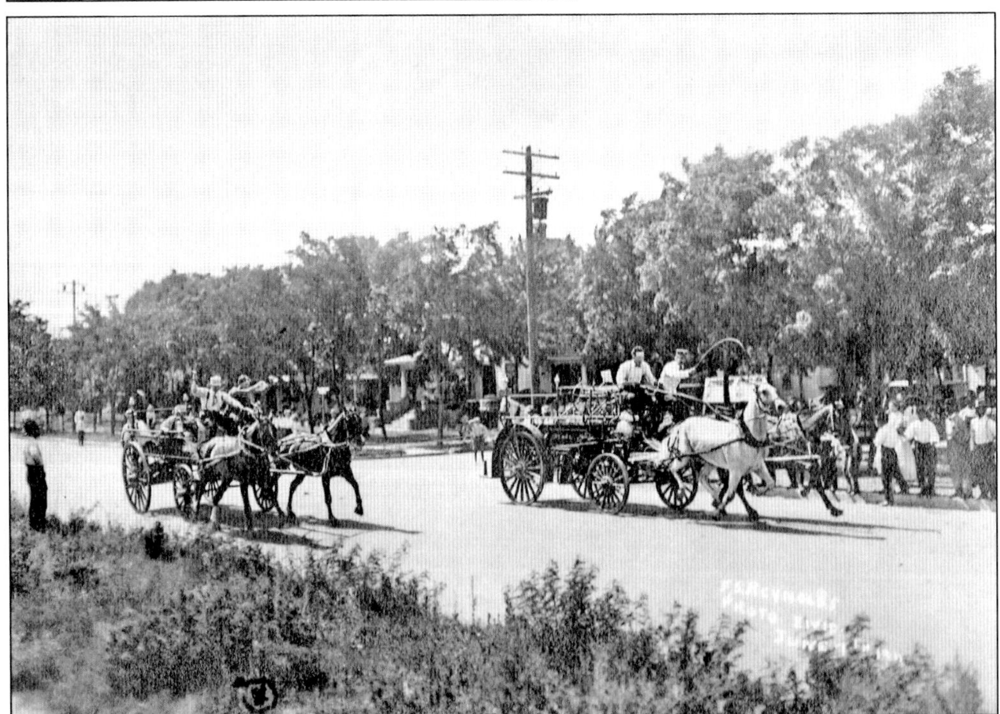

The Great Race. Two horse-drawn fire wagons race down Popular Street on July 6, 1908, probably in conjunction with Fourth of July activities. Teams competed against other departments across the state. The popular races helped firefighters hone their driving skills while keeping the horses and equipment fit. The Sapulpa team of Joe and Eagle won this great race.

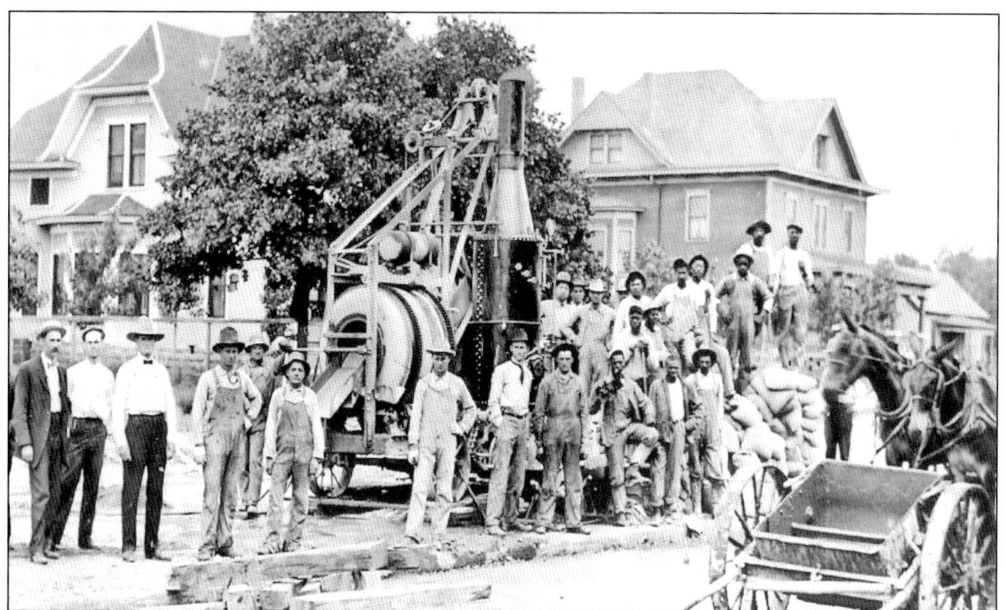

Street Paving Begins. As businesses burned, or were otherwise razed, along Sapulpa's first Main Street, they were replaced with masonry ones. Rails were laid for the electric trolley cars, and Main Street was paved. It was a big deal, as business and city leaders gathered to have their photographs taken with the cement, the machinery, mule teams, and a diverse work crew.

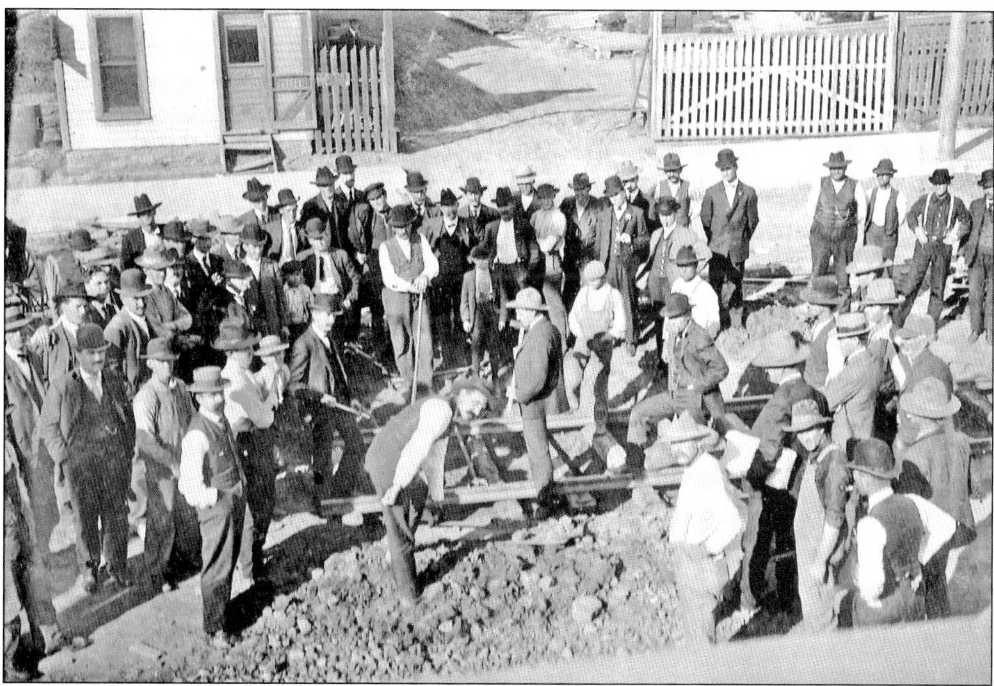

First Trolley Spike. The crew and a good crowd of citizens gather in downtown Sapulpa around 1902 to celebrate and witness the "first spike" driven for Sapulpa Electric Company's interurban trolley system. The electric streetcar was the mode of transportation between the horse-and-buggy era and the automobile. It connected Sapulpa to its neighbors, including Tulsa.

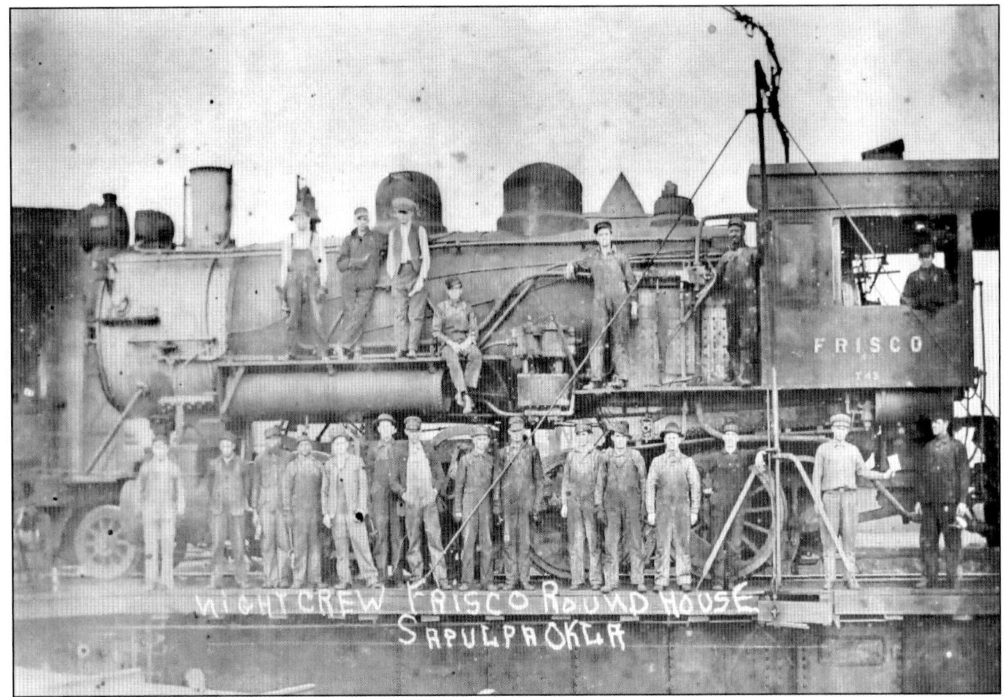

Working on the Railroad. The ever-expanding Frisco Railroad had made Sapulpa its division point, where it had its roundhouse and maintenance operation. This photograph of the night shift reflects the enormity of the operation in the early 1900s. At the time, it was the town's main industry.

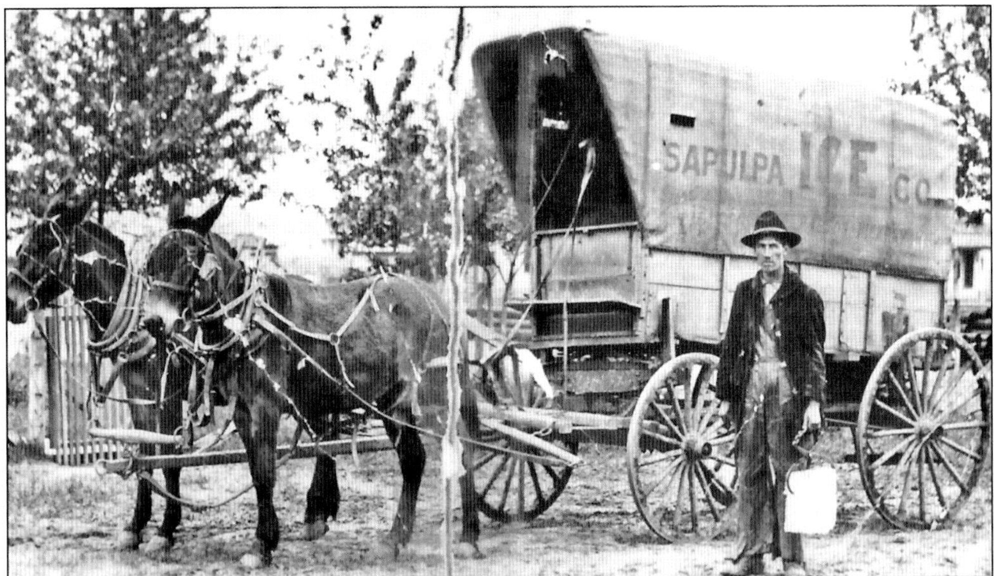

Ice Delivery Man. Early refrigeration in Sapulpa was dependent on the faithfulness of men like Charlie Wilson and his mule team. The earliest utility companies, even those selling electricity, were built around water and ice, as reflected in such names as Oklahoma Gas, Electric & Ice. Wilson delivered for Sapulpa Ice Company, as seen here around 1923. Ice tongs helped him carry a heavy block.

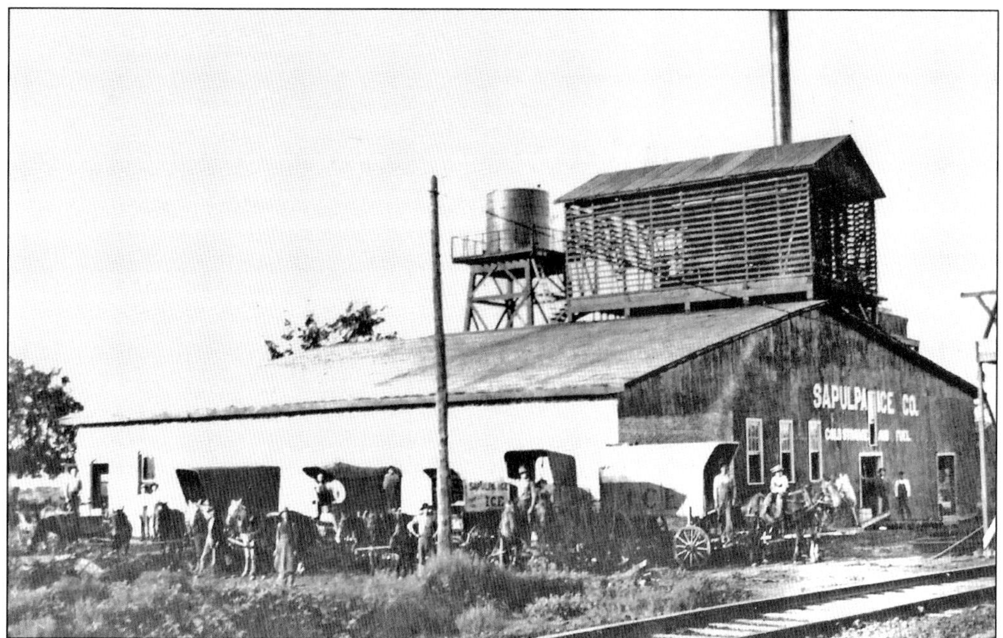

FIRST UTILITIES, 1900. Among the first industries in Sapulpa was the making of ice, which was often a top product of utility companies. Before there were just "gas and electric" companies, there were "ice, gas, and electric" companies. About the same time Sapulpa was becoming a town and Oklahoma Indian Territory was destined for statehood, ice plants like Sapulpa Ice Company on North Hickory Street were booming.

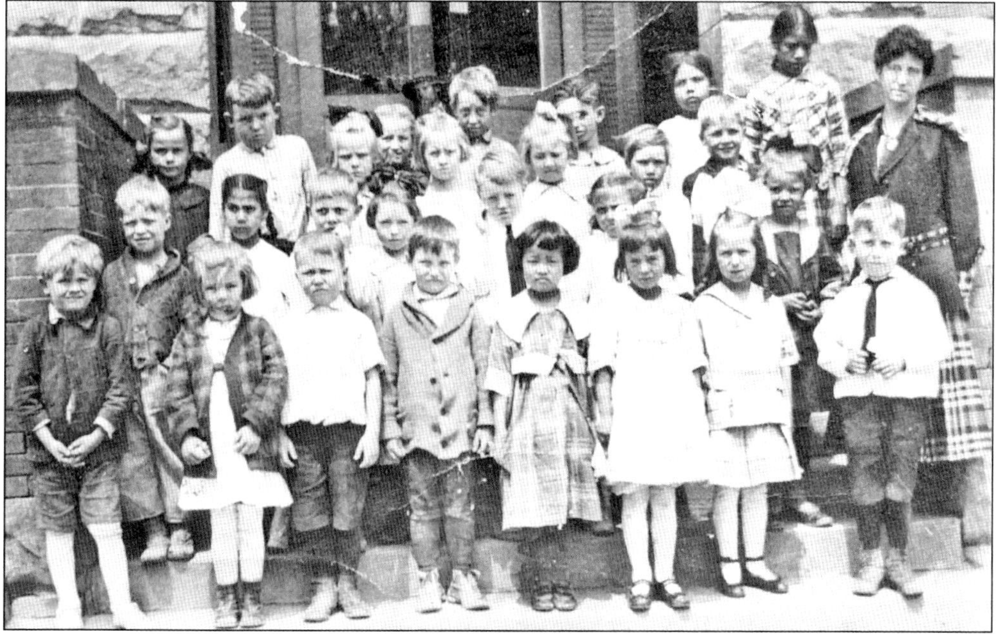

WASHINGTON SCHOOL FACES. Pupils attending early elementary school classes do not seem overly excited about stopping recess play to pose for a class picture. A lot can be seen in faces of Sapulpa's schoolkids in the early 1900s, including a representation of its diverse racial makeup. This was before government segregation policies took hold.

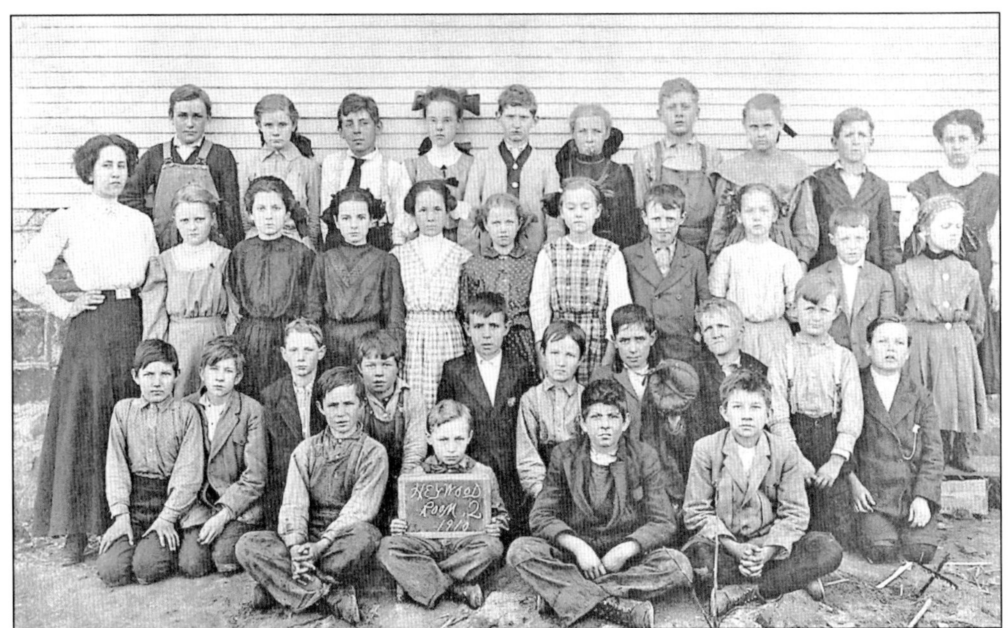

CLASS PHOTOGRAPH SAYS IT ALL. It is clear this is a photograph of Sapulpa School District's early-day Heywood School in 1910 because of the chalkboard held by the boy on first row. The teacher on the far left, the boy with the catcher's mitt, the girl at right in the third row, and the girl on the fourth row with an object in her mouth all seem to be making some kind of statement.

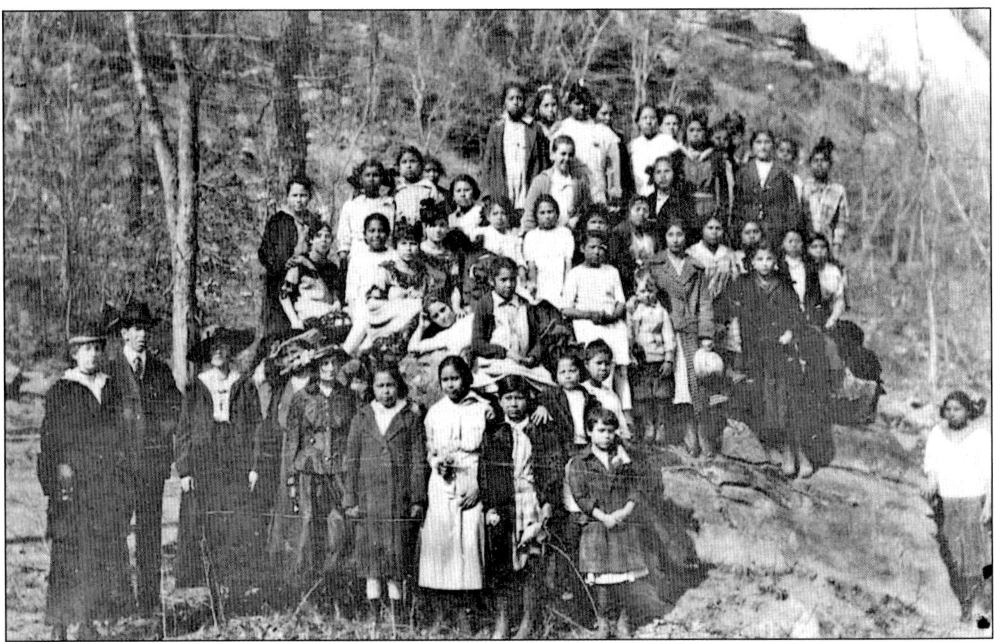

MISSION SCHOOL FIELD TRIP. Girls from the Euchee Mission School, along with teachers and superintendent, are pictured around 1924 at the legendary Moccasin Track Bluffs east of Sapulpa. A Romeo and Juliet story supposedly was played out here when one or both young lovers leaped to their deaths because their love could never be. It is said moccasin tracks were left behind in the stone formation.

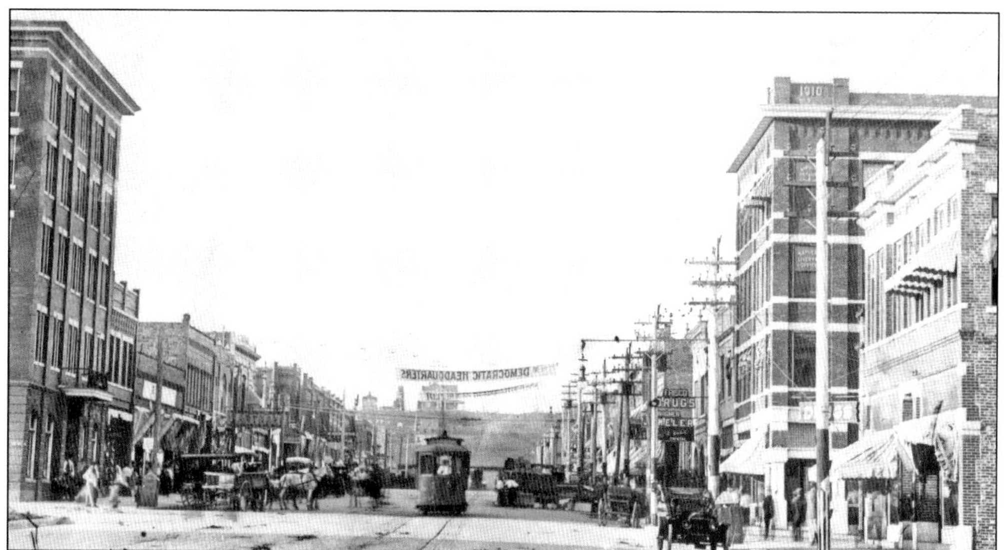

Town in Its Teens. The rapidly developing town of Sapulpa is shown in its infancy as Democrats and Republicans fly their banners above the horse-drawn buggies, Ford Model Ts, and electric streetcars. Looking north on Main Street, the second building at right displays the year 1910.

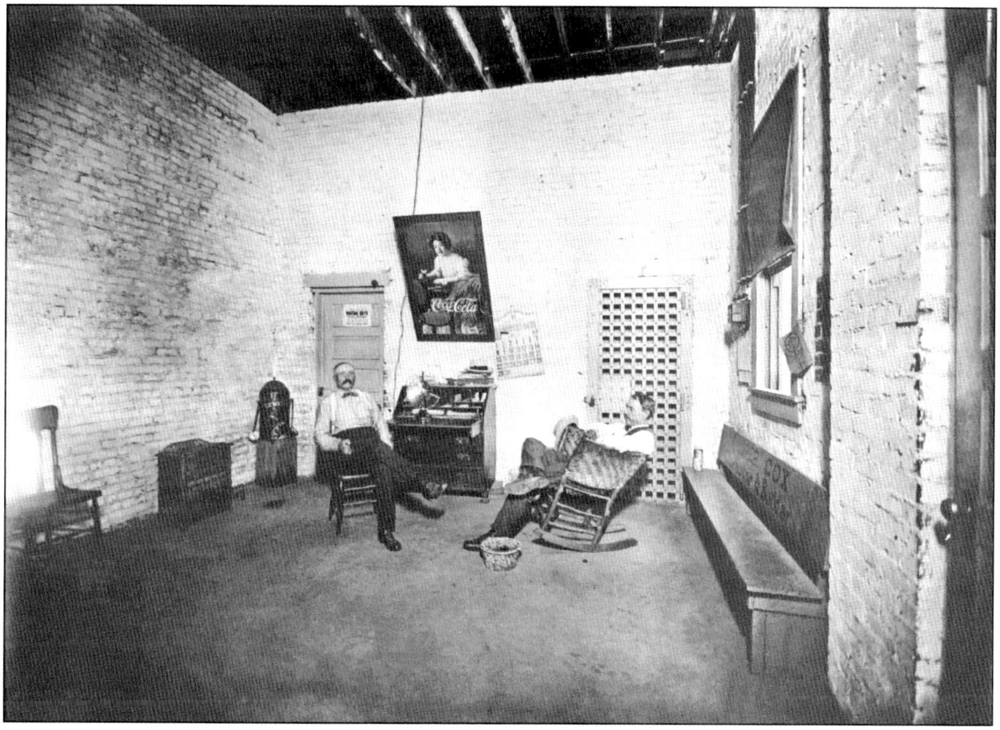

First Courthouse Built. Guy Hereford (left) and an unidentified man are pictured inside Sapulpa's first courthouse, on West Dewey Avenue. Hereford and John F. Egan built the two-story brick building and called it the Lucile Opera House after their daughters, both named Lucile. The first floor was the courthouse, and the upper floor was for entertainment events. Carrie Nation gave a talk in the opera house in May 1906 on the evils of alcohol. The building was razed in 1935.

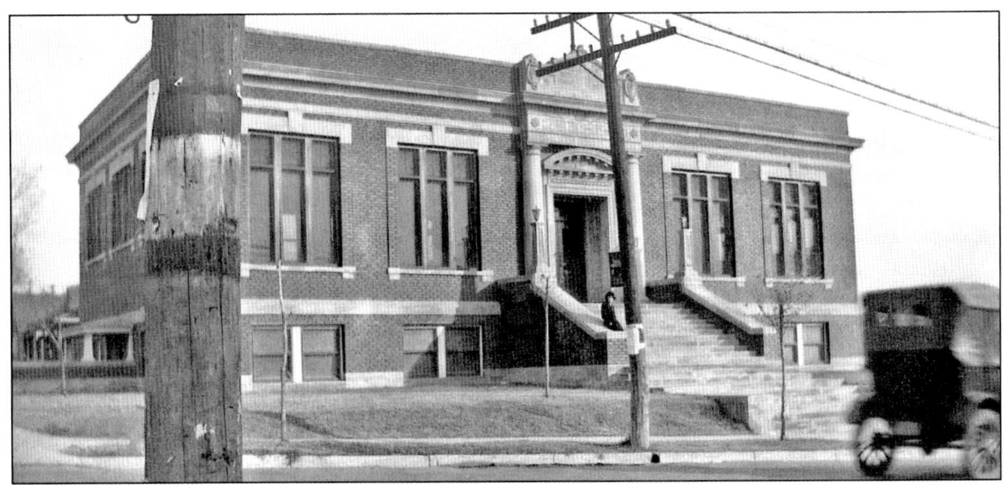

Sapulpa's Fine Library. The Carnegie Sapulpa Public Library was built in 1917 at 27 West Dewey Avenue with $25,000 gift from the Andrew Carnegie Trust. This historical landmark has continually maintained the reputation of being one of the finest resource centers in the county. In 1997, the Edward E. and Helen Turner Bartlett Foundation donated funds to restore and expand the library. The name changed to Bartlett-Carnegie.

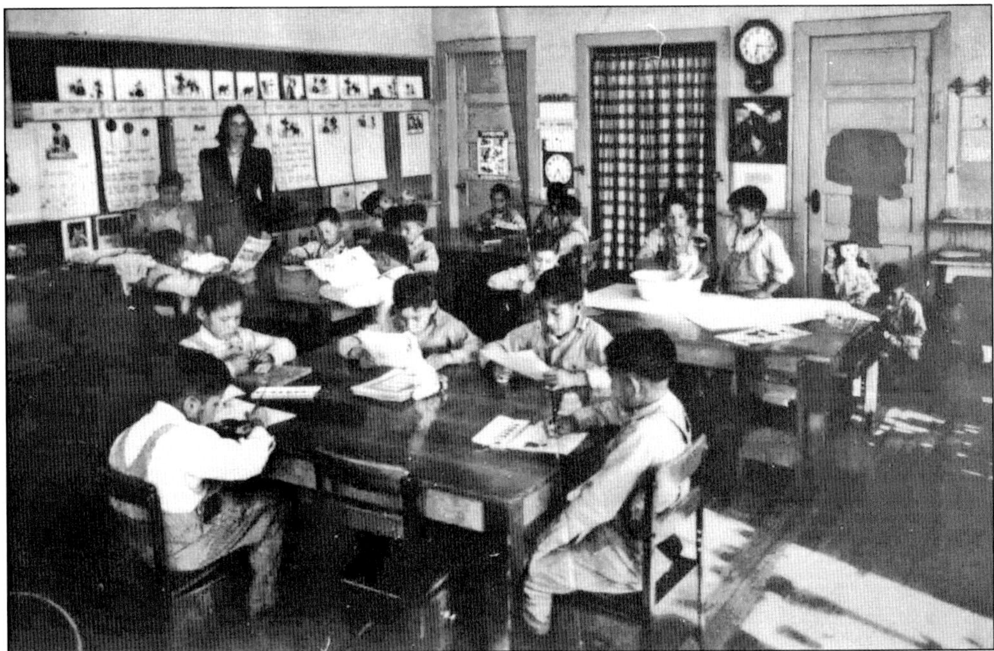

Class at Euchee Mission. The first education system in Sapulpa was developed by and for its Native Americans (Creek and Euchee) as early as 1891. Euchee Mission and Boarding School was built in 1894 when an appropriation was made from Creek tribal funds at the request of S.W. Brown, chief of the Euchees. The campus, where Sapulpa High and Junior High Schools are today, had three buildings, made up of two dormitories and a three-room school. The first superintendent was Noah Gregory, a full-blood Euchee. From 1895 to 1899, J.H. Land, a minister and one of Sapulpa's key founders, was superintendent. William A. Sapulpa, son of Chief Sapulpa, succeeded Land. The school was abolished in 1947 by governmental order. The tribe sold the land and buildings to the Sapulpa Public Schools for $50,000. The buildings were eventually razed.

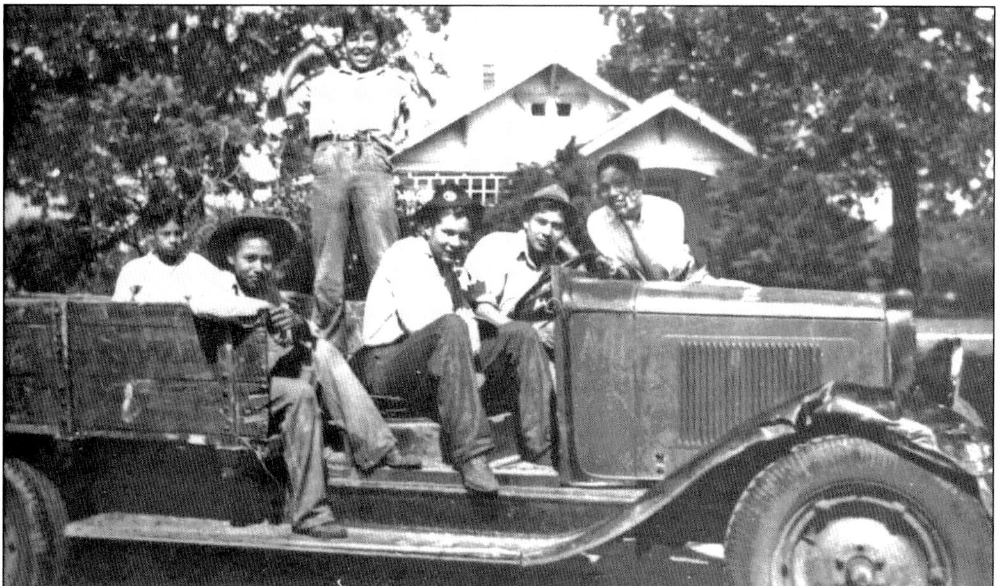

First Sapulpa Cruisers. Some of Sapulpa's first teenage cruisers were likely these Native American students at the Euchee Mission Boarding School in the early 1920s. The school, operated by the Creek Indian Council, enrolled both boys and girls, principally from Creek and Euchee Indian families. It became an all-boys school in 1925 and integrated with public schools in 1947.

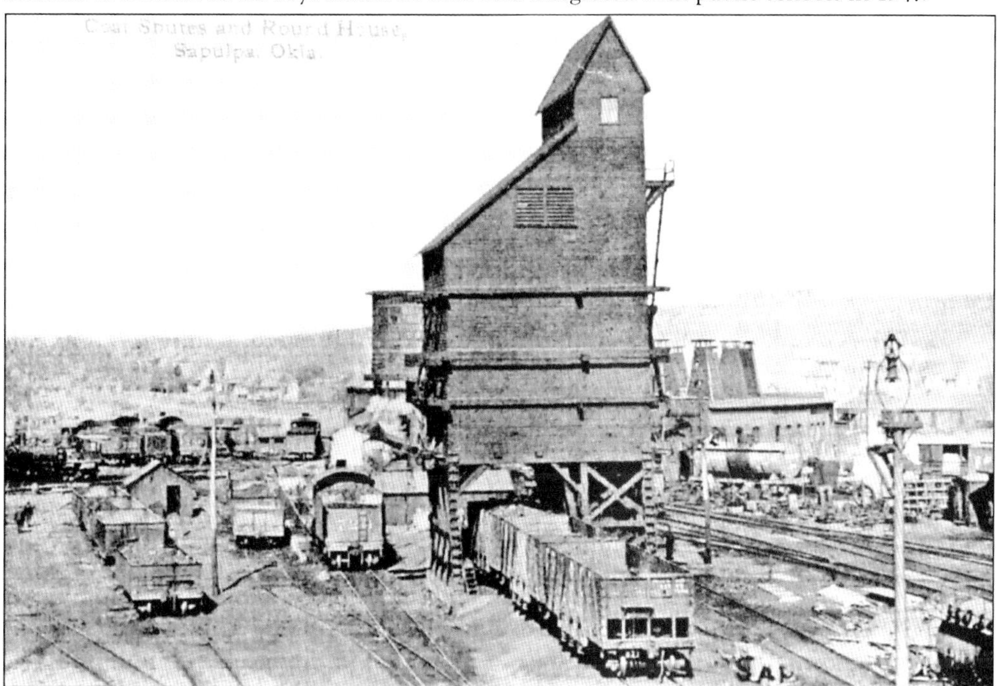

The Frisco Yard. This old photograph shows the turn-of-the-century Frisco Railroad headquarters at Sapulpa, complete with coal chutes and water tanks to fill and fuel its large steam locomotives. Also noted is the massive roundhouse where the engines were serviced and turned around. Early locomotives did not easily operate in reverse. These facilities were about where Farmers' Feed is today, eastward to the railroad wye.

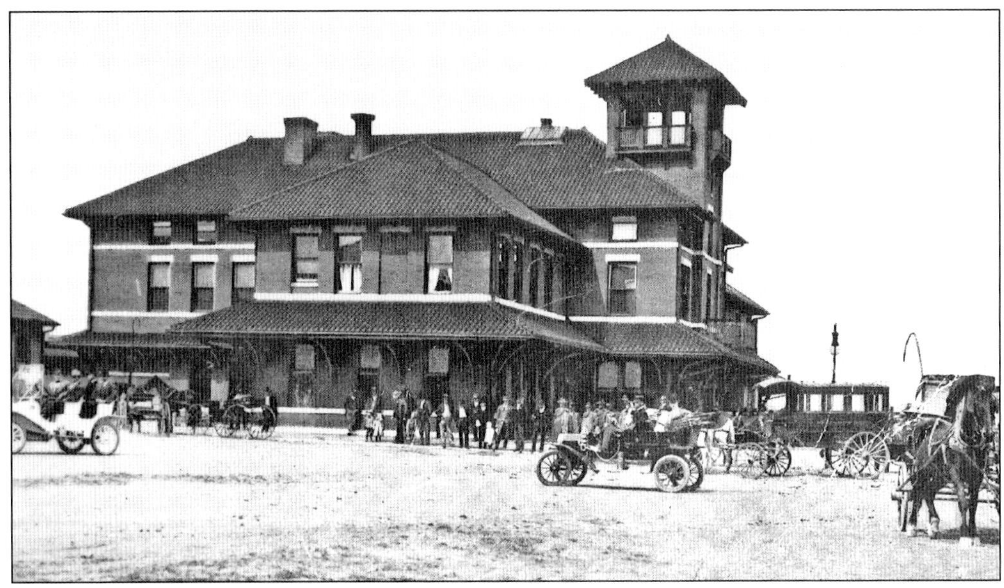

DEPOT AND HARVEY HOUSE. The Frisco Depot, with its iconic Harvey House restaurant and hotel on Hobson Street, was built in 1907 and enlarged in 1912. Harvey Houses were mainly on the Santa Fe line, which owned the Frisco at the time. Fred Harvey was awarded the contract to build and operate the Sapulpa edifice. The Harvey House closed in 1930, and the building was razed in 1963.

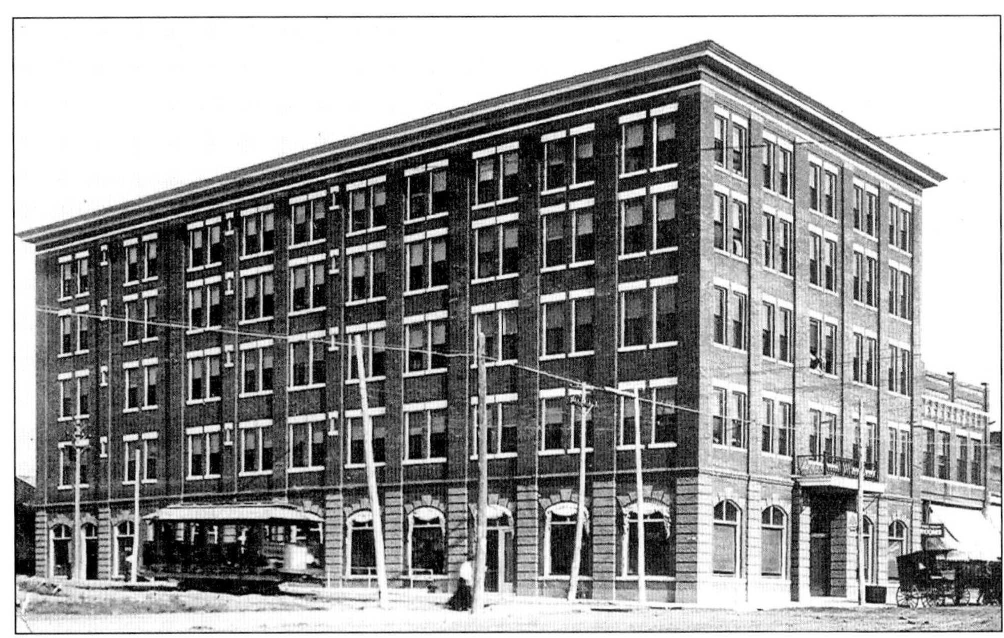

ST. JAMES TROLLEY STOP. Known simply as "the St. James," this quality hotel was built by Bates Burnett in 1907 and was named for his son William James at a cost of $100,000. The five-story building at Lee and Main Streets was said to have been Sapulpa's original truly first-class hotel. The interurban trolley stopped here and carried passengers to area parks and towns.

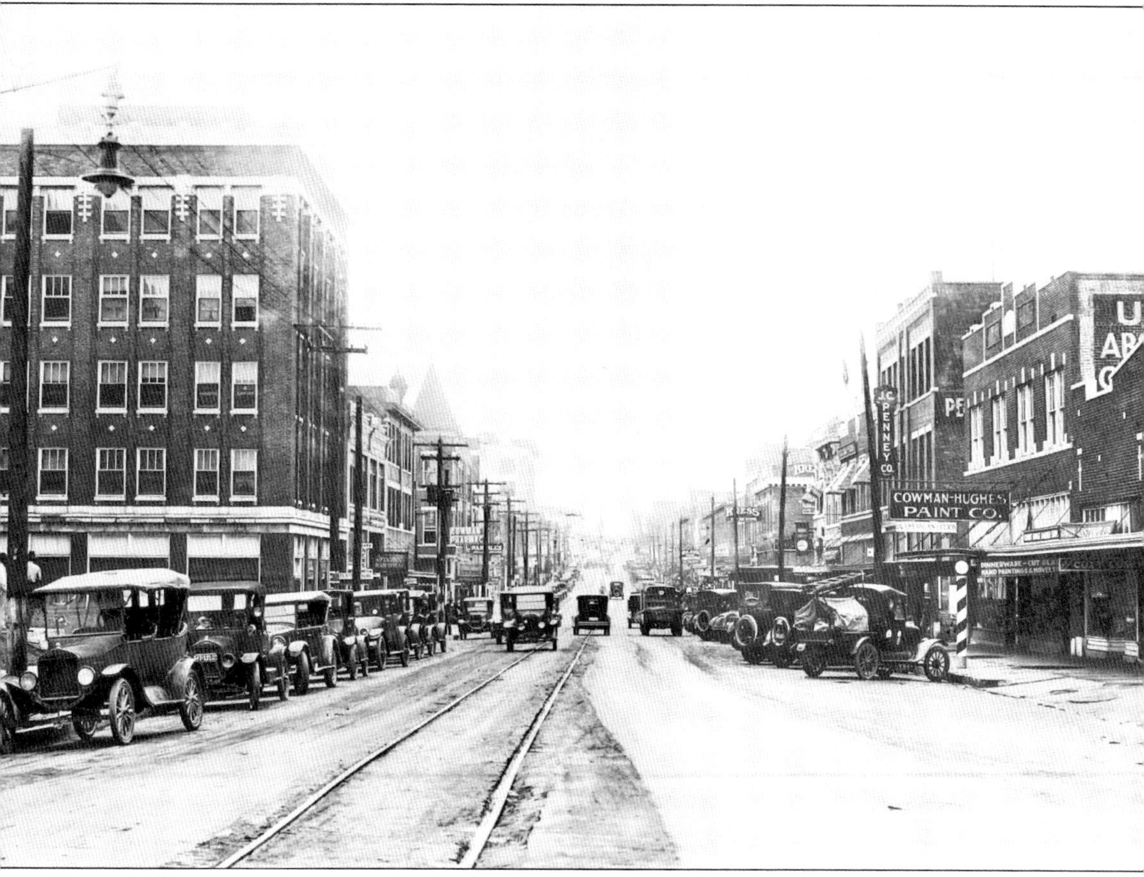

Model T Takeover. It appears that by the 1920s everyone in Sapulpa had a Model T. Here, the automobiles fill up parking spaces and straddle the trolley rails along East Dewey Avenue. Fewer and fewer folks were using the streetcar. Except as a converted diner and a filling station office, streetcars disappeared locally in the early 1930s. Automobiles had been around for decades but were scarce and expensive until the Model T's introduction in 1908. The Model T was produced through 1927.

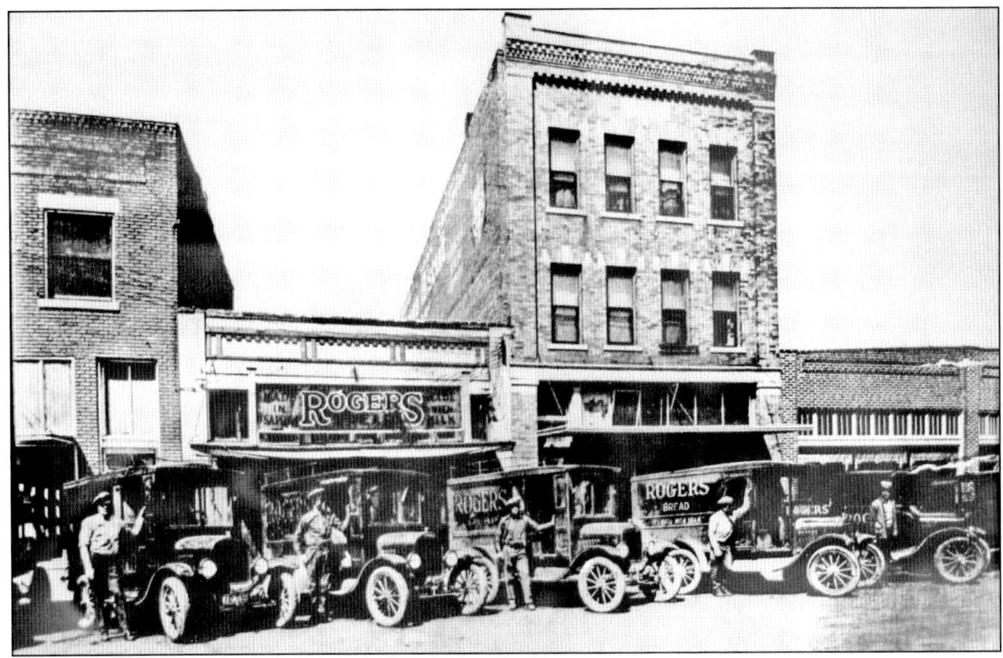

DELIVERING THE BAKED GOODS. Harry and Elizabeth Rogers came to town in the 1920s and bought the Vienna Bakery at 317 East Dewey Avenue. It would be one of several popular Sapulpa bakeries over the years. With their breads, cakes, and other pastry specialties, they not only hired additional bakers but also extended from 5 routes to 35 during the next 25 years.

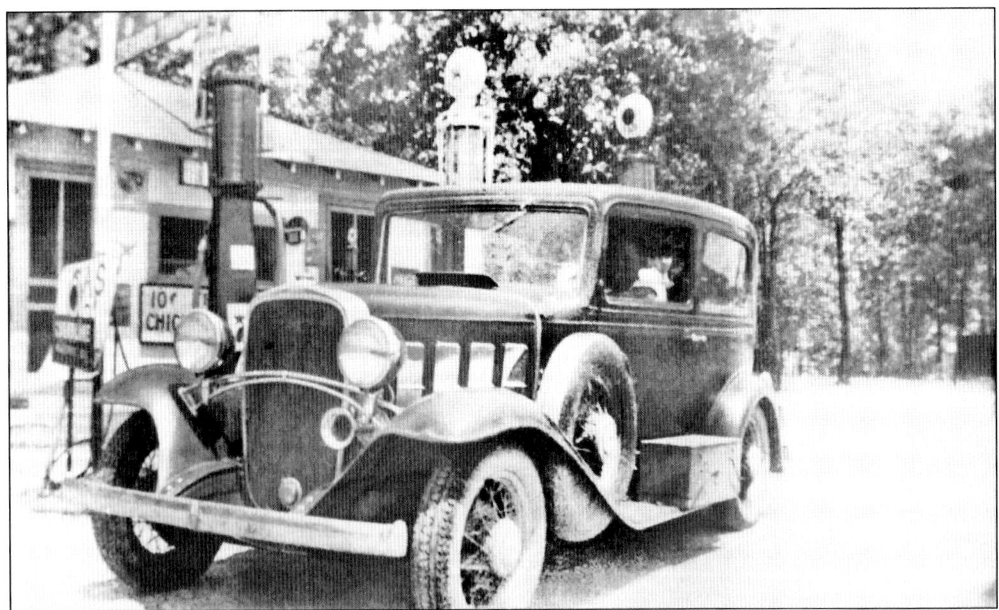

DUSTY MODEL A. A dust-covered Ford Model A pulls into an old corner filling station in Sapulpa as the prosperous days of the 1920s roll into the 1930s, when folk began to feel the impact of economic woes, dust storms, and the like. Ford made Models A through T and began again in 1928 with the Model A. The times they were a'changing.

Two

Building Community
Early Homes, Infrastructure, and Businesses

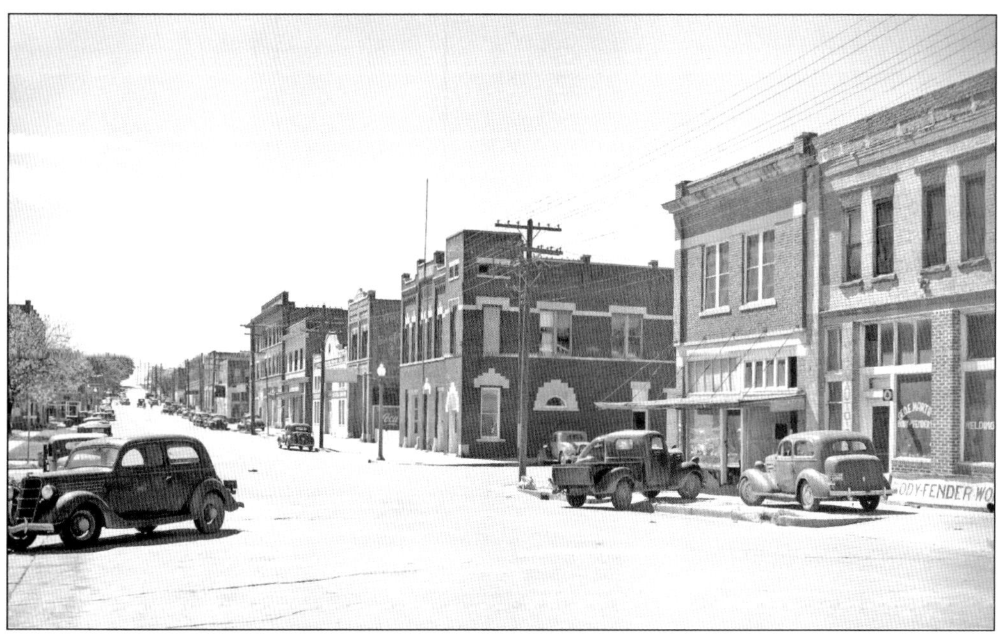

Automobiles, Buildings, Streets Change. For a time, it seemed Sapulpa's main thoroughfare could be Hobson Street, a block north of Dewey Avenue and eventual Route 66. Here, on the corner of Hobson Street and Park Street, city hall (second building on right) had lost its dome atop the fire hose drying tower. City hall today is on Dewey Avenue, as are the central fire and police stations.

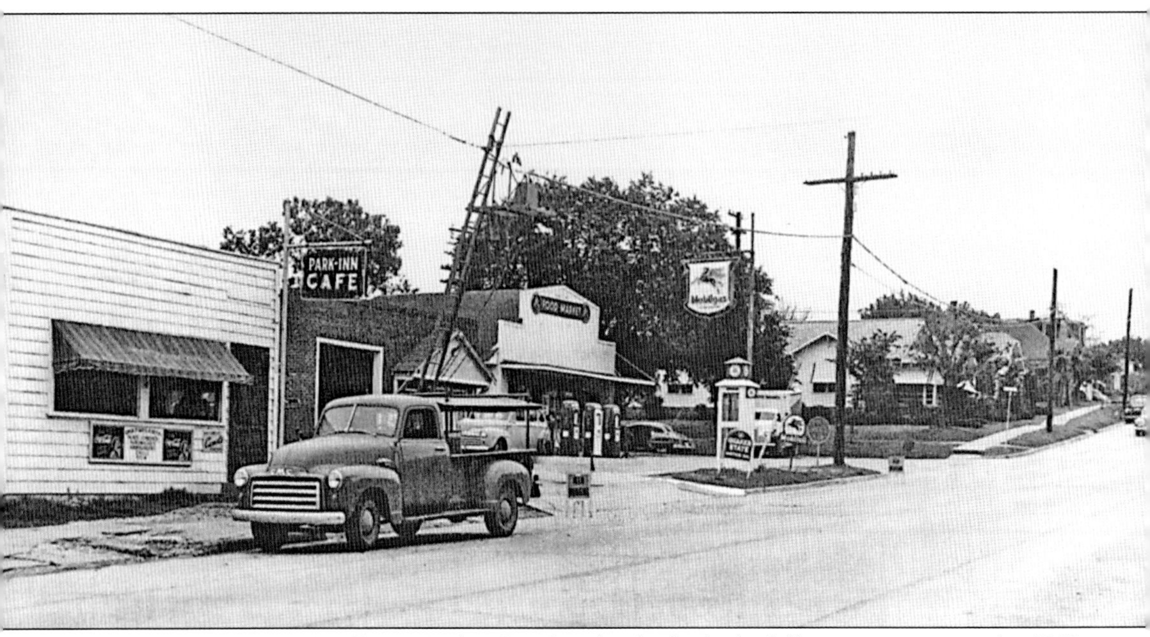

ONLINE IN THE 1950S. Being "online" in Sapulpa had a little different meaning in the 1950s. "Most Connected," however, is still the town's motto. Before there were fast-speed Internet and cell towers, workmen in pickups with ladders had to reach the main Southwestern Bell phone line connecting Sapulpa businesses and residences along West Dewey Avenue.

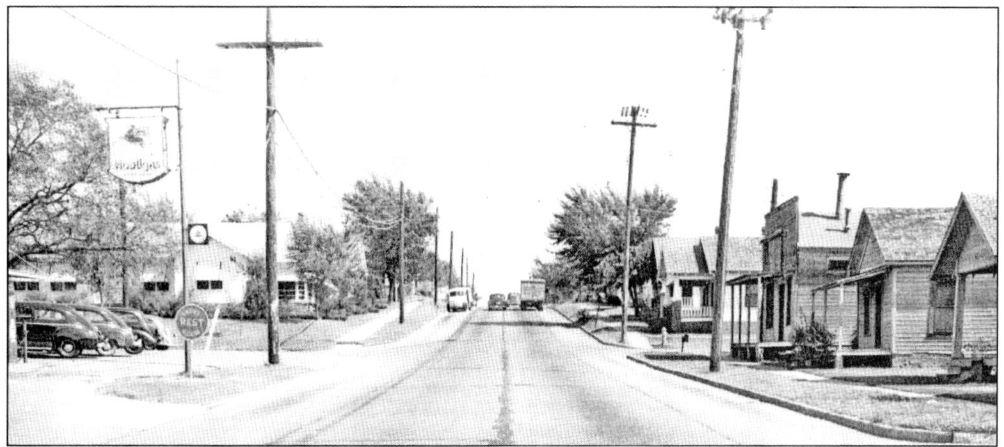

GOING MODERN ALL THE WAY. There was still old cars and old houses, but in the 1940s, Sapulpa was going modern. The filling station at one of the city's gateways offered a public telephone and ladies' restroom. There appear to be delivery trucks and vans and even some drivers passing on a hill.

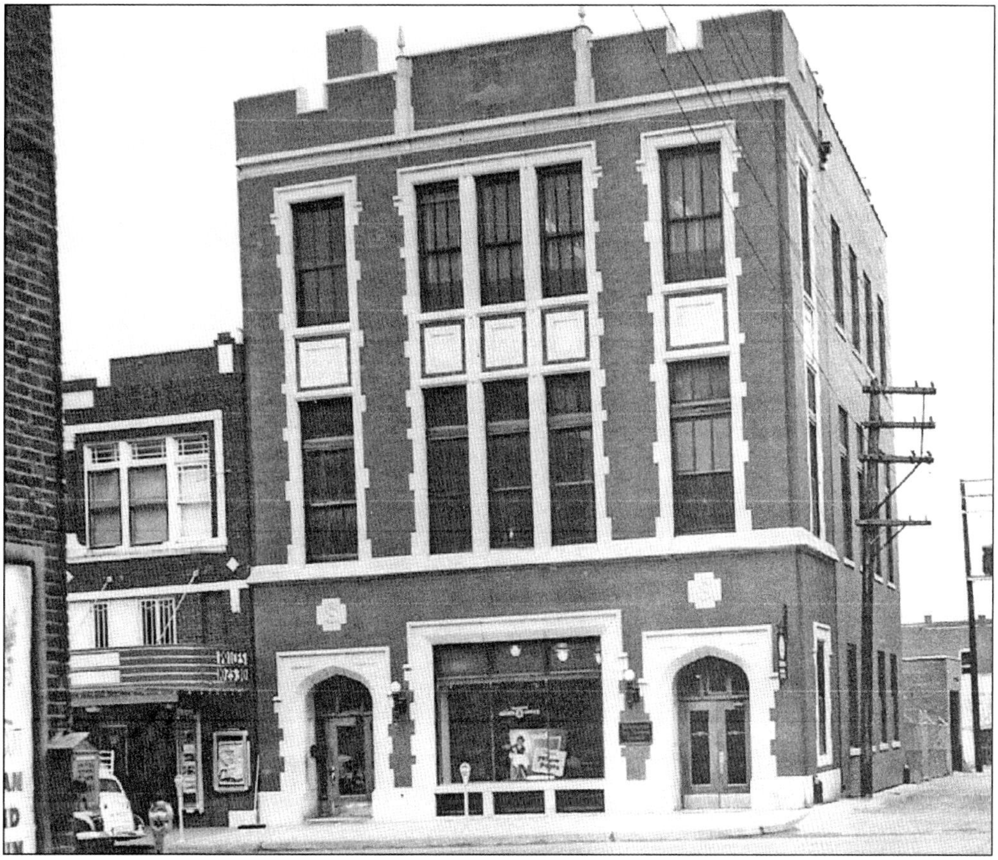

PHONE COMPANY BUILDING. Constructed in 1918 for the Pioneer Telephone Company, this building was later home to Southwestern Bell Telephone Company, which remained in the building until 1960. It was acquired by the city and was used as a city hall and police station until 1985. The police station was in the rear of the main building in the alley.

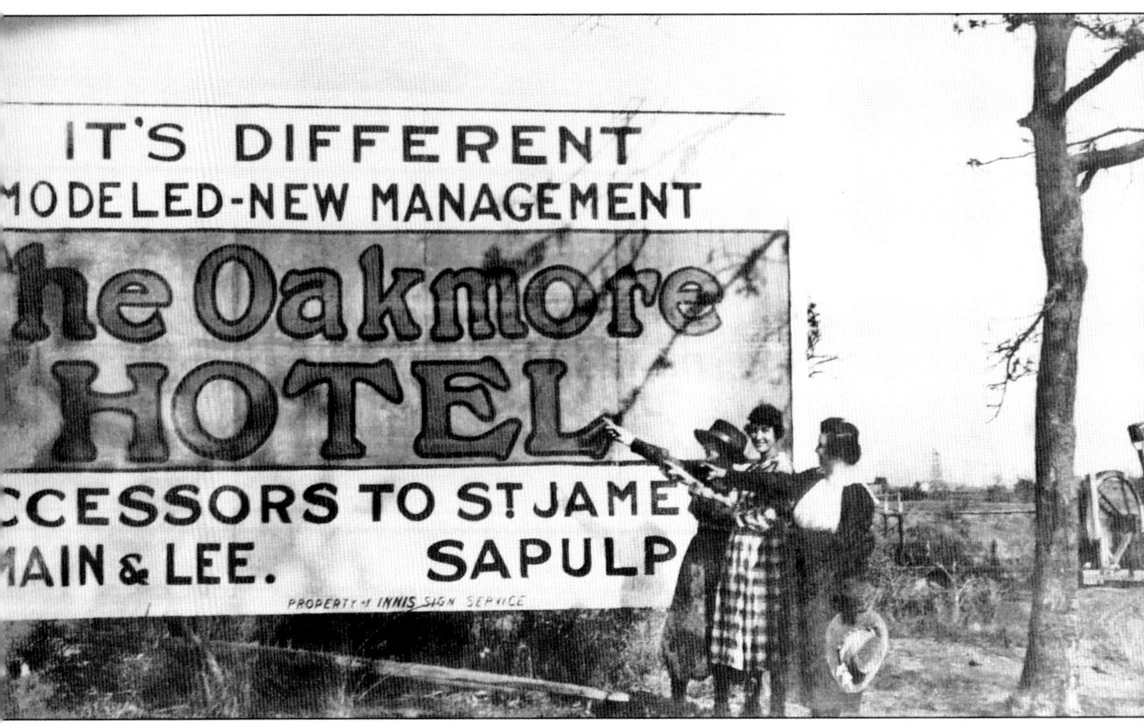

HOTEL TRIES NEW NAME. Because it was first a railroad town, then a manufacturing and oil boomtown, and finally a tourist destination—or at least a stop along the way—Sapulpa built a lot of hotels and places to stay over a night or so. Here, three women (perhaps the owners or representatives thereof) promote the temporary renaming of the magnificent St. James Hotel. Competition was keen not only locally but also across the Arkansas in Tulsa, where skyscraper hotels also stood.

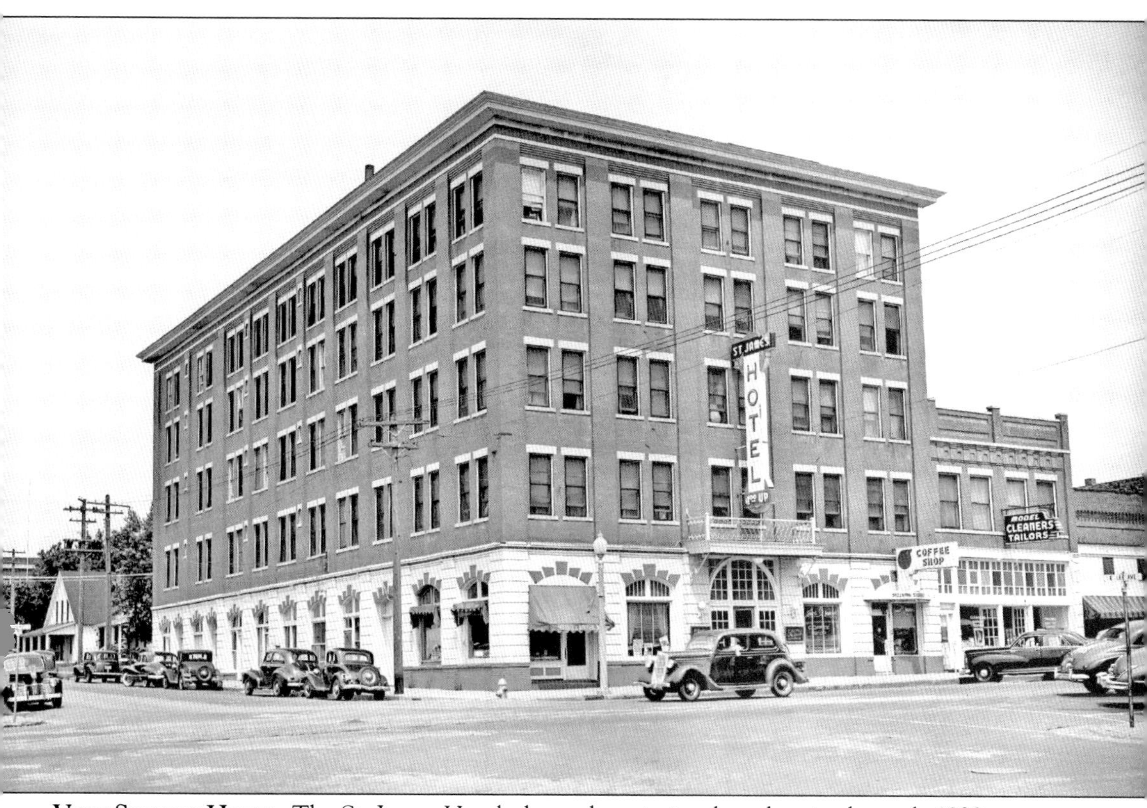

VERY STATELY HOTEL. The St. James Hotel, shown here in its glory days in the early 1930s, was truly first class. It was five stories and had 100 rooms with hot and cold water in each, with 75 rooms connected to a private bath. It also had a restaurant and a ballroom. The trolley tracks are still visible in this mid-1930s photograph, but the electric streetcars shown in an earlier photograph are gone.

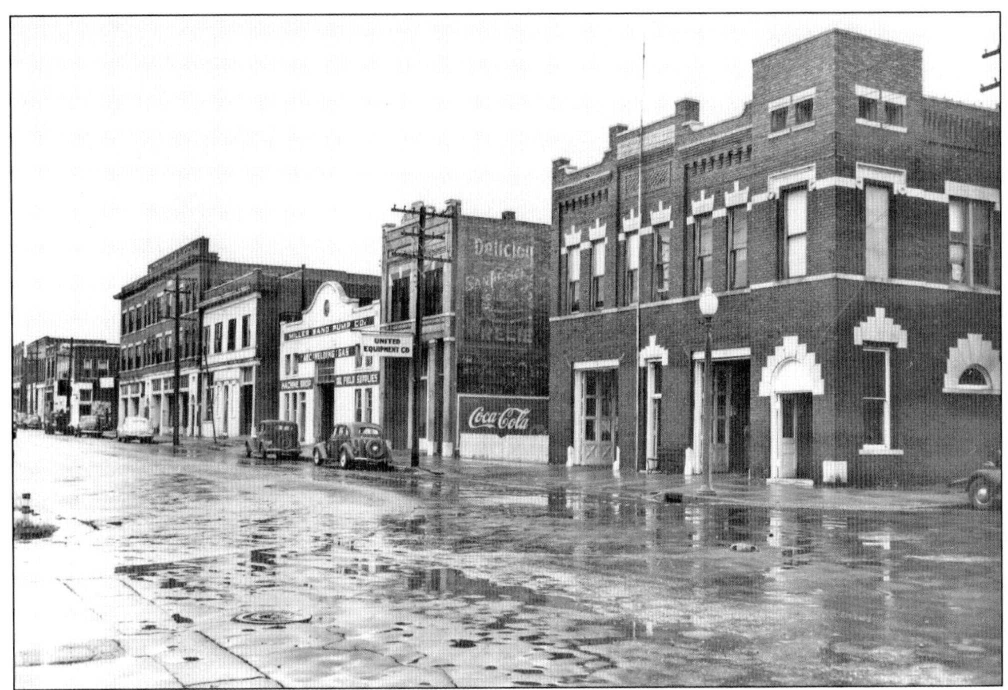

Potholes and Slick Streets. But automobiles wear on streets, too. Sometimes, even potholes created over the winter months by freezing rain and ice became historic along Hobson Street, which had to be kept clear in front of city hall so fire trucks could get a running start when alarms sounded.

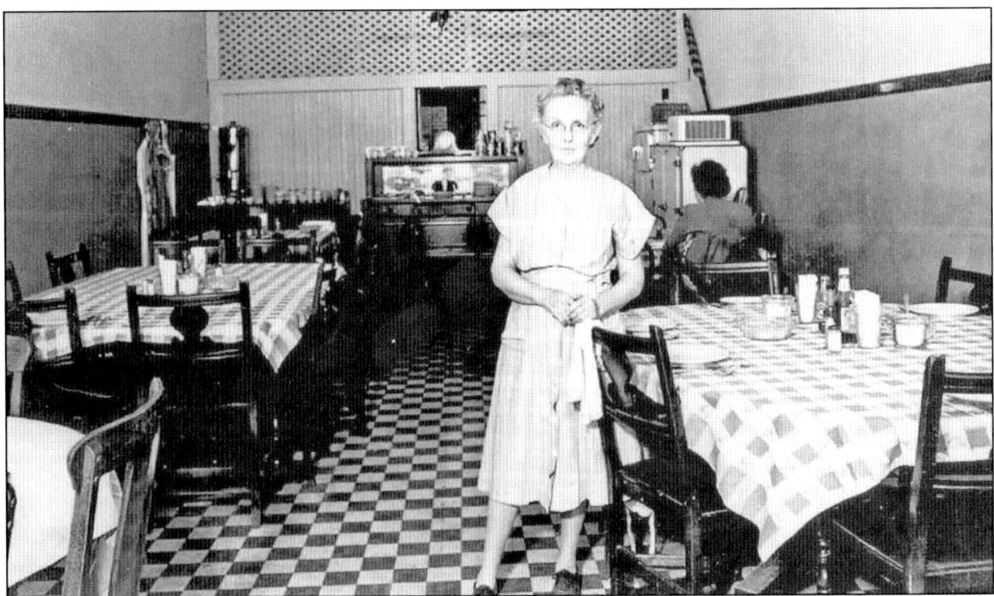

Cooking for the Public. It was a good recipe when Lilly Thompson married Charlie Warner and moved to Sapulpa. She had grown up in the restaurant business, which proved a good fit at Woods and Sapulpa (later Loraine) Hotels and then at her own restaurant in 1933. She operated the popular Ferndale Café on Water Street for years. Lilly also was the source for the character "Aunt Eller" in the musical *Oklahoma*.

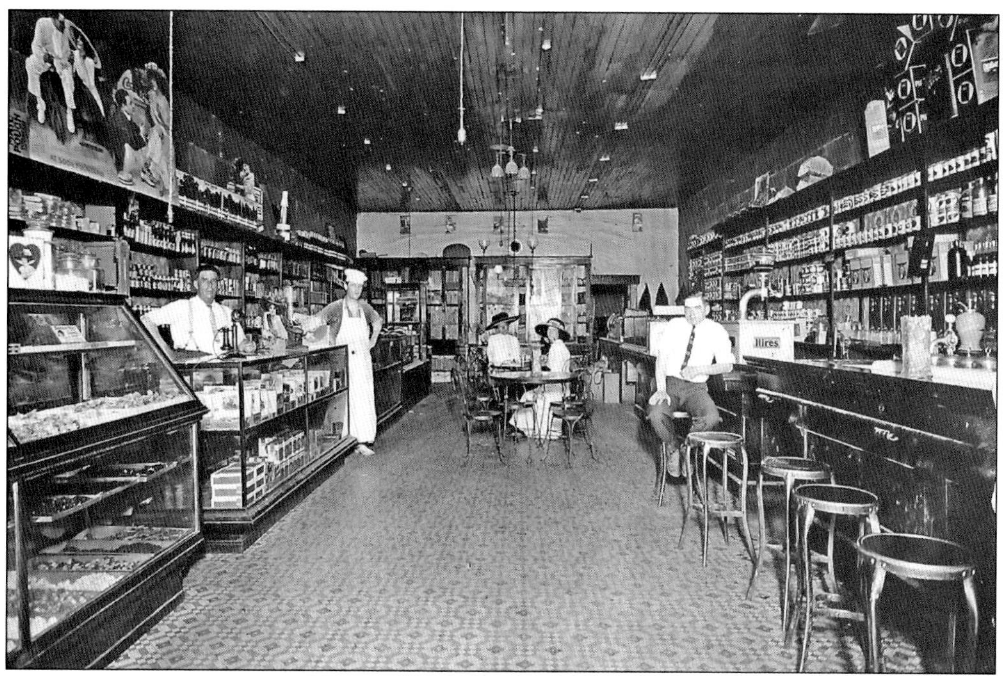

Not Sundaes, but Sundries? Most people of yesteryear associate the word "sundry" with the old-fashioned drugstore in their neighborhood that used to sell all sorts of odds and ends, from magazines to hairbrushes; combs, clippers, comic books, cards, candy, and cosmetics; tobacco products, remedies, salves, and lotions; and of course, medicine, as well as those with soda fountain counters offering ice cream sundaes. Among Sapulpa's popular drugstores are Humes' Rexall, Lawrence's City Drug, and Moore's, located at corner of Dewey Avenue and Oak Street. One of the last was Plymouth Drug, operated locally until recent years and competition of chains and box stores like Walgreens and Walmart, where one can find sundries.

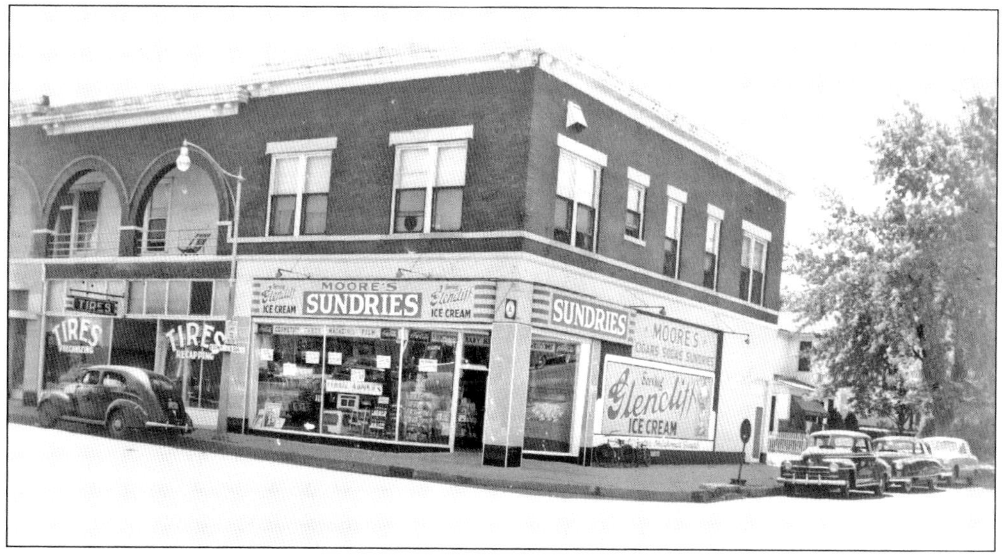

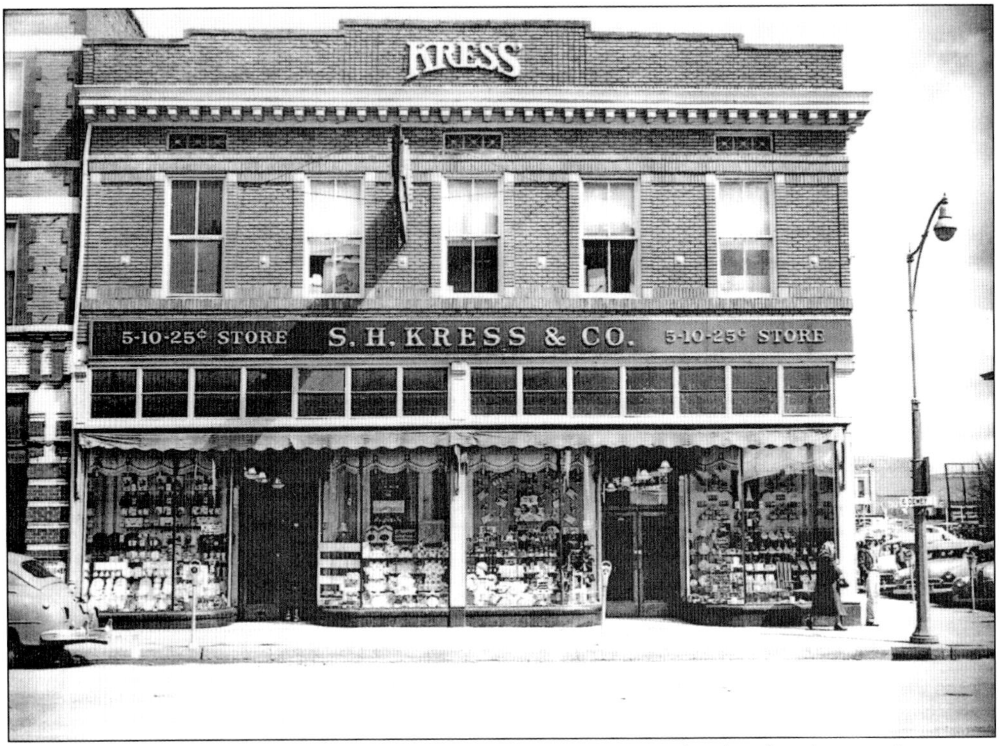

THOSE WONDERFUL FIVE-AND-DIMES. The Kress' Building remains a landmark in historic downtown Sapulpa, but the merchandise has changed since this 1950s photograph, when the popular department store offered its variety at 5¢, 10¢ and 25¢. Kress', Newberry's, J.C. Penney, OTASCO, Montgomery Ward, and the rest were all downtown.

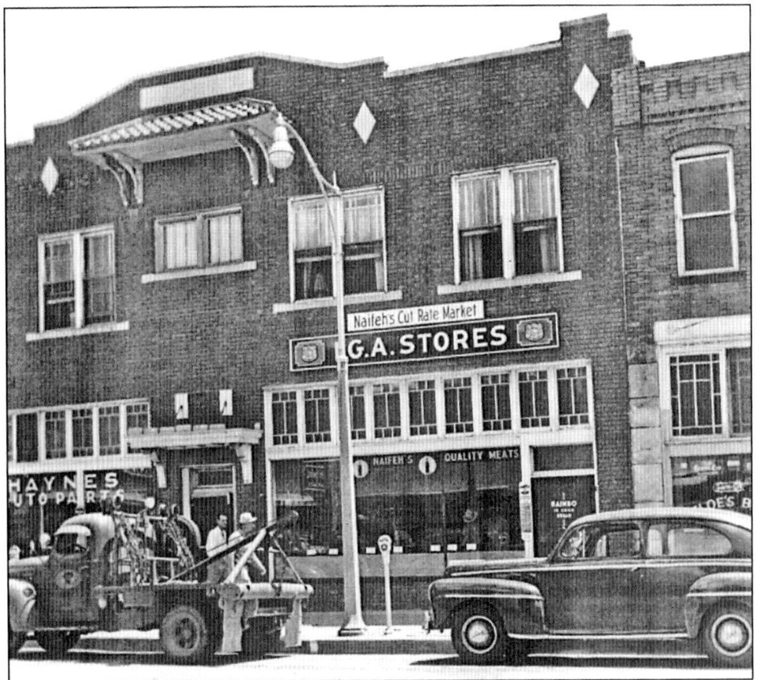

MEAT AND GROCERIES. Naifeh is a well-known name in the Sapulpa business community in both retail and wholesale. In the 1950s, the name was associated with this downtown IGA grocery store and meat market. The brand name "Rainbo" on the front door is correct and not to be confused with Rainbow swirl bread.

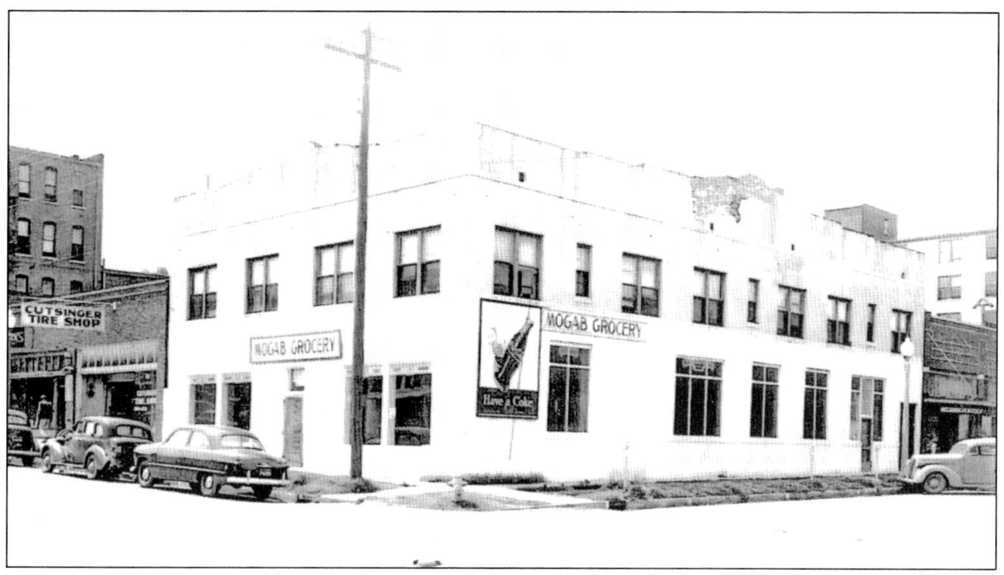

The Corner Grocery. In the 1950s, there were grocery stores—some swankier than others—on nearly every corner in downtown Sapulpa and scattered across the community. Many offered the essentials: meat, produce, other groceries, and bread as well as some clothing items (dry goods).

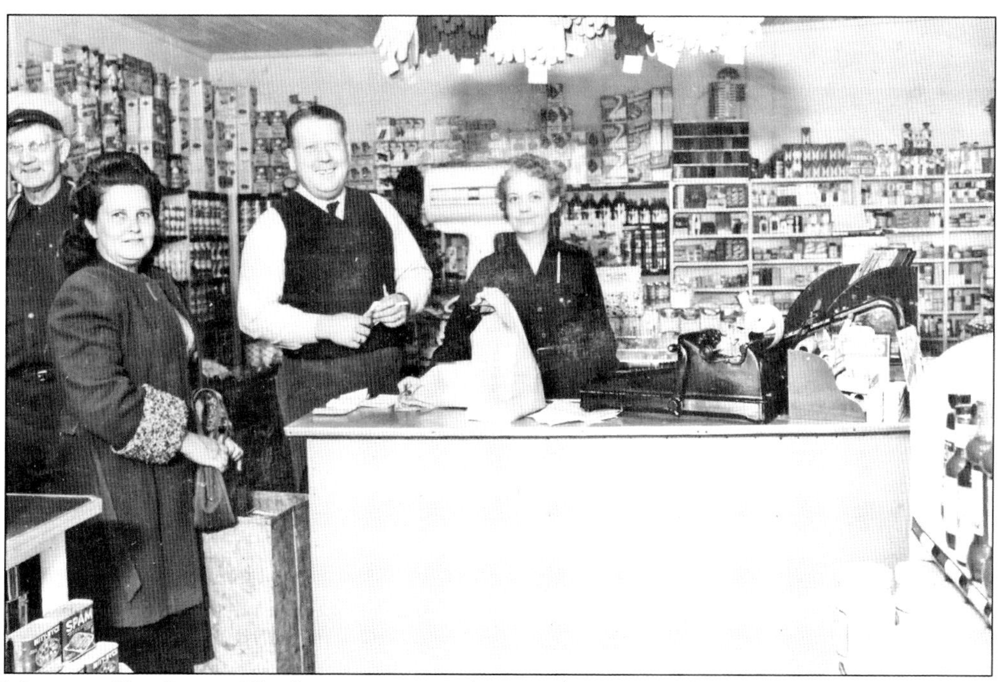

Mom-and-Pop Store. The forerunners to today's quick "stop and shop" convenience stores were the community mom-and-pop grocery stores like this one found all over town. As evident in this photograph, the operations offered just about everything one would need to get by—and most times on credit.

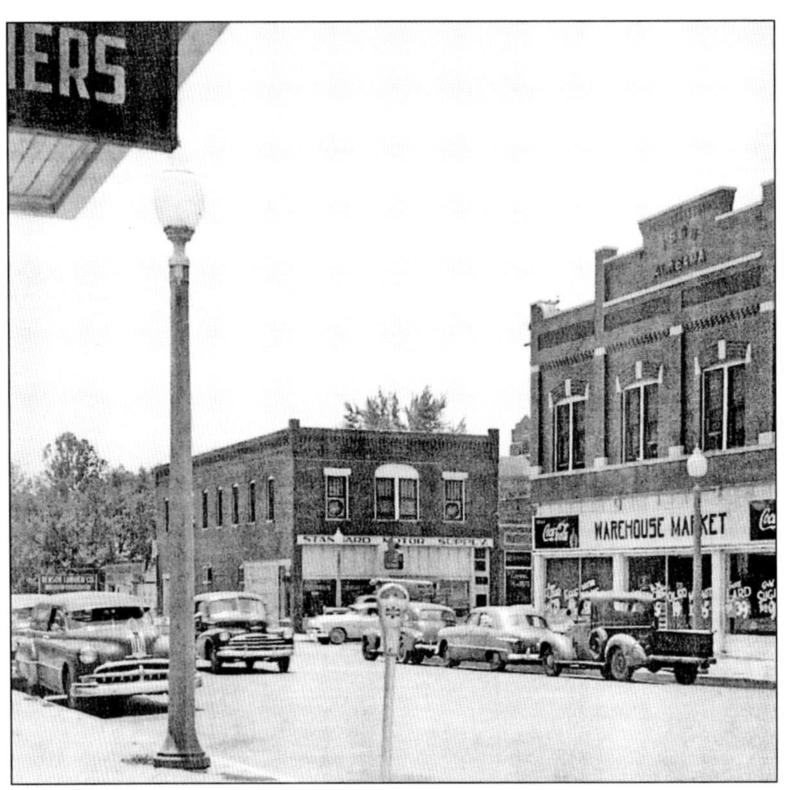

Warehouse Market Back Then. The Warehouse Market now is an area chain of grocery stores. It still has a strong presence here, but some can recall that back in the 1950s, it was one of several grocery stores located in the thick of things right downtown.

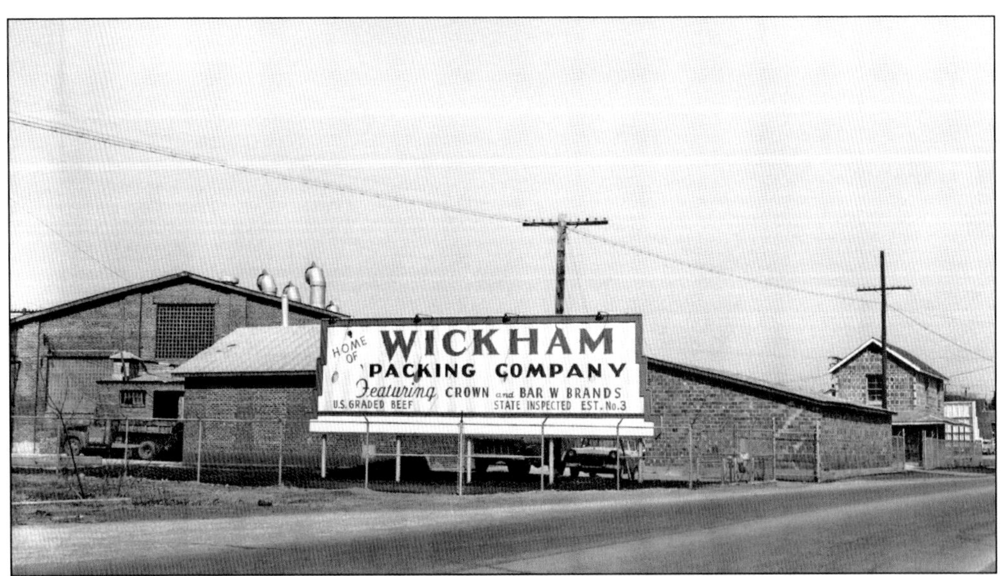

Meat Packing and Shipping. The coming and modernization of the railroad, along with methods of refrigeration and preservation, allowed the emergence of several meat-packing plants in Sapulpa. Wickham Packing Company slaughtered, processed, packaged, and distributed a wide range of meat products, "Featuring Crown and Bar W Brands."

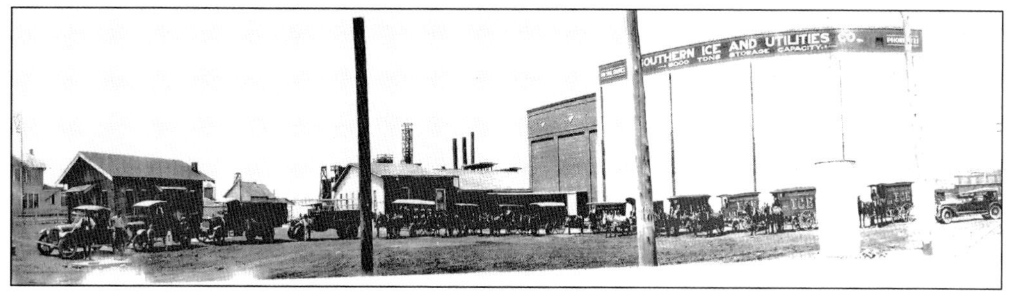

Ice, a Big Industry. Among the first booming industries in Sapulpa were ice plants. In fact, ice was often the chief product offered by local utility companies. About the same time Sapulpa was becoming a town in Indian Territory, ice plants were proliferating. By 1900, those springing up in Sapulpa were among hundreds across the country delivering ice to shippers of beef and other perishables to restaurants and homes, where everyone had an icebox.

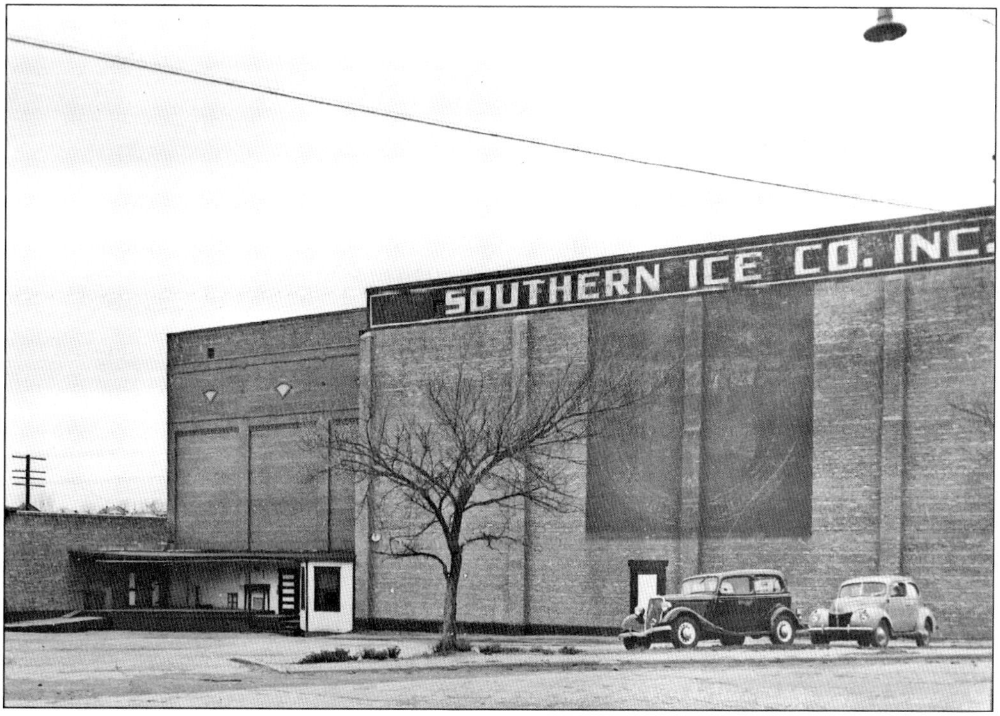

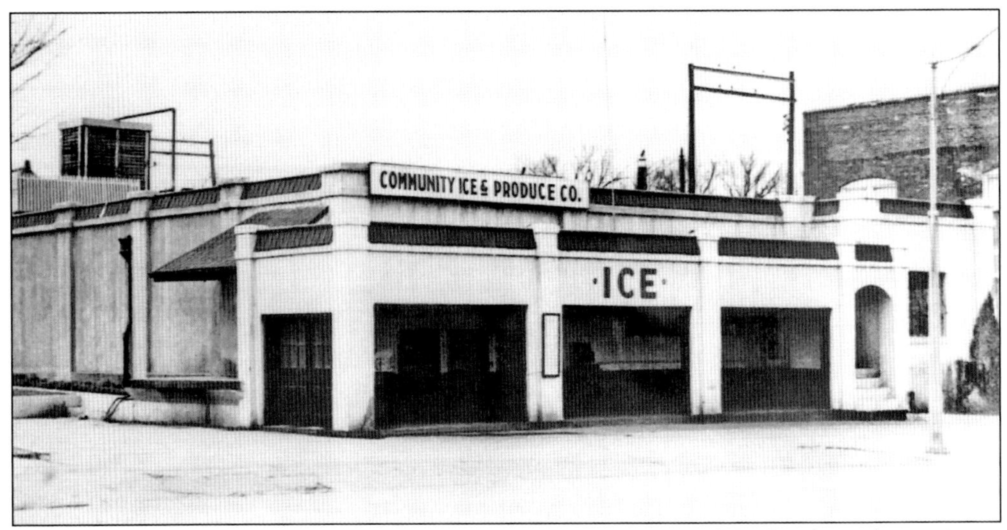

Manufacturing Ice. Before the arrival of modern refrigeration, people had to depend on iceboxes to keep food cool. The icebox like the one on display at the Sapulpa museum held both food and large blocks of ice. Plants like Community Ice and Southern Ice met the demand. Southern operated well into the 1950s. Portable ice-making and vending machines and freezer boxes filled with bagged ice do the trick today.

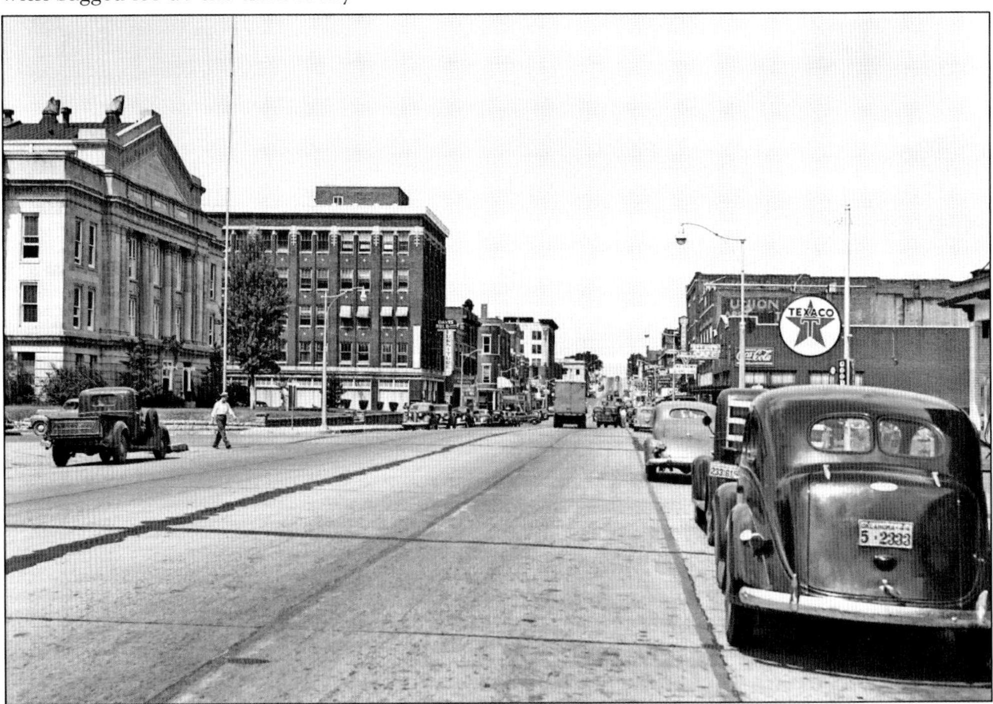

County Courthouse. Creek County's courthouse (left), in this street scene at 218 East Dewey Avenue, was built in 1914 after a bitter fight with Bristow for the county seat designation. Built by Manhattan Construction Co. of Muskogee for $132.350, it was designed by Solomon Layton, the same architect who designed Oklahoma's state capitol building in Oklahoma City. Sapulpa, Indian Territory, became a town in 1898. The first courthouse was built by J.O. Hereford and John F. Egan in 1903 at Dewey Avenue and Mounds Street before statehood.

Three

TRANSPORTATION
TRAILS, RAILS, SKIES, AND TRAVELING DOWN ROUTE 66

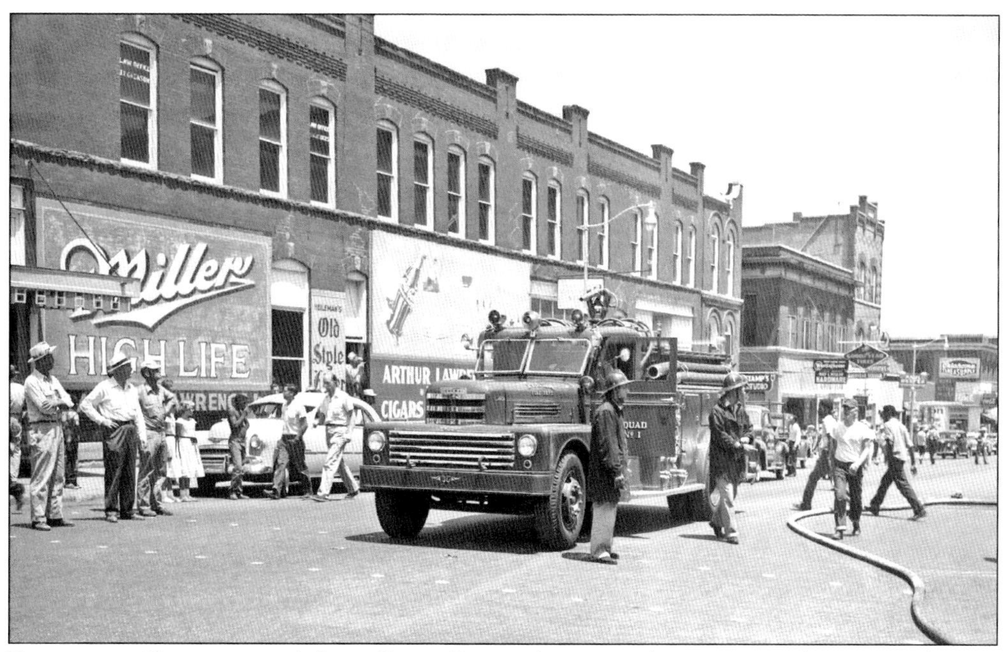

FIRE AT THE CROSSROADS. A fire call near Dewey Avenue and Main Street drew a crowd in the early 1950s. In the background is Lawrence Cigar Store, where the then-famous proclamation "Sapulpa—The Crossroads of America" is seen on the Coca-Cola sign painted on the exterior bricks. The nation's east–west and north–south highways Routes 66 and US 75 met here.

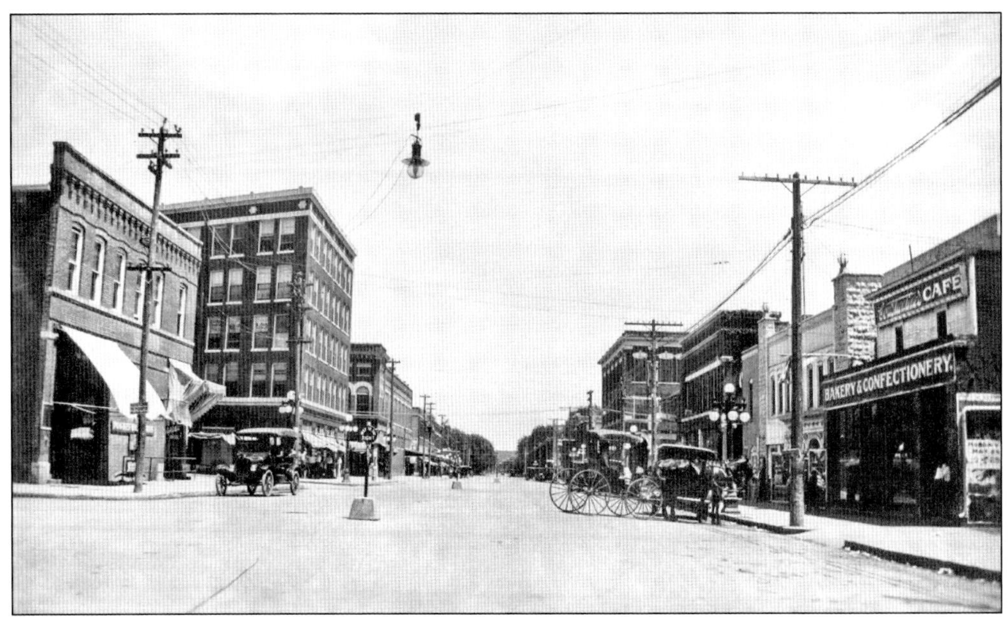

Horse or Horseless? There was still a preference for horse and buggy in Sapulpa in the teens and beyond, while some chose to give the horseless carriage a try. Soon, the Ford Model T—and later, the Model A and the competing Chevrolet—was all the rage.

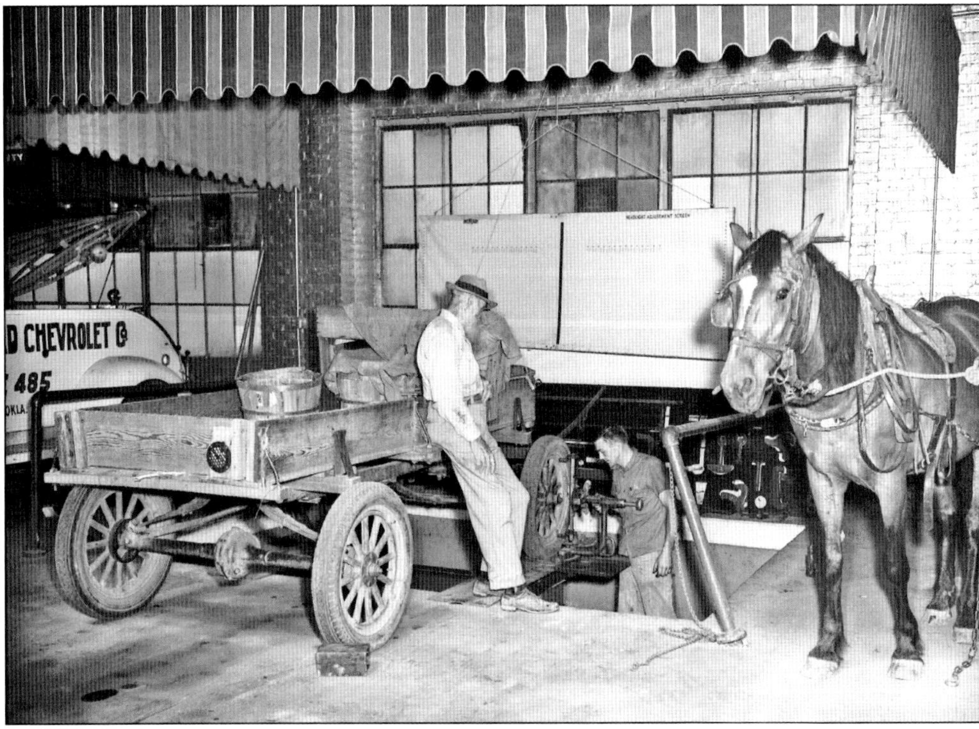

Wagon Mechanic. Pete Belk was one of the young mechanics learning the trade at Standard Chevrolet in the 1950s. Working on the latest models was cool, but from time to time, one had to be "old school" and pack or replace wheel bearings on a wooden-spoked wagon. The older, unidentified gentleman enjoys the conversation as the horse waits patiently.

Rather Choice Parking. This photograph, taken in downtown Sapulpa, shows transportation in transition and gives real meaning to the phrase "plug the meter," as an old horse and wagon utilizes a metered space. Parking meters were invented in Oklahoma by a newspaper reporter and first placed in Oklahoma City in 1935.

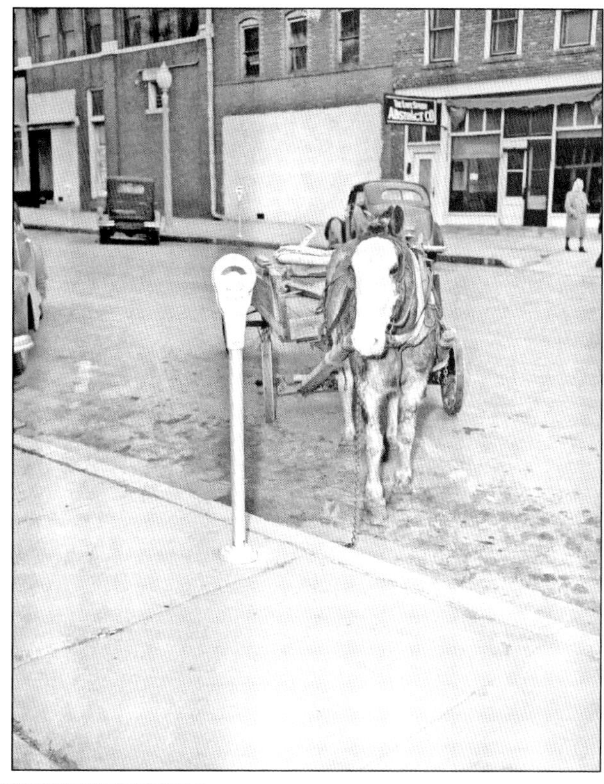

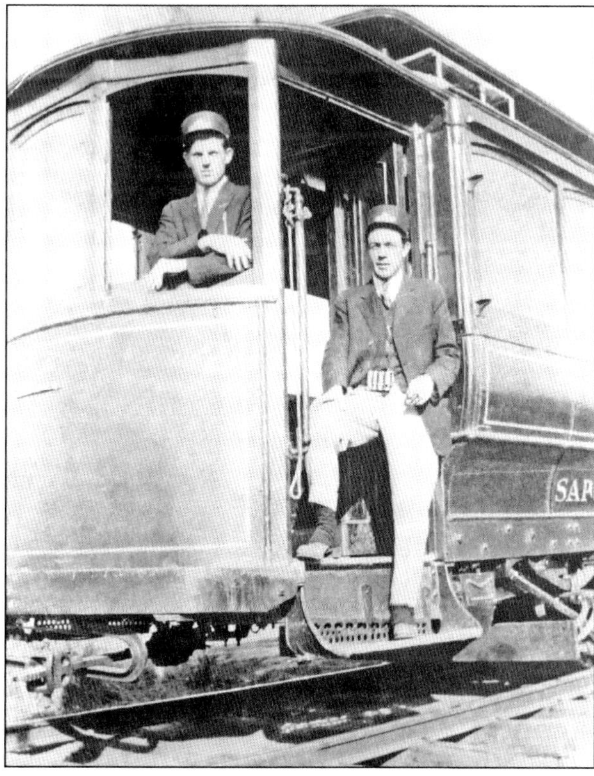

Happy Trolley Operators. In the 1920s, the Sapulpa Interurban Trolley system had a fleet of electric streetcars running all over town as well as to Tulsa, Kiefer, and Mounds. Birney Safety Cars like this one could be operated by one person, but two happy conductor/operators made an ideal crew. Trollies did not turn around. Drivers simply switched trolley poles and took the control handle to the box on the other end of trolley while passengers flipped seats to face the other direction.

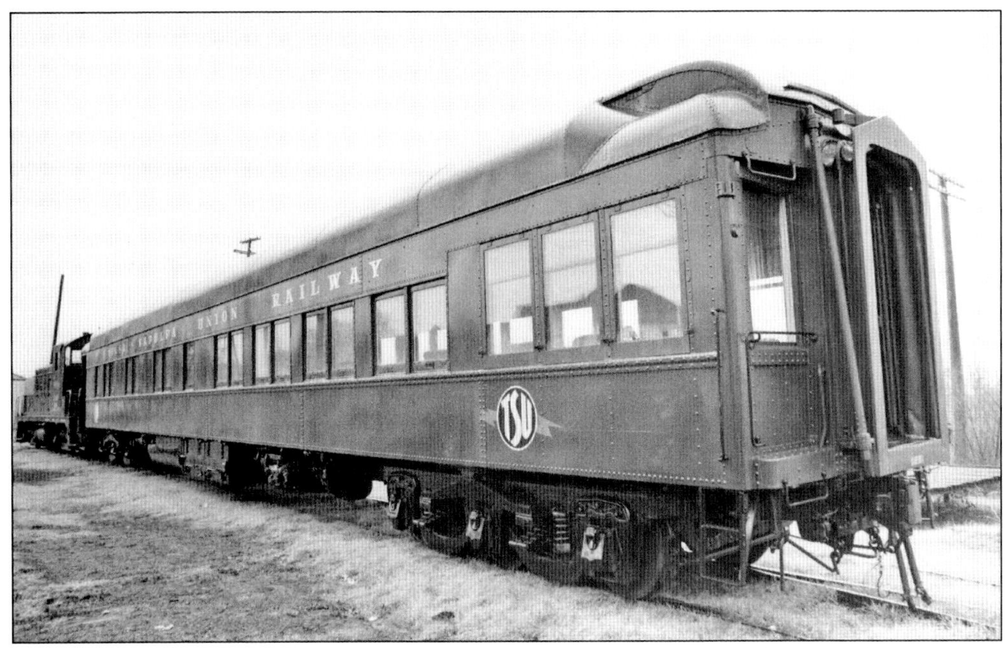

The TSU *Murray Hill*. Before the days of private jets to help make business deals happen, corporations acquired their own private railway business cars. That was not a difficult feat for Sapulpa's Collins family, which not only owned Liberty Glass but also the Tulsa-Sapulpa Union (TSU) Railway. The *Murray Hill* could be added to the make-up of a train or pulled by its own private locomotive. The car was plush, with splendid upholstered privacy for its passengers. Such cars also were used for travel and entertainment. Today, the car is preserved at a railroad park and tourist stop in West Tulsa along Route 66.

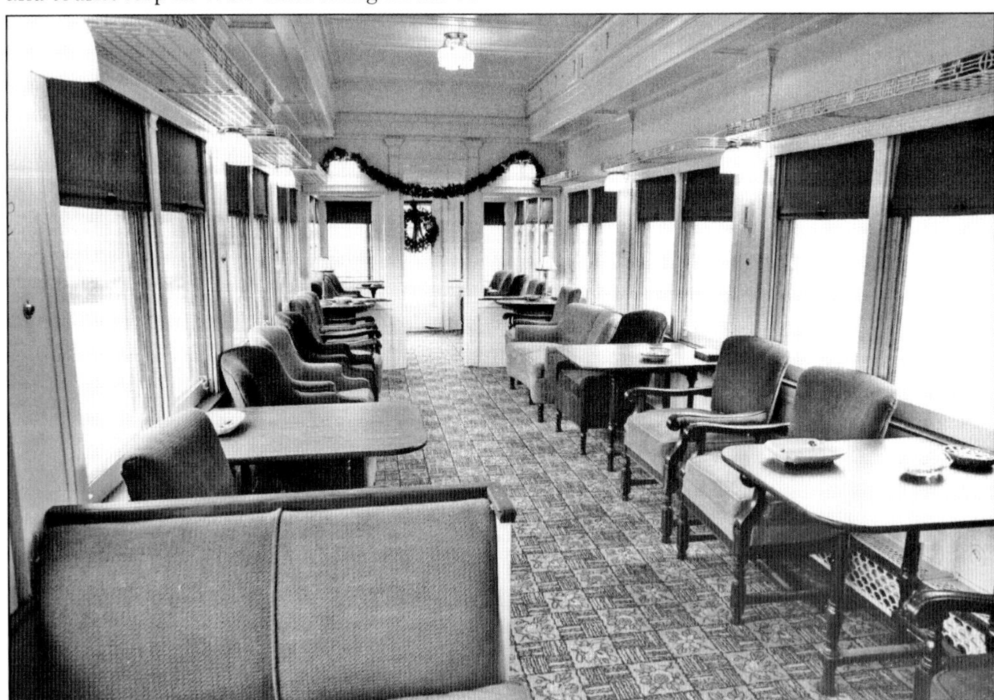

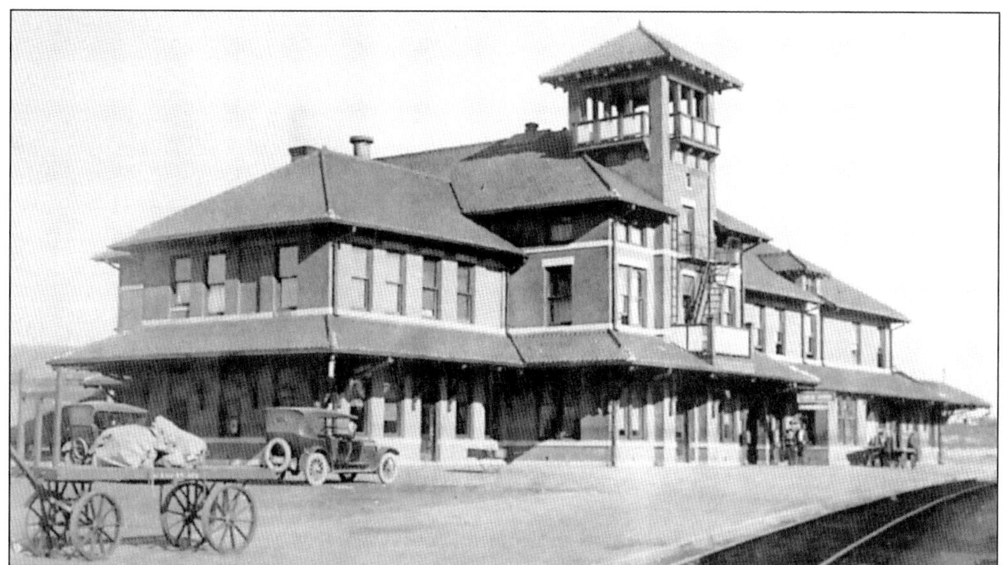

Frisco Depot and Harvey House. The beautiful Frisco Railroad Depot and Harvey House restaurant building was constructed in the spring of 1907 between the two Frisco tracks near the 700 block of East Hobson Avenue. Fred Harvey opened restaurants in many railroad towns, and Sapulpa had one of the finest dining houses west of St. Louis, Missouri. Besides the train passengers, locals and those from across the area came to eat at the Harvey House. It closed in 1930, and the whole structure was razed in 1963. Before its move to Tulsa, Frisco had made Sapulpa a division point. The yards contained a roundhouse and 16 stalls for repairs of locomotives.

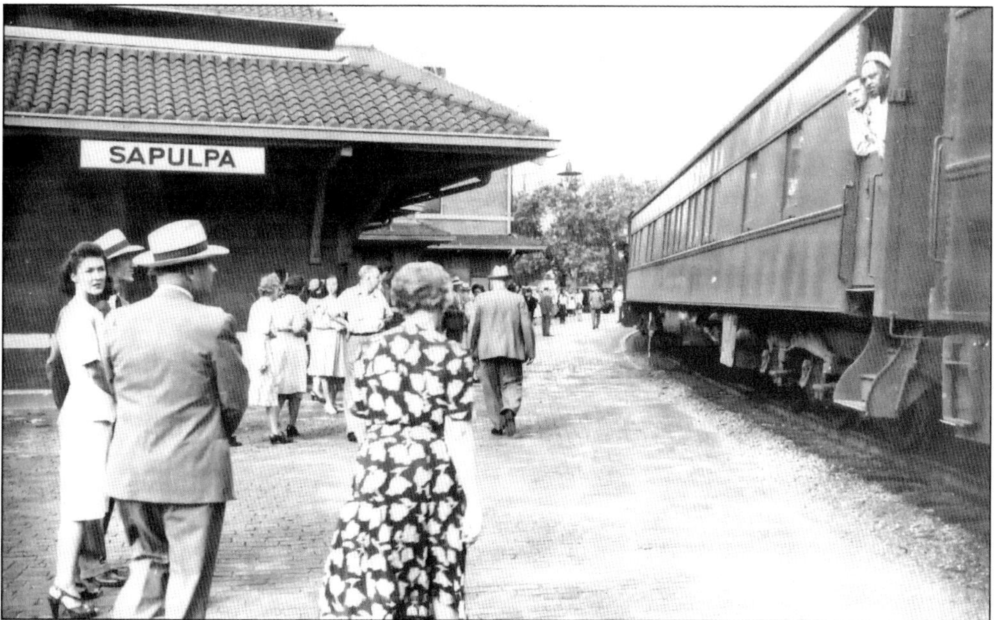

Last Passengers "All Aboard!" In recent years, there have been several excursions and lots of talk about revival of passenger trains between Tulsa and Oklahoma City, with Sapulpa serving as a terminal on the Tulsa end. But for the most part, passenger trains began to wane in the 1940s and were gone in the 1960s. This c. 1950s photograph reflects the days of Sapulpa train travel. The last passenger train left Sapulpa in 1959.

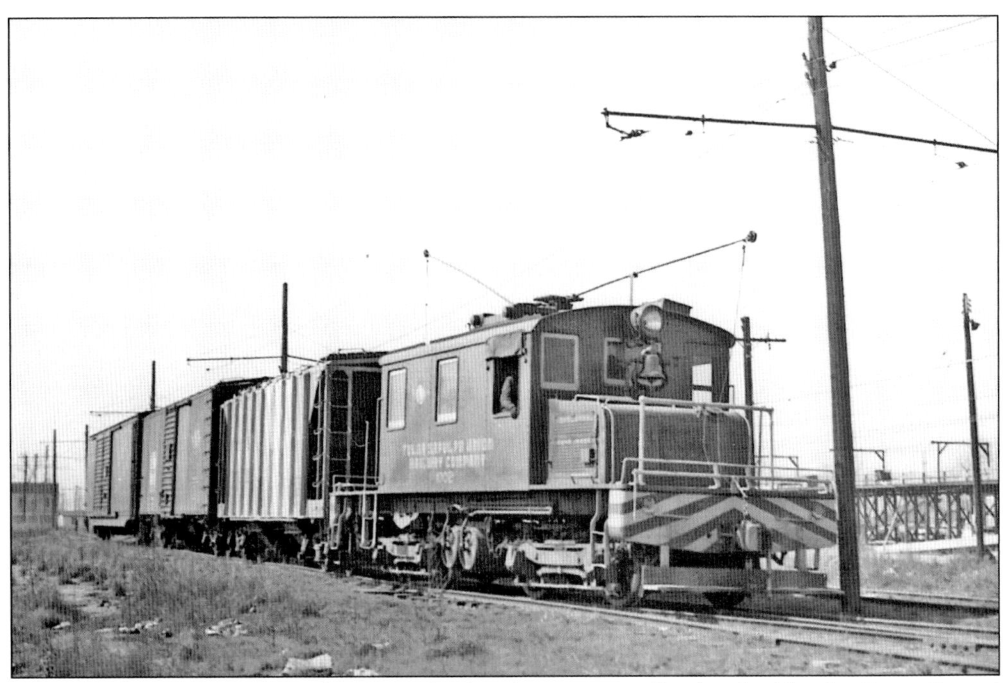

Sapulpa's Two Railroads. The Frisco Railroad was eventually absorbed by the Santa Fe and today is the BNSF (Burlington Northern Santa Fe). Numerous freight trains run through Sapulpa daily. But local and Tulsa-area manufacturers are also served by the Tulsa-Sapulpa Union short line. Pictured is one of TSU's early electric-powered engines.

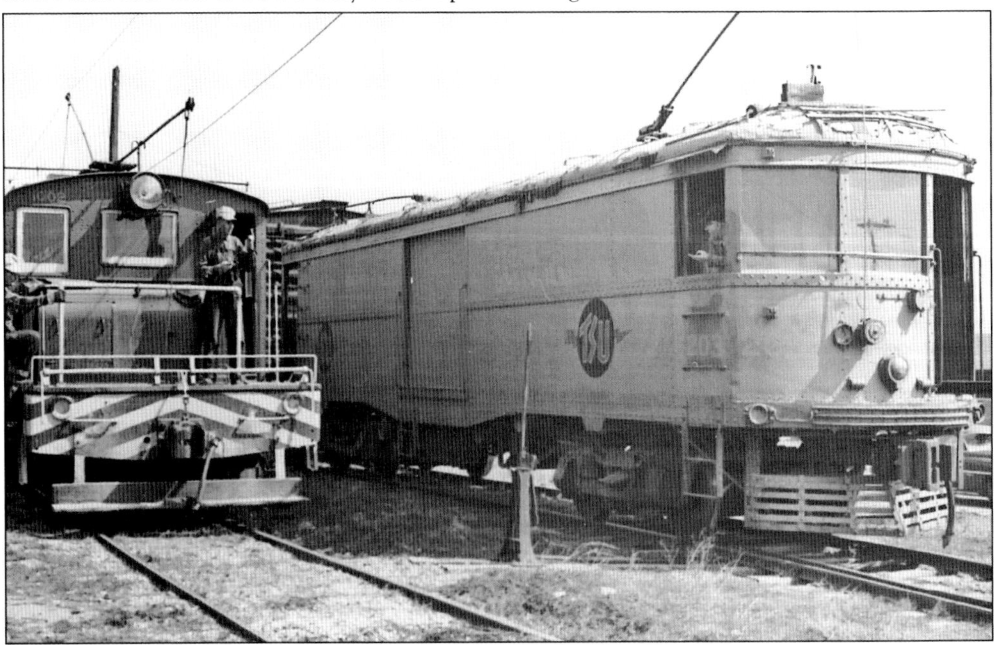

Electric Trains. After Tulsa-Sapulpa Union Railway acquired the interurban trolley system, it converted from passenger service between Tulsa and Sapulpa to freight, but it continued to be powered from the overhead electric lines. TSU employees Ben (left) and Rodney Robbins are pictured here. The electric train generators today are diesel-fueled.

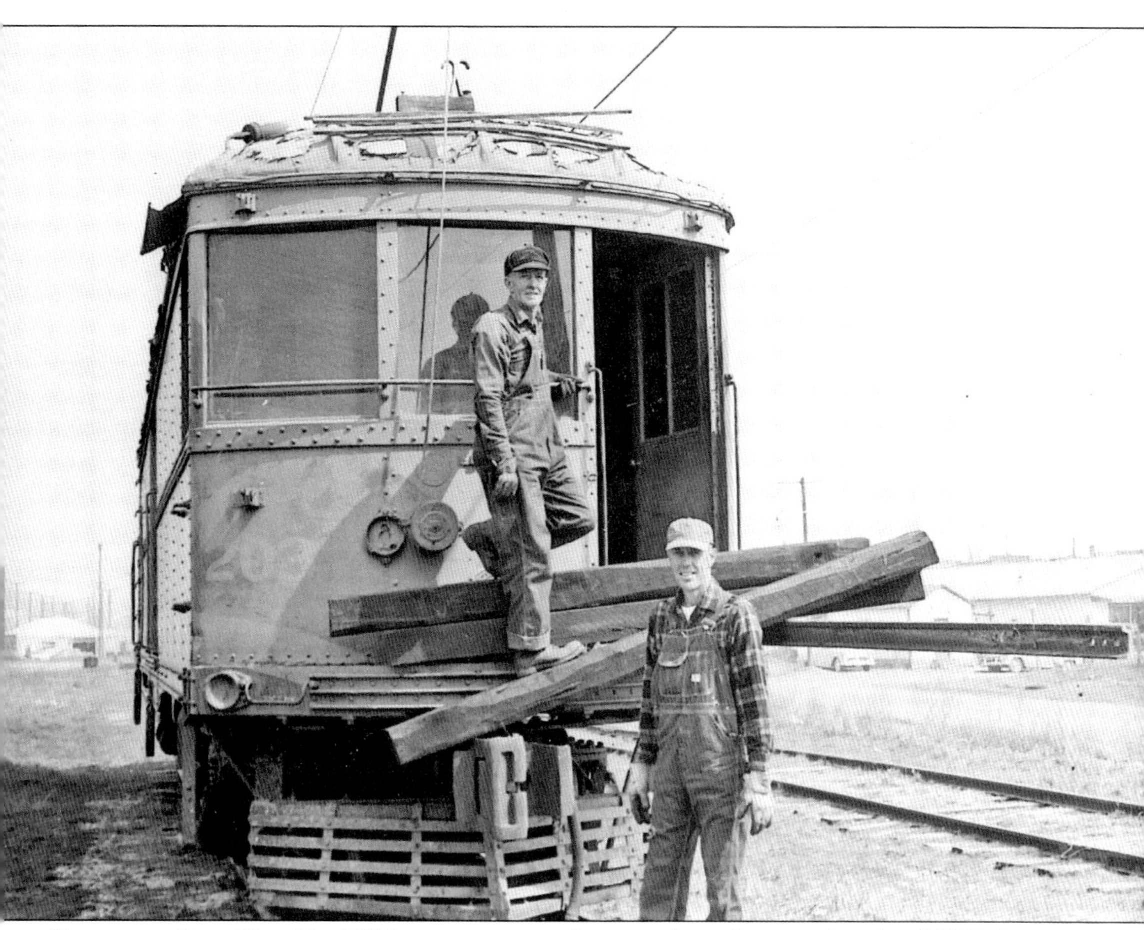

Replacing Some Ties. Two TSU section crew workers stop for a photograph in April 1957 along track just north of downtown Sapulpa as they replace railroad ties. TSU utilizes the same route of the old interurban trolley system between Sapulpa and Tulsa. The man on the car is unidentified. Standing on the ground is George Boaz, section foreman.

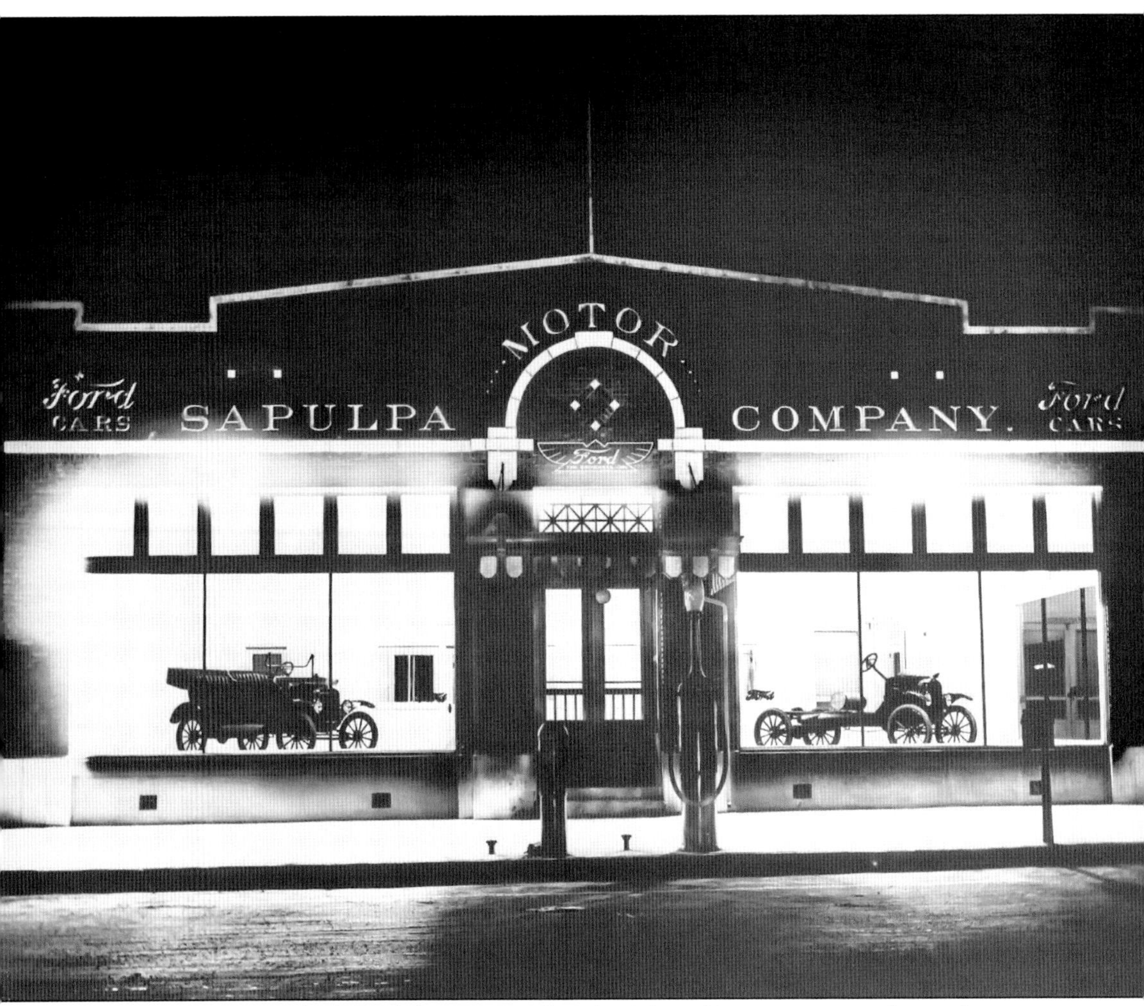

FORDS AT NIGHT. The lighted showroom at Sapulpa Motor Company was on the southwest corner of Main Street and Hobson Avenue in downtown Sapulpa. Seen here sometime between 1917 and 1922, it gave passersby a good view of offerings by Ford. The Sapulpa Motor Company, opened by Stanley Leachman in 1917, was the first Ford dealership in Sapulpa. Features of the 1915 building on the southwest corner of Main and Hobson included tracks and pulleys to assemble the Model T bodies to the chassis. The early Fords were shipped to Sapulpa on the nearby Frisco rails and assembled in the plant.

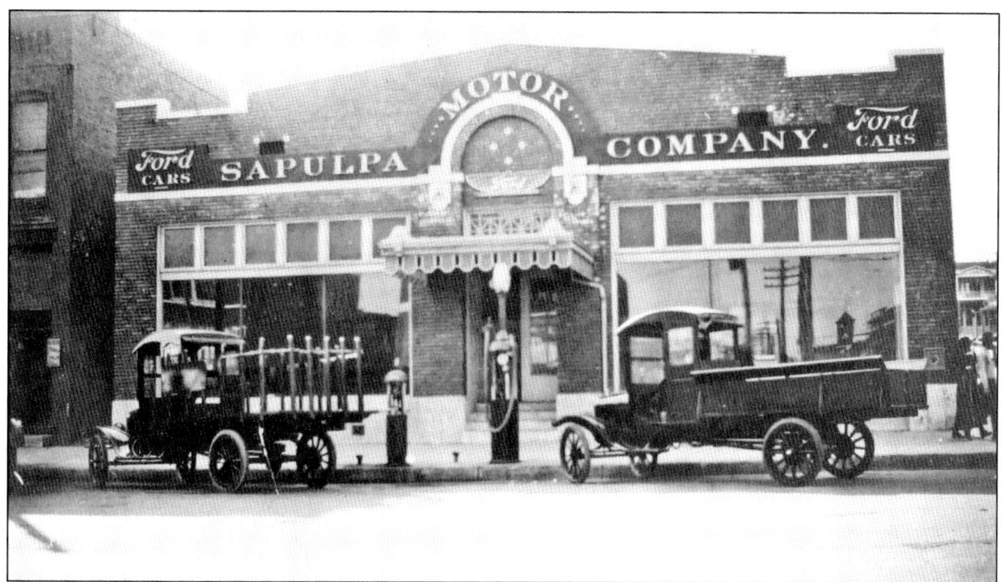

Ready to Roll. Ford trucks parked in front of the showroom were gassed up and ready to be driven off the lot. Today, the building is home to Gasoline Alley, which markets replica gas pumps like those seen here, along with accessories and collector oil cans.

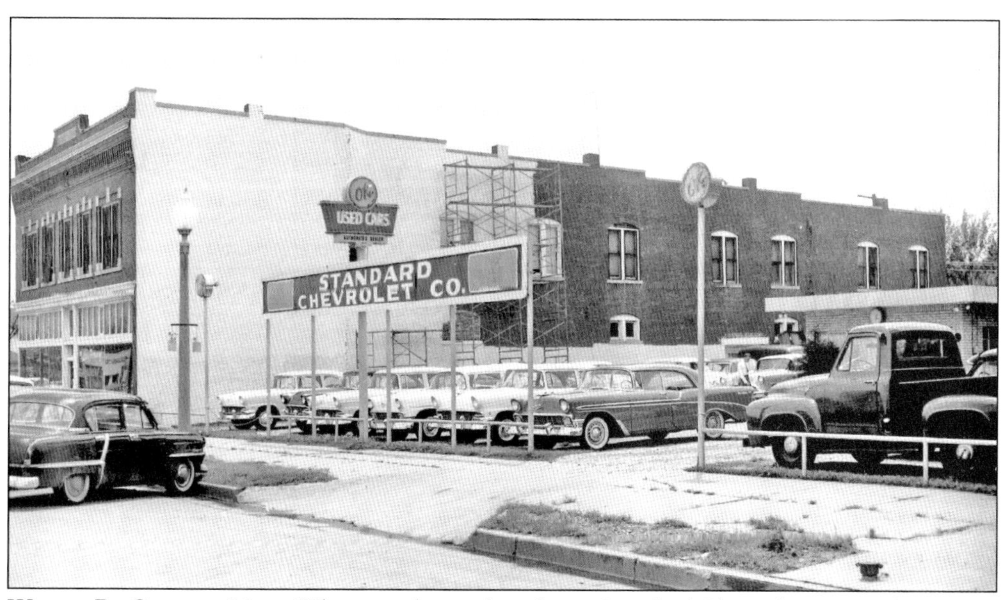

Would-Be Classics Now. What was the used car lot at Standard Chevrolet on Sapulpa's Main Street in the mid-1950s would be a classic car show today. These year models of Chevrolets, Fords, and pickups are still popular, as evidenced at the town's annual Route 66 Blowout that attracts thousands.

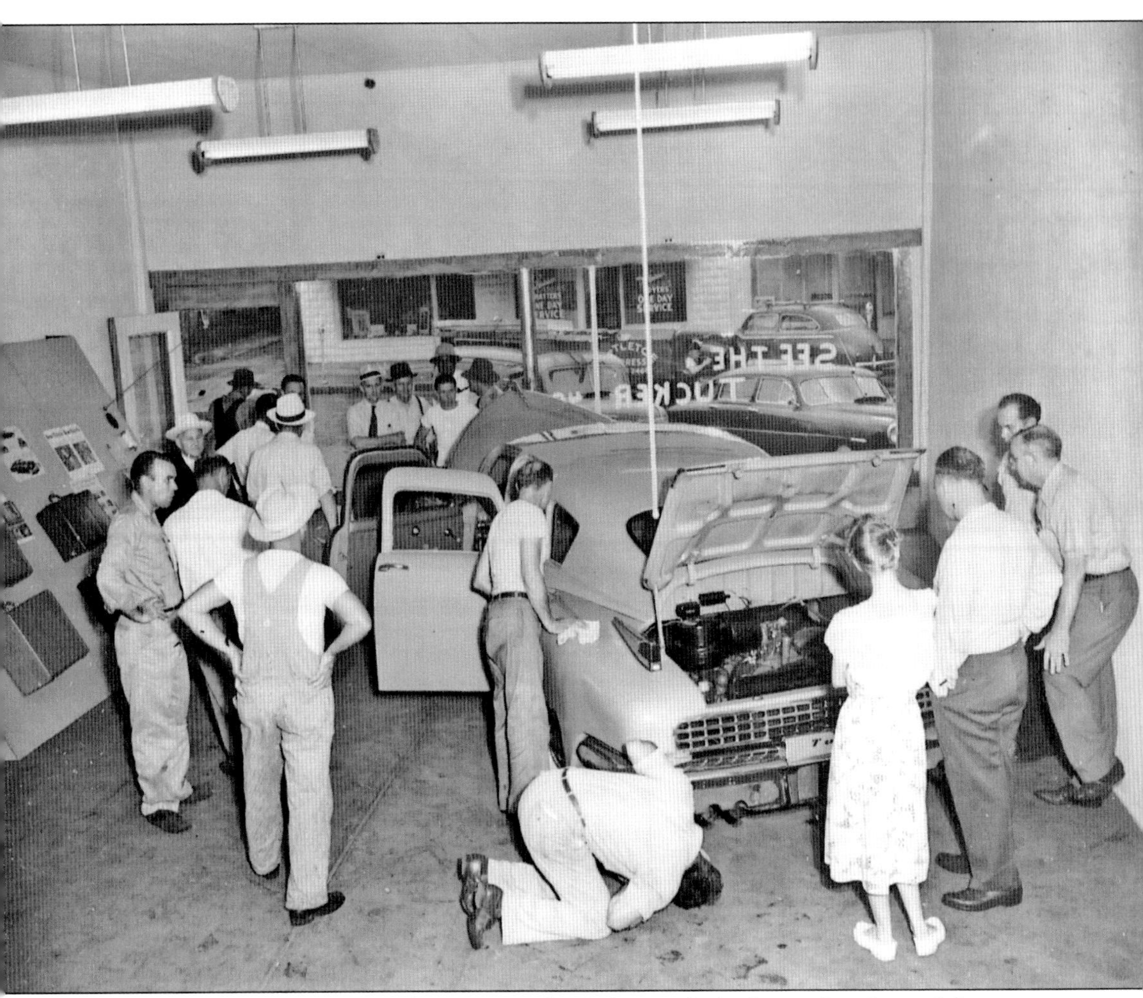

TUCKER AUTOMOBILE TOUR. The prospect of a Tucker car dealership in Sapulpa and the innovative post–World War II car itself attracted a crowd at the Collier Agency at 18 South Park Street in 1948. There were only 51 Tuckers made. Chapman Motor Company was in line to be a dealer, but Tucker financing did not jell, and the company halted. This building later became the Harmony-Woodruff printing plant.

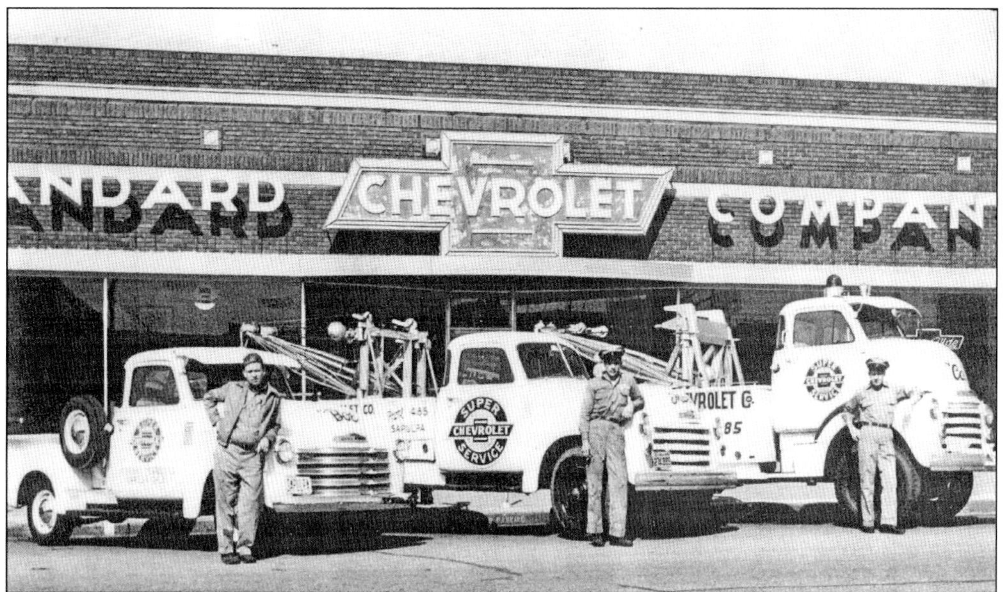

Wrecker Operators. The roads were busy and the cars were getting faster in 1951. These three local wrecker operators with Standard Chevrolet, from left to right, Joy Bacon, Pete Belk, and Bob Wadle, stayed plenty busy. This building was home to various car dealerships and then tire stores.

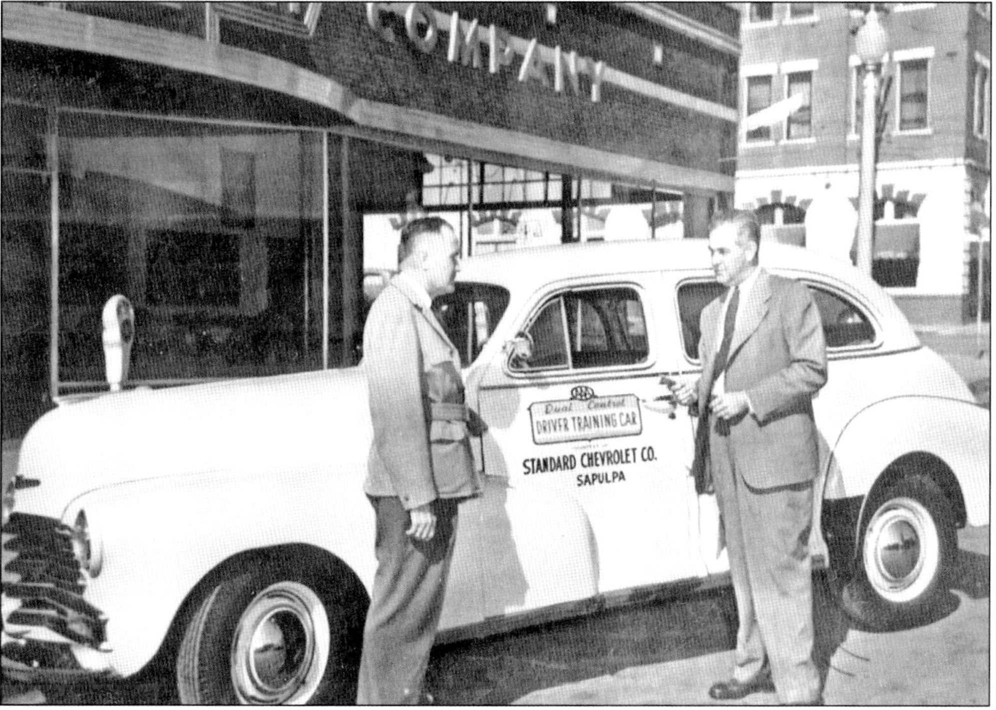

Learn to Drive First. This "Driver Training Car," seen around 1948, may have been a first for Sapulpa. It was supplied by Standard Chevrolet of Sapulpa when the dealership was at 100 South Main Street. Salesman Fred Cowden is shown presenting the keys to the instructor or school official. Earl Berryhill was owner of the agency, which later would be turned over to son-in-law John Bingman.

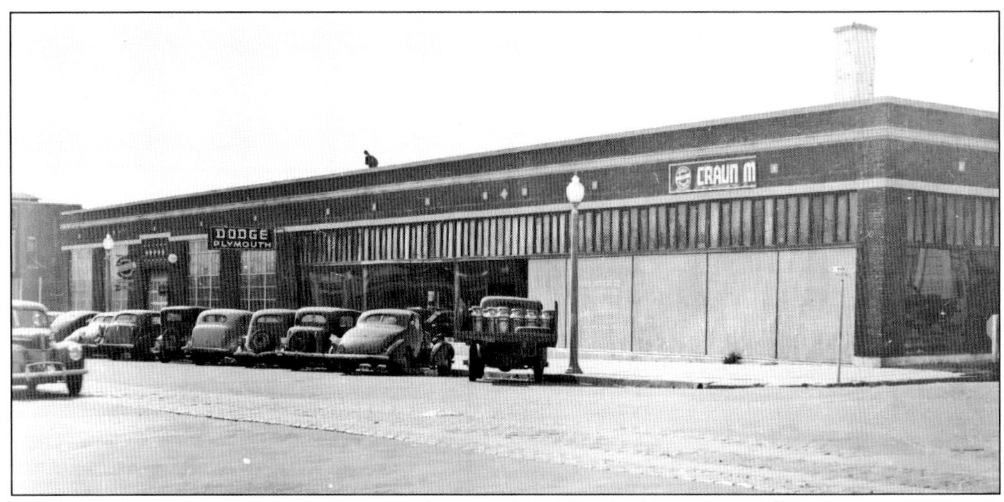

SAME BUILDING, DIFFERENT DEALERS. What was first a Ford sales and assembly plant at 100 South Main Street became a Dodge-Plymouth agency, followed by Standard Chevrolet. This c. 1940s photograph shows a nice assortment of cars and a milk truck parked in front of the Craun Motor Company. Other dealerships would take up residence just across the street.

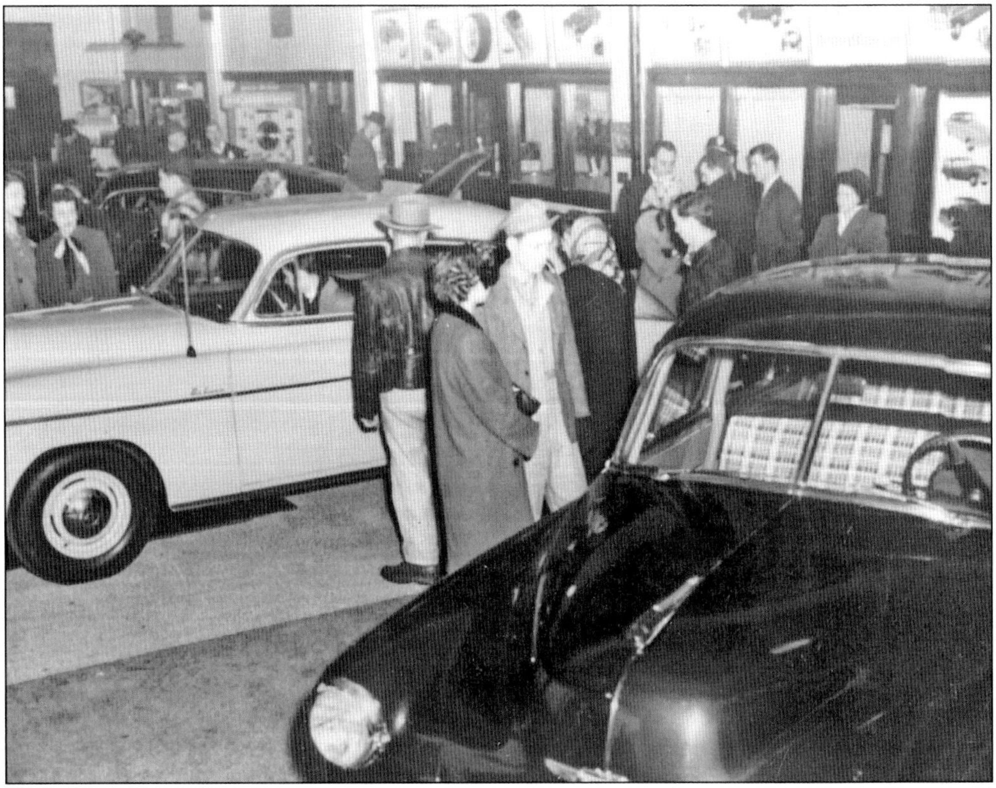

SHOWING NEW CHEVROLETS. When Standard Chevrolet occupied the building at 100 South Main Street, the city had apparently installed the recently Oklahoma-invented parking meter to help with retail parking space. On the inside, people come to the showroom to see the new 1951 Chevrolets. The plaid seat covers may have been installed to protect the newness of the car until it was sold or custom ordered by buyer.

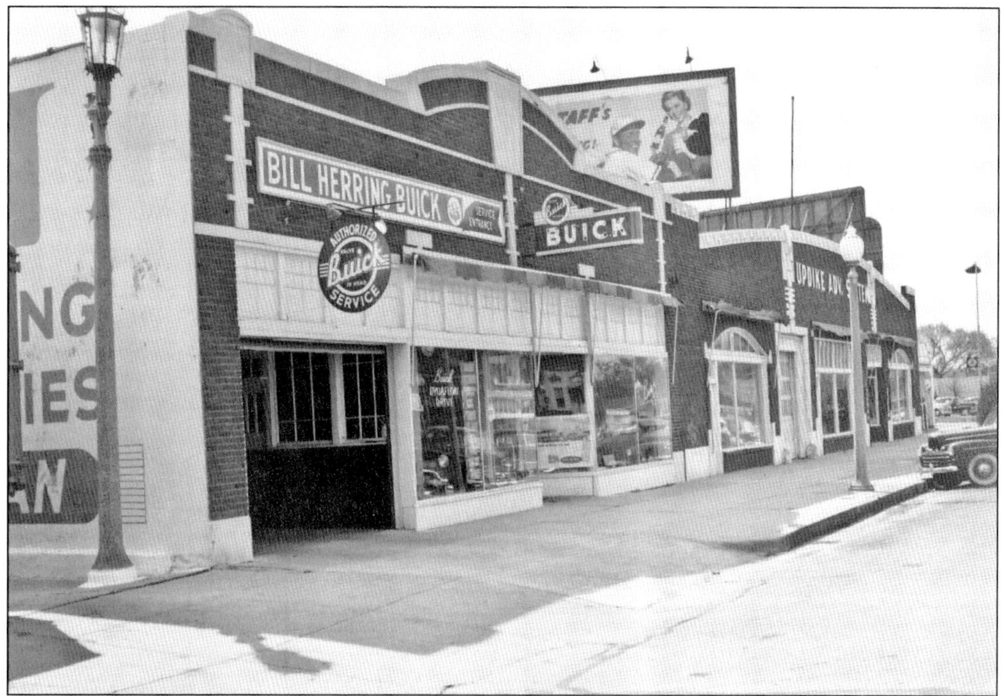

Town of Car Dealers. In the ever-changing makeup of car dealerships in Sapulpa in the late 1940s and early 1950s came the Hendrix Motor Company at 321 East Dewey Avenue, where First United Bank is today. Standard Chevrolet had earlier occupied this same site. Sapulpa-area motorists had a full range of car brands. Besides Chrysler, Dodge, and Plymouth, Ford, and Chevrolet, there were Buick-Pontiac-Oldsmobile, DeSoto, Nash, Studebaker, Packard-Willys, Kaiser-Frazier, and Henry J. One could buy everything from the Hudson to International trucks and jeeps. There were Lincolns, Cadillacs, Clippers, and Ramblers. Tucker did not make it, but there were a few other startups, including one at Tulsa named The Tulsa Four.

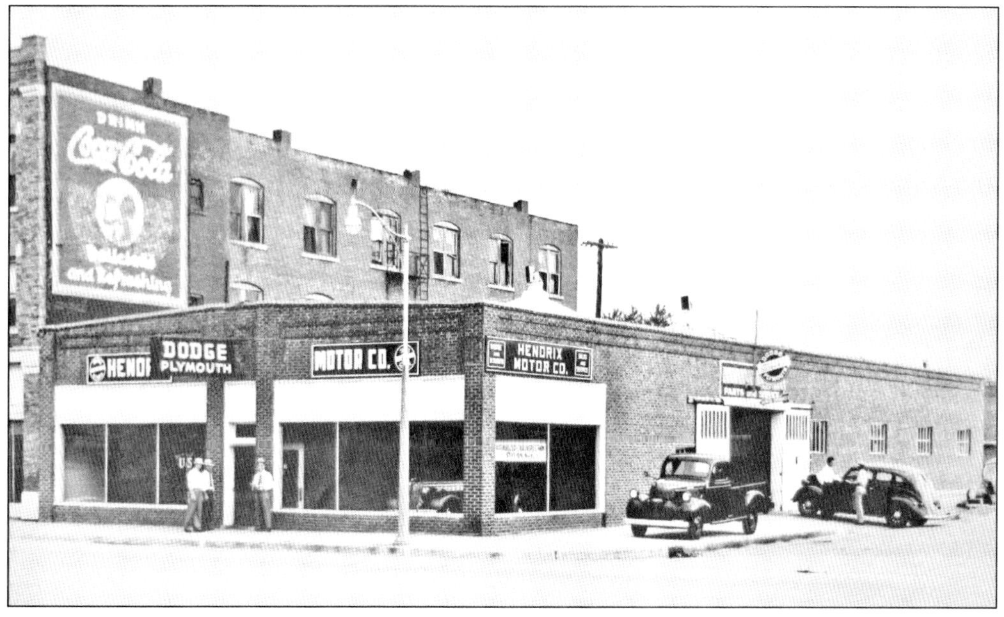

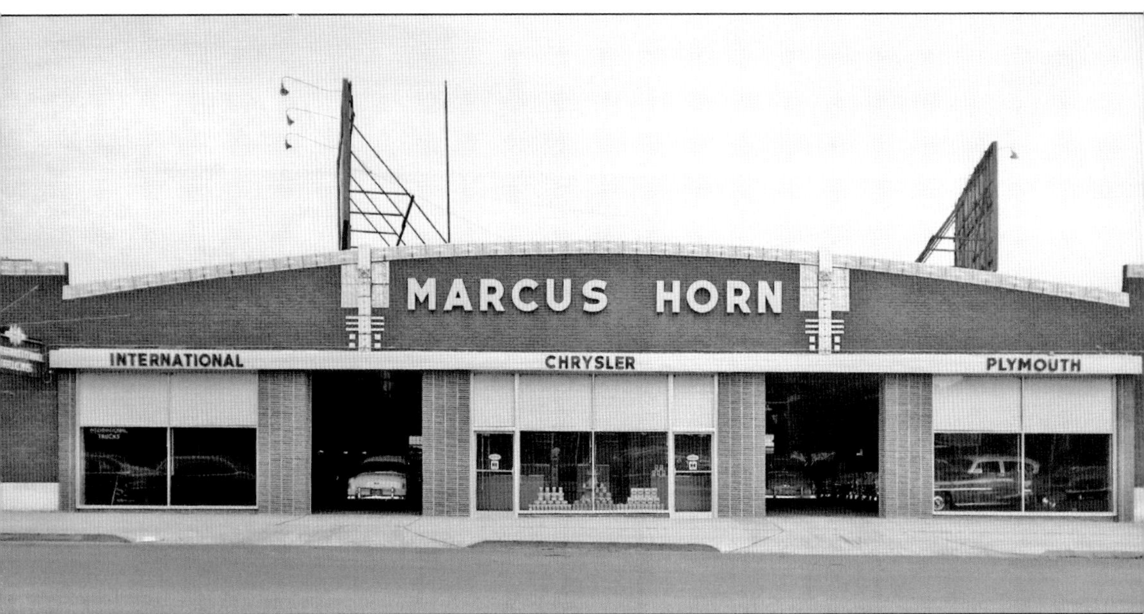

ROLLING INTO MODERN TIMES. Sapulpa's Marcus Horn Chrysler dealership at 115 South Main Street sharpened the new-car competition into the 1960s. More dealers and expanded car lots would soon occupy the burned Updike Advertising Agency building. Ironically, the Updikes had perished in an automobile accident north of Sapulpa.

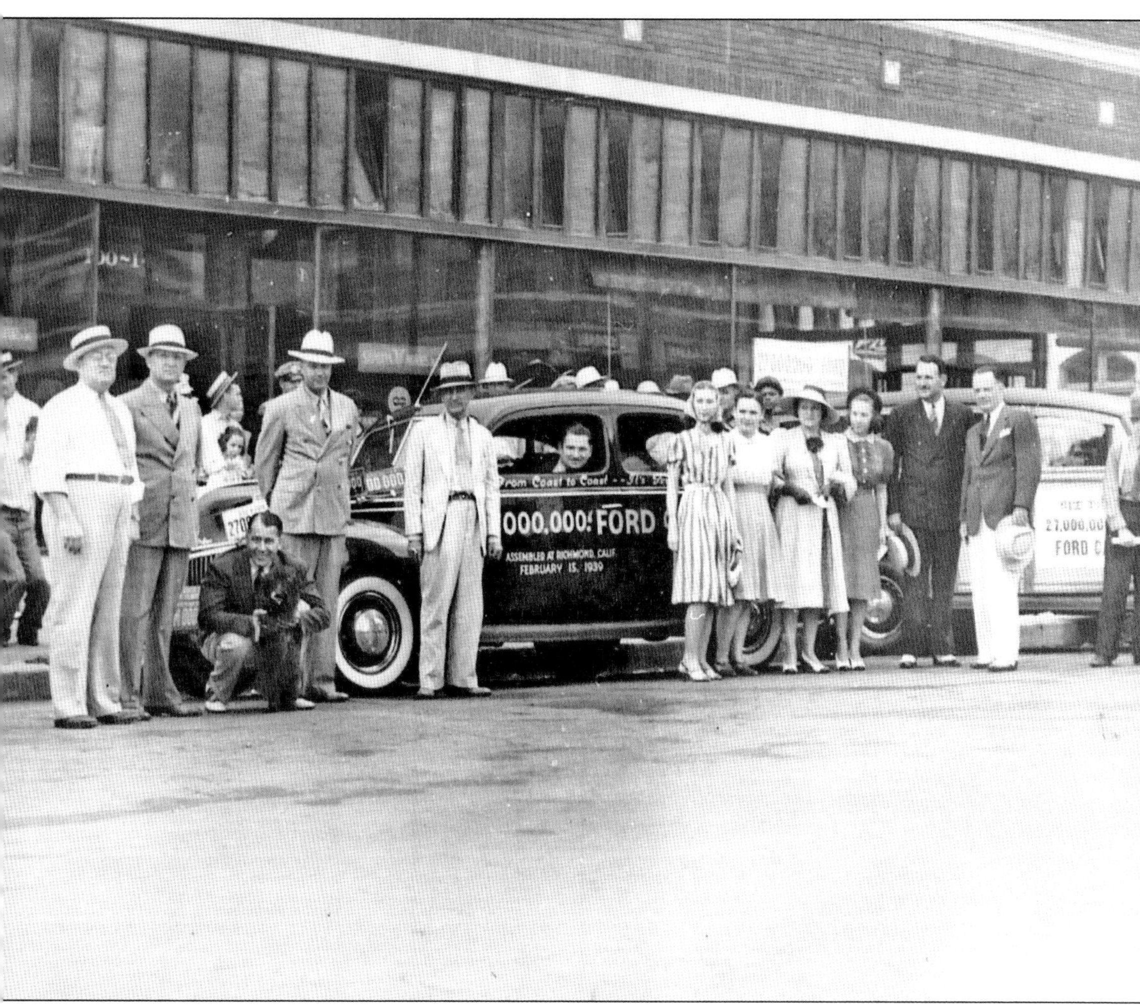

Twenty-Seven Million Fords. While Stanley Leachman owned the Ford agency in Sapulpa in 1939, Detroit produced the 27-millionth Ford. The sedan toured dealerships across the nation and was a photographic event when it came to Sapulpa. The State of Oklahoma issued a license plate numbered 27000000. Leachman (left) was joined by personnel and local businesspeople. Daughter Lucille Leachman stands to the right of the man in the driver's seat.

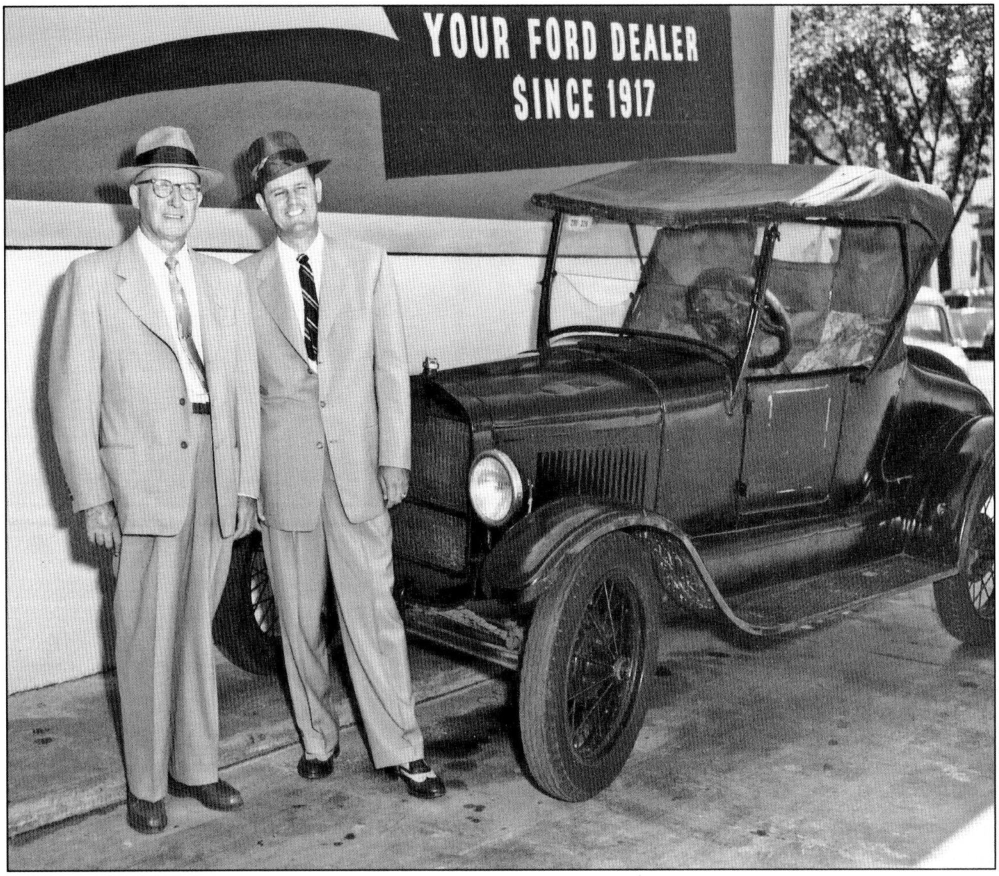

EVER-CHANGING AUTOMOBILE DEALERSHIPS. Pictured above, ford dealer Stanley Leachman (left) sold his dealership to Lee Eller (right) in 1955. As noted in phonebooks at the time, Sapulpa could boast of a dozen new automobile dealerships in the downtown area. There are none today. Eller sold his dealership in the 1960s to the Denton-Easterly agency, who would later move to the Turner Turnpike Gate north of Sapulpa. Currently, Sapulpa's only two new-car dealerships, Mark Allen (formerly Danny Beck) Chevrolet and Bob Hurley Ford, are on New Sapulpa Road (close to original Route 66 and Interstate 44) where Sapulpa and Tulsa join.

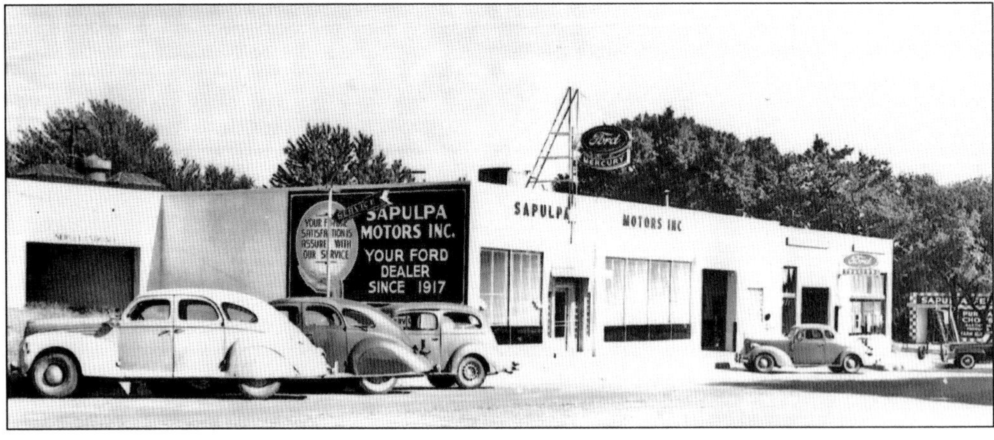

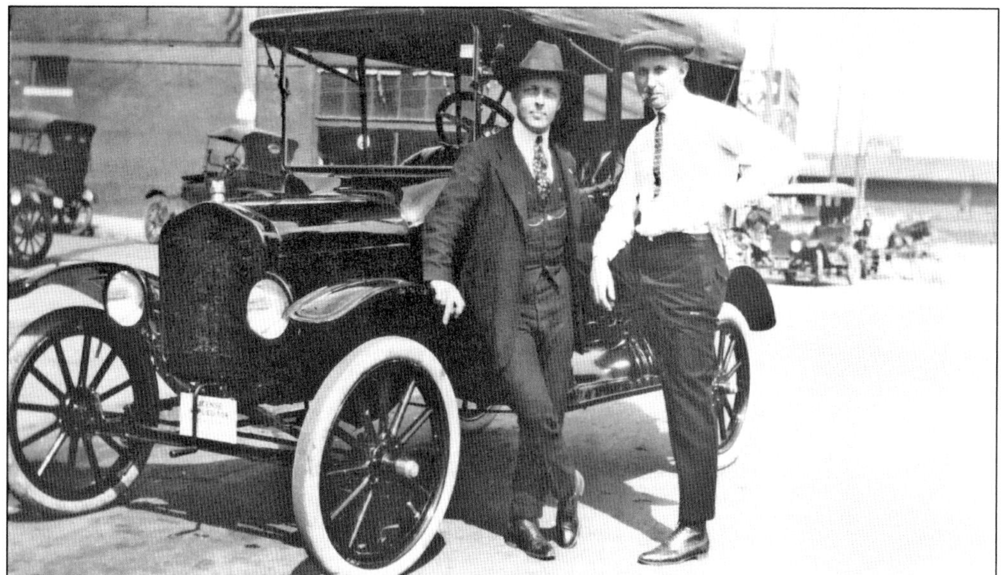

Automobile Salesmen. Early Sapulpa car salesmen dressed rather fine and, after a sale, might have celebrated by sharing a cigar they bought down on the corner. Competition was keen in downtown Sapulpa in the 1940s and 1950s, with at least a dozen or so dealerships vying for business.

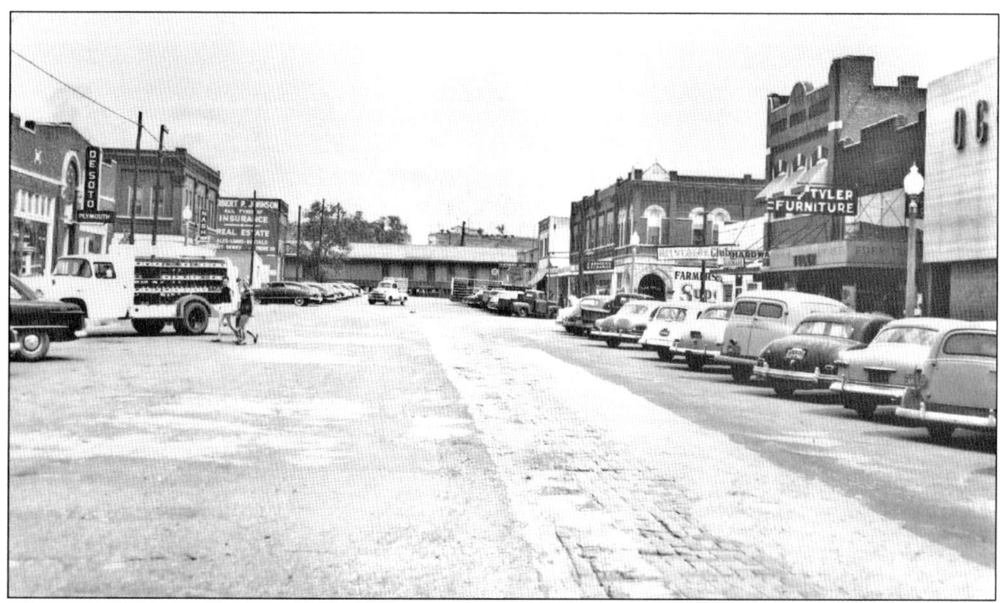

Where Main Street Ended. Here is a show-all picture that identifies Tyler Furniture when it was on Main Street and the old railroad freight station when it was at the end of Main Street. There was no Highway 97 going up the hill. That building, since moved to the west, is part of the Farmers' Feed complex. The photograph also shows the Ray Martin Motor Co. at 24 North Main Street, a DeSoto-Plymouth dealer, and Sapulpa Nash, at 100 North Main Street.

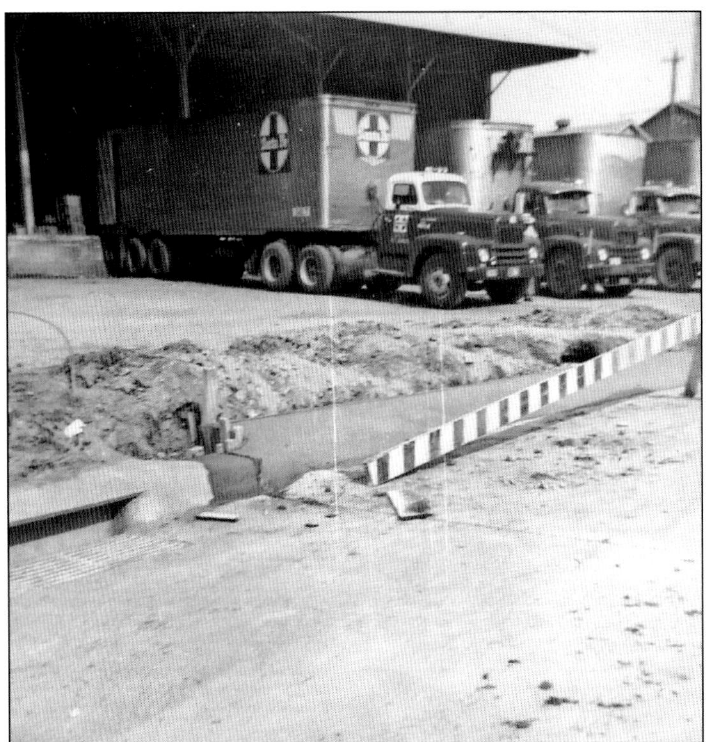

ROLLING STOCK. This photograph may have been taken to show some of the curb and gutter work being performed by the Sapulpa Street Department, but it also captured the Santa Fe trucks loading manufactured goods at a local plant. The term "rolling stock" had before been used when referencing trains. By the 1950s and advent of the highway system, 18-wheelers shared the load as well as the term. Today, many of the raw supplies still come in by train but leave by truck.

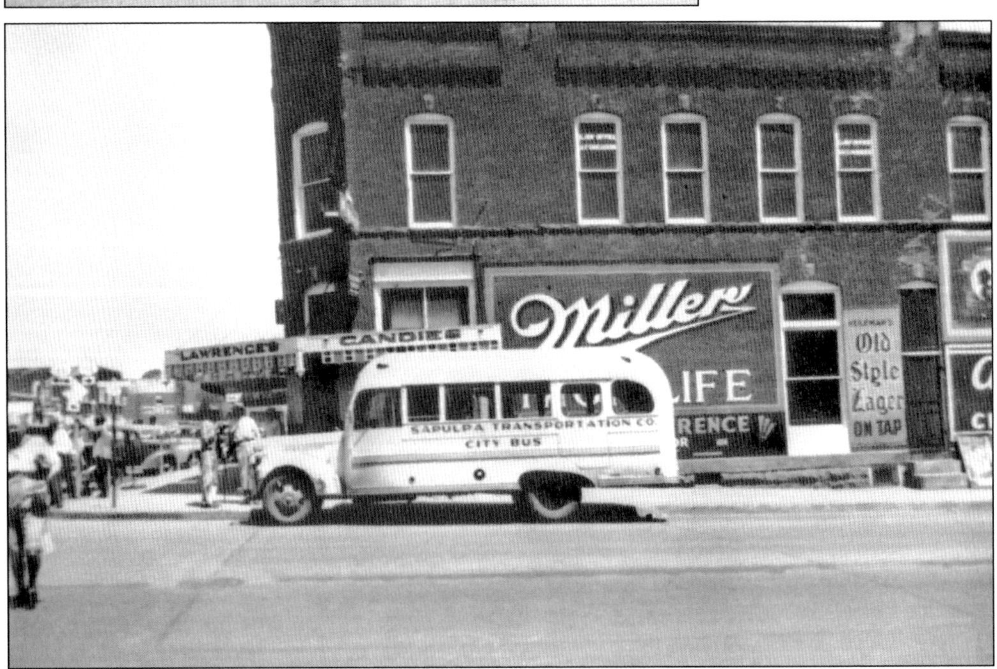

DAYS OF THE CITY BUS. Sapulpa's interurban trolley ceased operation in the early 1930s. It seems almost everyone had an automobile, and those who did not could always take Sapulpa Transportation Company's city bus. Like the trolley, buses ran between Sapulpa to Tulsa. There also was a bus station where the Greyhound stopped. The Turner Turnpike opened in 1953. Passenger trains ceased, and buses in town these days are of the tourist variety.

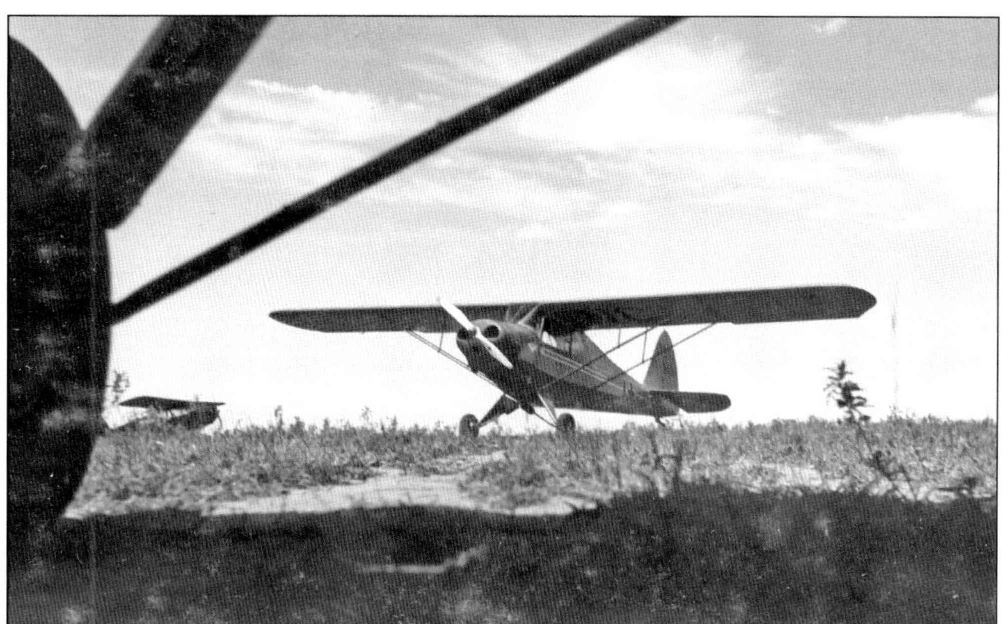

Sapulpa Had an Airport. Planes are shown in front of the hangar at the Sapulpa Airfield in the 1950s. The strip was on city property once dedicated for fairgrounds. It was north of Line Street and east of Brown Street in the Liberty School area, east of Liberty Glass. Some locals learned to fly and do mechanic work here. It became headquarters for several local pilots, like John Sawyer and Clyde Kirby, who lived nearby. Al Bradley of the historic Bradley Radiator Shop erected a hangar here for his taildragger. City leaders had less and less interest in developing the airport. It faded, and local pilots began using Tulsa's Riverside facility at nearby Jenks.

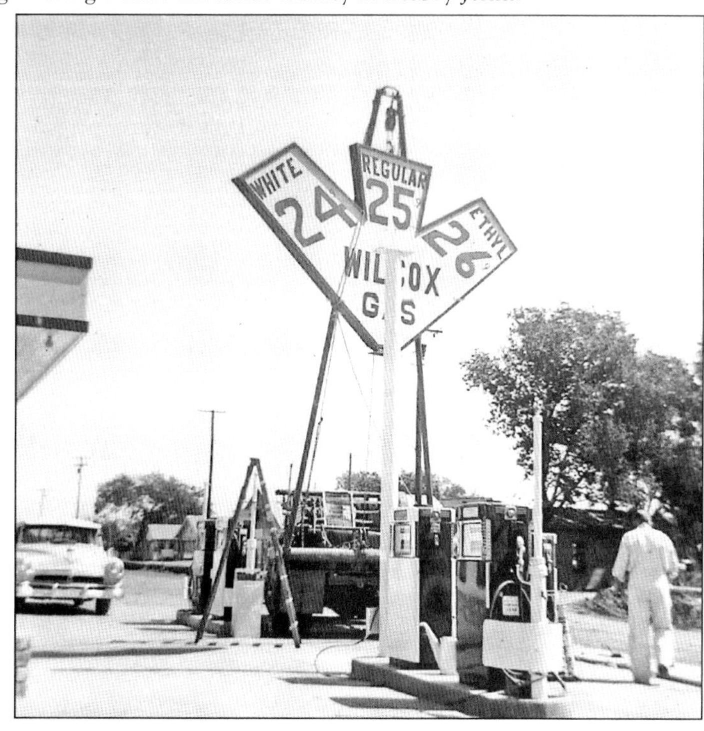

Sapulpa and Gas Prices in 1953. Advertising of gas prices and hoisting the signs higher to attract customers was most important in Sapulpa as more and more motorists took to the roads. The Turner Turnpike, a toll road connecting the state's two largest cities, Oklahoma City and Tulsa, opened in May 1953. The turnpike was named after Gov. Roy J. Turner, who along with *Sapulpa Herald Newspaper* editor R.P. Matthews pushed to build the toll road. Matthews would also run for governor.

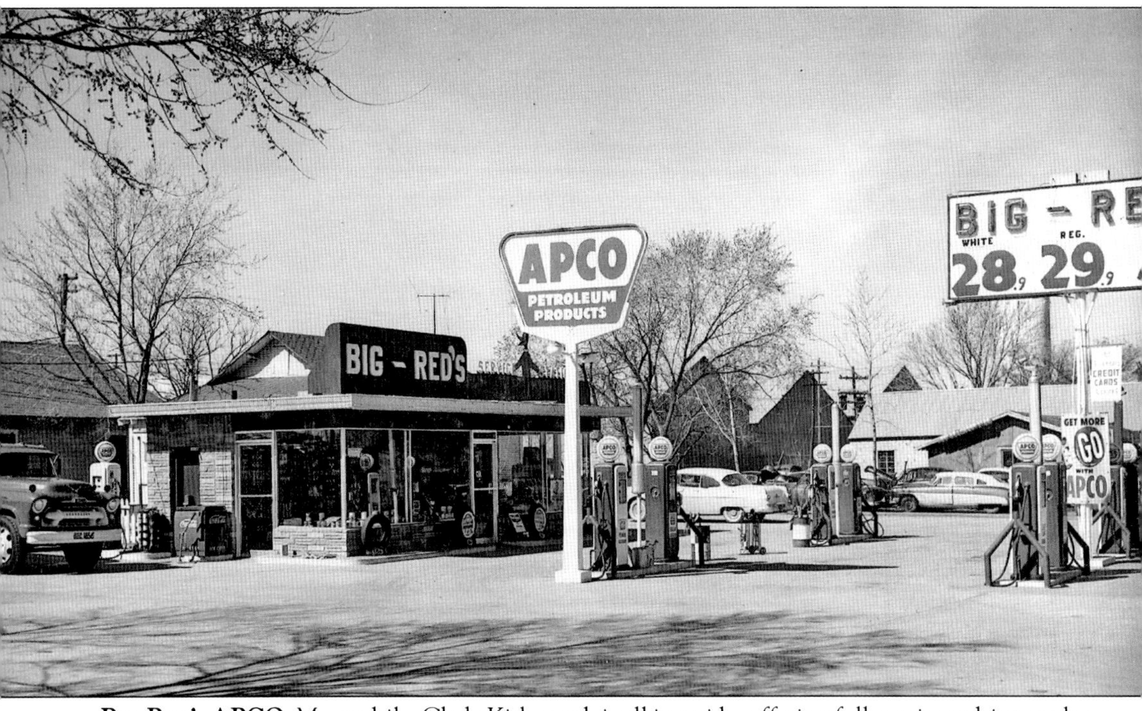

BIG-RED'S APCO. Meanwhile, Clyde Kirby took it all in stride, offering full service at his popular Big-Red's APCO on Mission Street, also known as Route 66, for those taking the turnpike or remaining on the Mother Road.

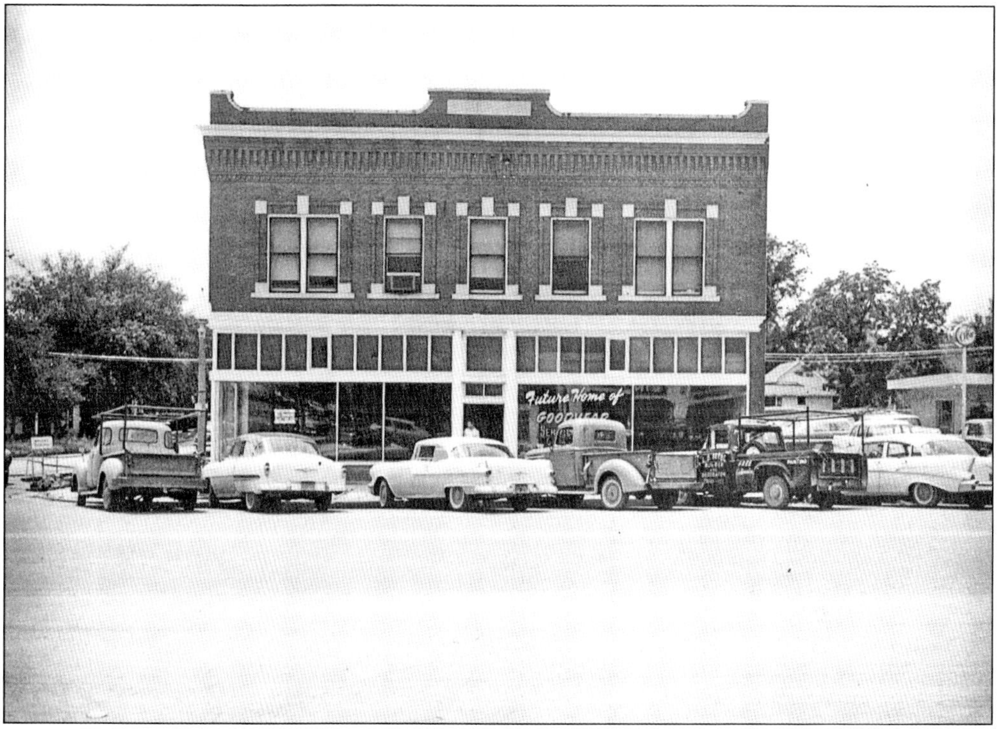

Where the Rubber Meets the Road. From the beginning, Sapulpa has been a "road" town, where automobiles and everything about them has been the main business on the main drag. Major brands like Firestone and this Goodyear retailer operated flourishing tire stores in Sapulpa, as did local men like Bob Davis. There also have been battery shops like the one operated out of the old Waite Phillips 66 Service Station on East Lee Avenue and those like O.K. Rubber Welders on East Dewey Avenue who could recap tires "within 24 hours." The phone number was rather easy to remember, as it was just two digits: "64." Also, take note of the width of those whitewalls back when.

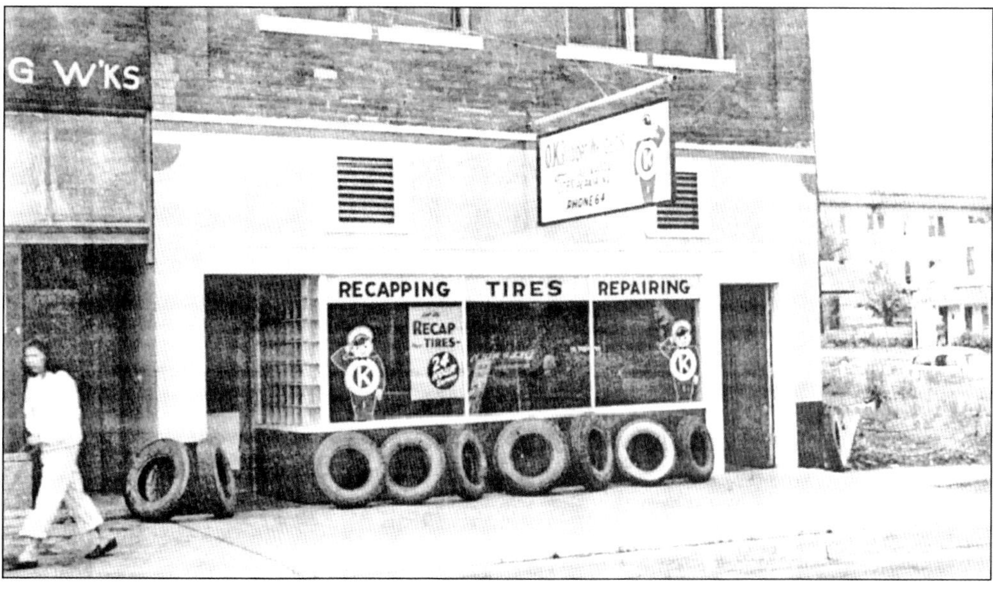

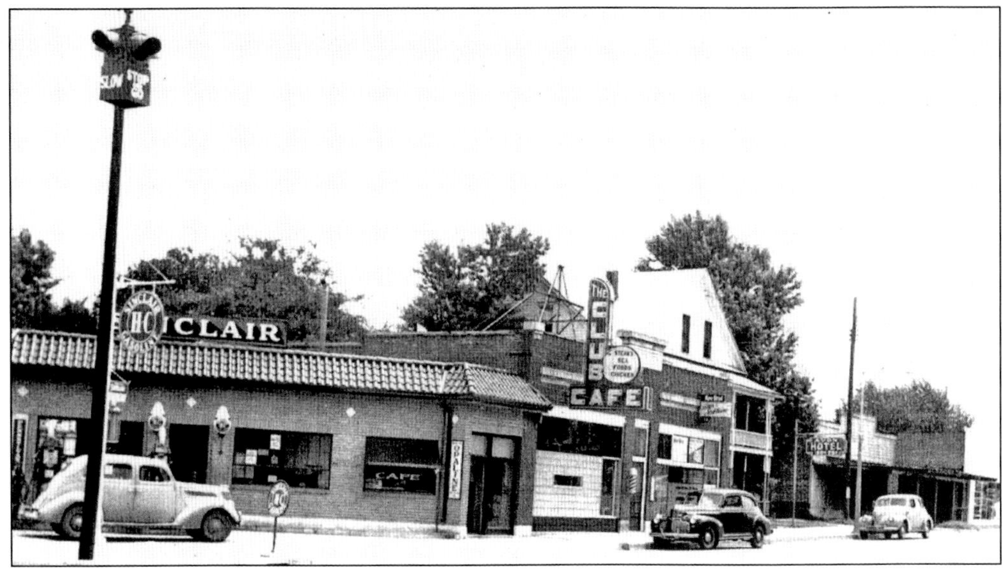

Ideal Tourist Stop. Among the big industries in Sapulpa in the 1930s through 1950s was travel and tourism. In the 1940s, an ideal stop would include a filling station, café, and hotel. Passenger rail service was declining, and travel by plane was on the horizon. Families, individuals, tourists, and salesmen traveled by automobile without GPS but with map in hand, as they read the signs along the way. Sometimes, "one stops" would appear as a strip mall or expanded service station, like this one on Mission Street (below), to include groceries, a meat and fish market, and a sit-down restaurant.

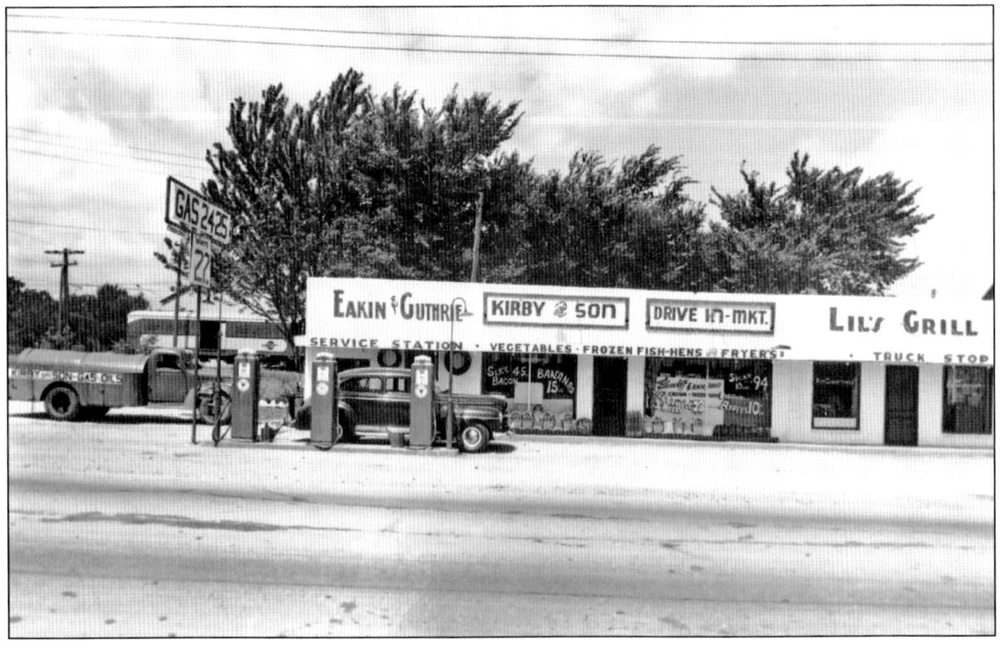

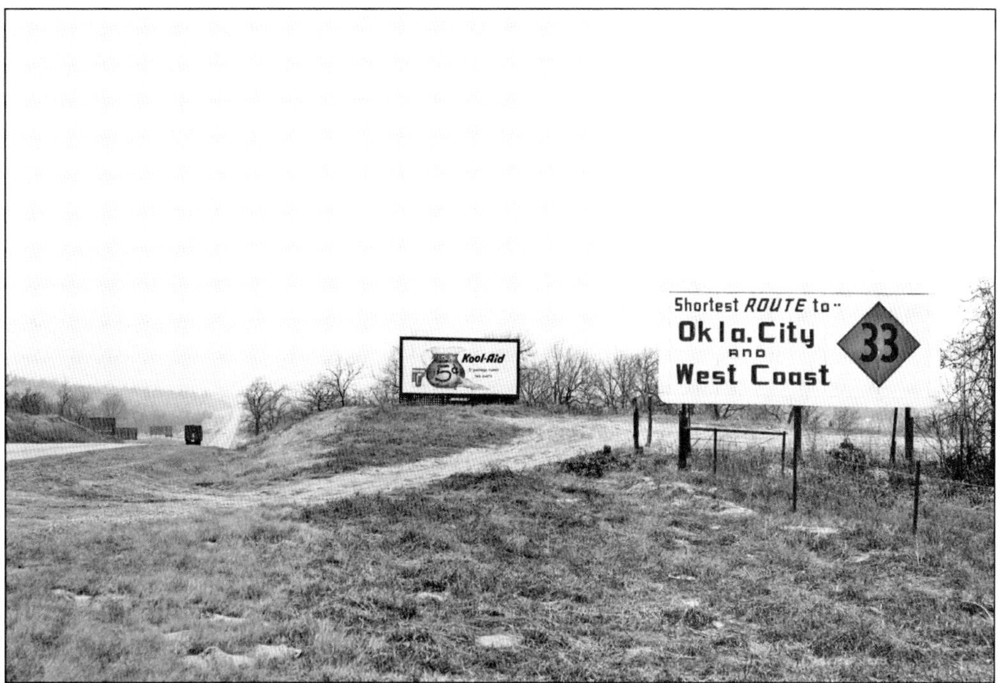

Then There Was Highway 33. Even today, Sapulpa markets itself as "most-connected" because of the major highways that come through town. Business associations had learned from the Route 66 phenomenon the value of promoting the route, on which their business was located. For instance, consider the wide-open Highway 33.

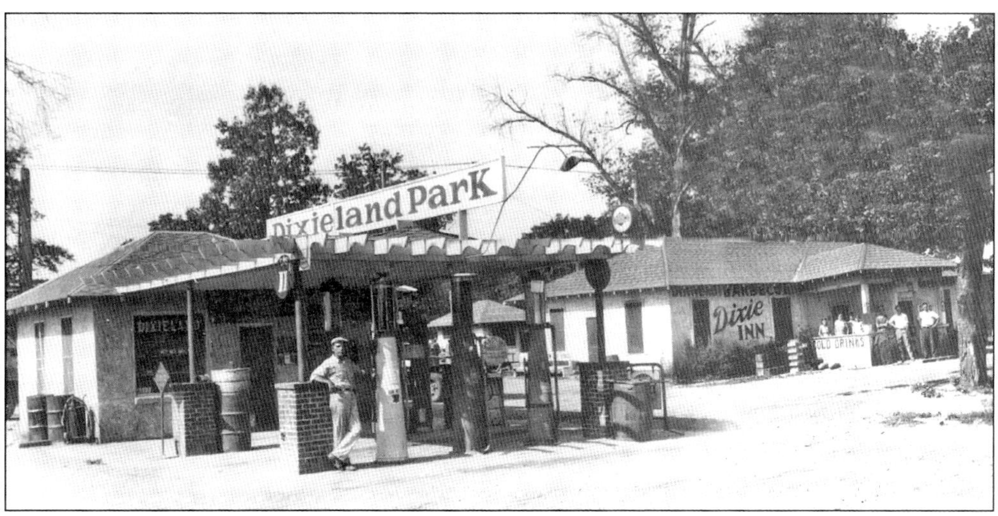

Mother Road Stop. Among the favorite places for Route 66 motorists to stop and fill up, eat a bite, maybe stay over a night or two, take a swim, and go roller skating was Dixieland Park, just west of downtown on the Mother Road. It was one of several motor courts in the Sapulpa area. It closed in the early 1950s, when a new US 66 was built and construction was underway on the Turner Turnpike.

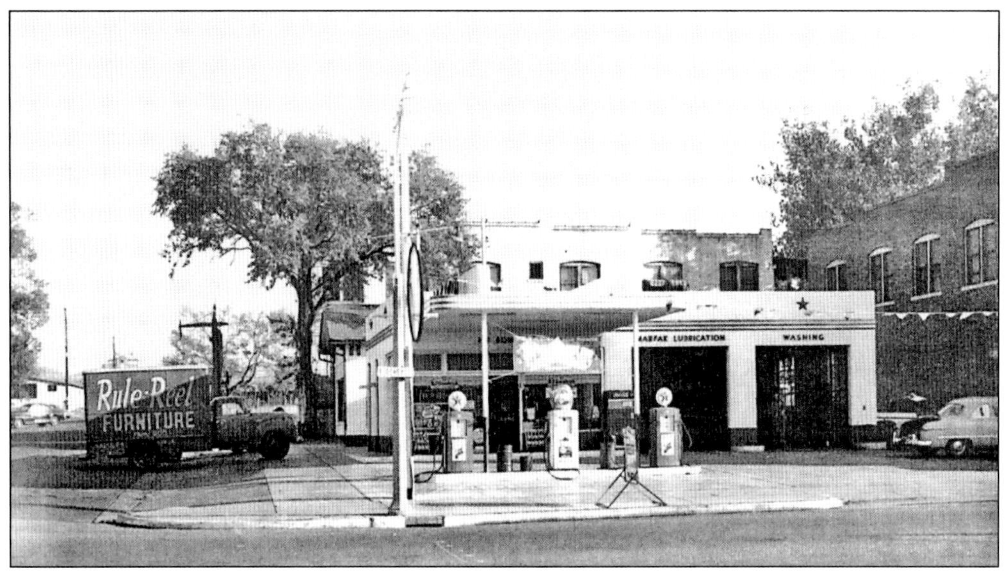

Corner Filling Stations, Convenience Stores. One may still find a gas station where tires can be aired up, windshields washed, and tanks filled, with gas and oil checked, but one has to do it all themselves. The "selfie" generation may not believe this, but there was a time in Sapulpa—it seems like on every second corner along the main drag—when "service station" meant just that. If they were not waiting as one drove up, they would be there before one could get the key turned off to take care of business while showing a whole lot of friendliness. Inside, one could get a cold soda pop. "Groceries" usually meant bread, milk, lunch meat, cookies, and candy bars, and sometimes more—and maybe S&H Green Stamps.

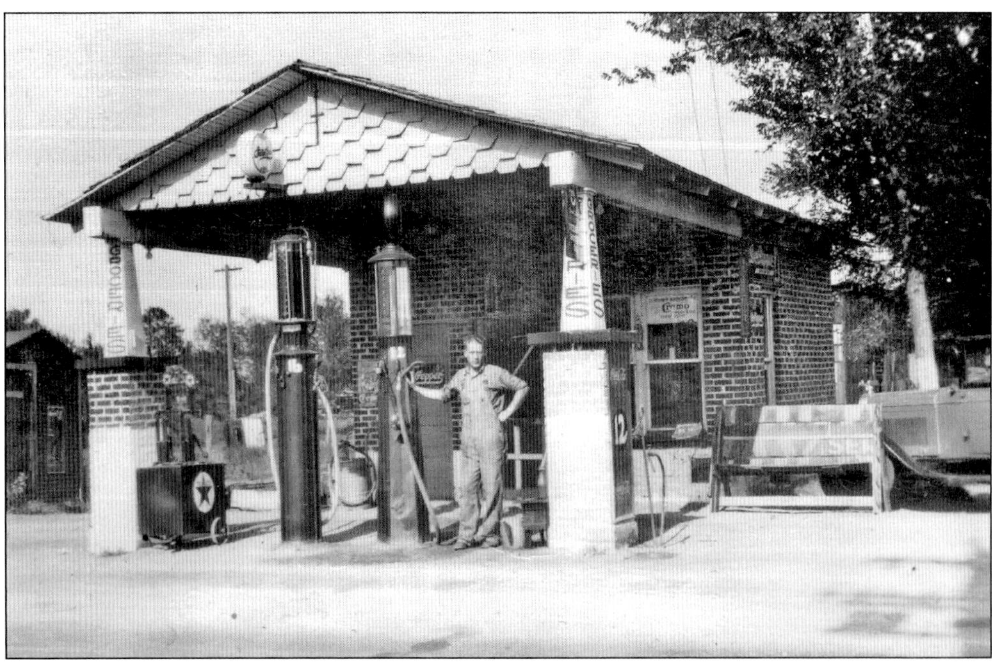

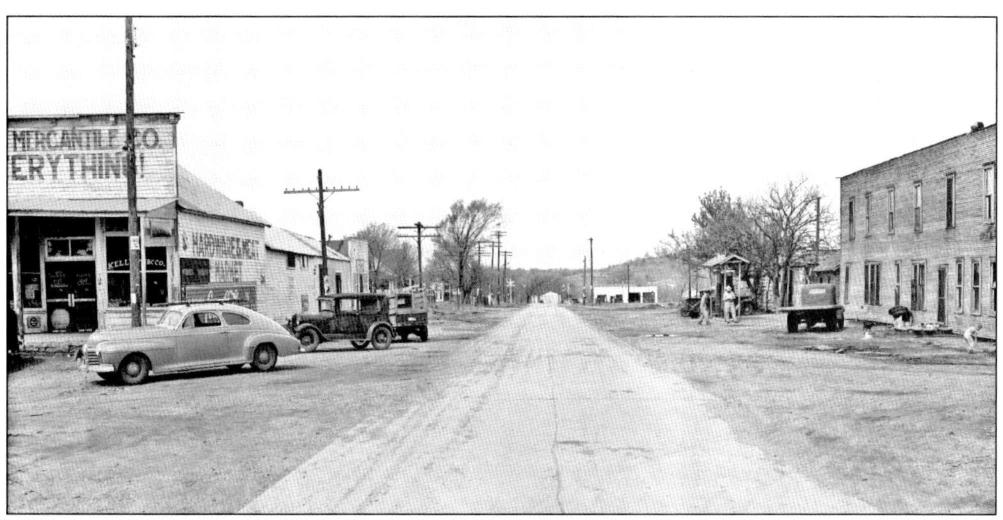

PLANNING AND ZONING? Before there were a lot of (or any) planning and zoning requirements, businesses would diversify to the extent of mixing hardware stores and meat markets. Discarding old tires meant stacking them out of the way. It was not always easy for property owners—especially during the Great Depression and recovery of the 1930s.

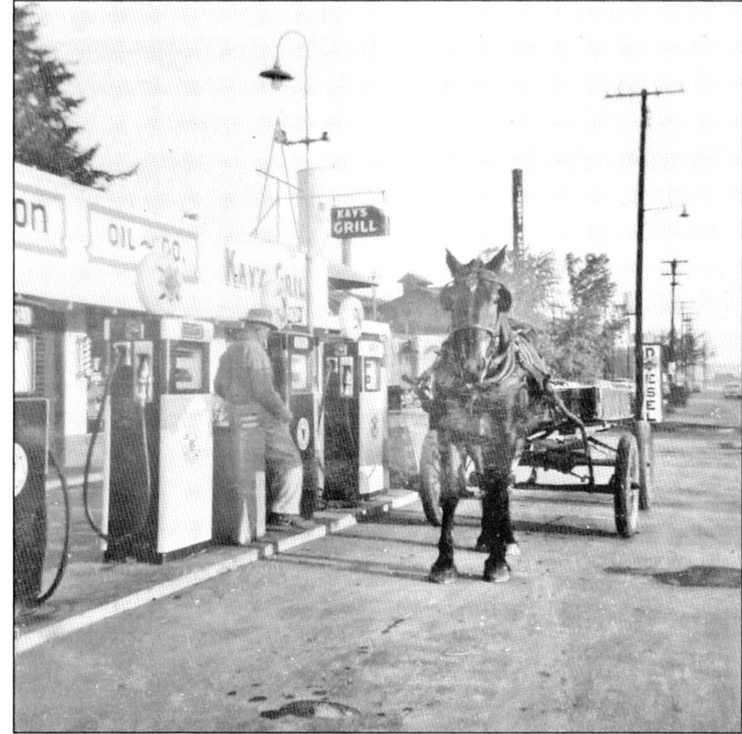

NO OATS TODAY. A filling station on North Mission Street adjacent to Kay's Grill offered full service, but that did not include fuel for horse-drawn vehicles. Automobiles had all but taken over as the mode of transportation by the 1930s, but a lot of local folks still utilized "old dependable" horsepower to get things done effectively and efficiently, albeit rubber tires and soon-to-come rubber horseshoes were a plus on the concrete.

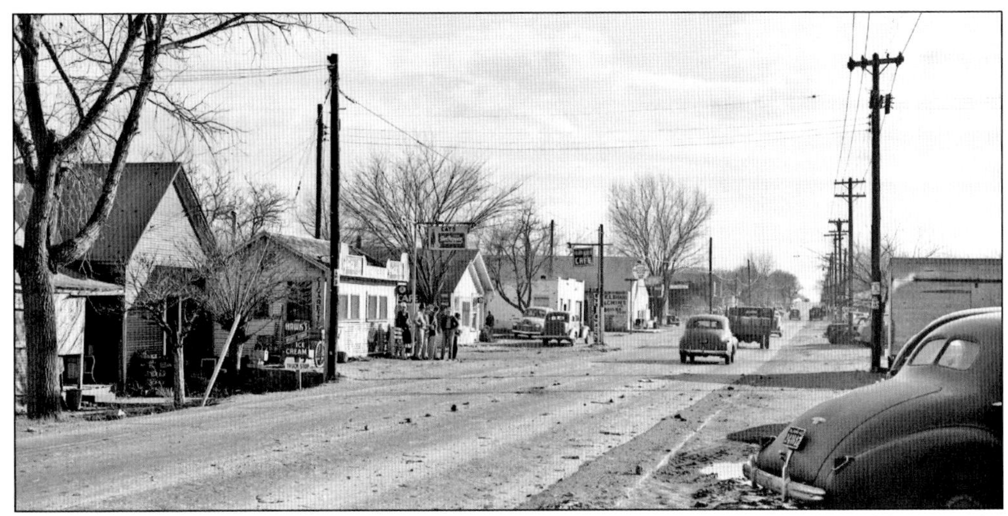

Dirty Thirties Discussion. Sometimes, it seemed easier to solve the world's problems in the 1930s with meeting of the minds and some street conversation after a cup of morning coffee at the L&G Cafe. The ecological disaster coined "the Dust Bowl" caused massive dust storms across Oklahoma; they were heavier in the western part of the state, as well as in and around Sapulpa. The economic impact also was devastating.

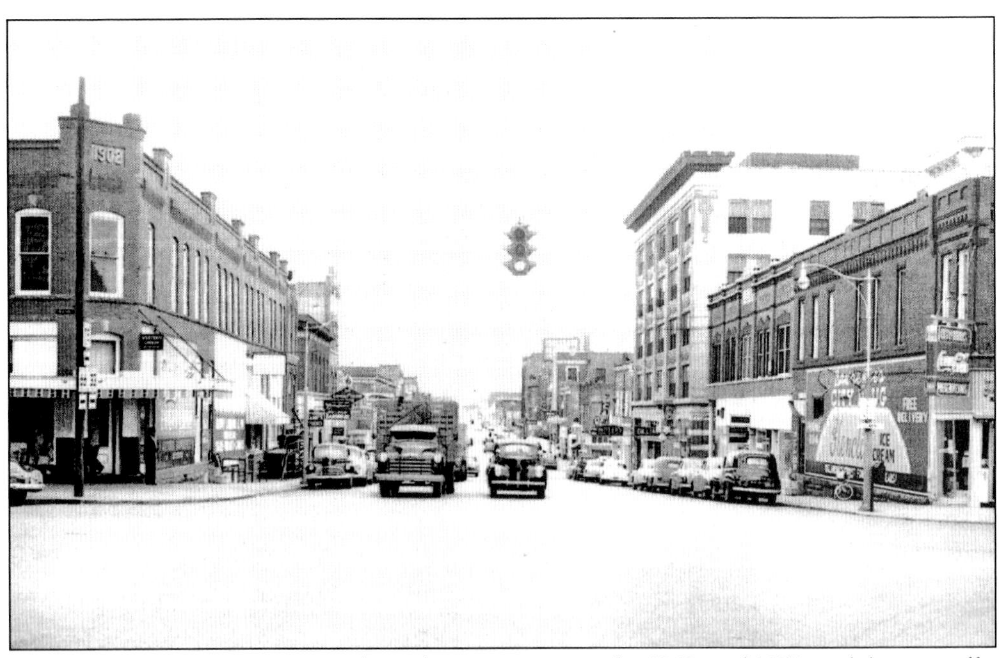

Fast Roads and Wide Streets. Things begin to revive in the 1940s and 1950s with better traffic ways. Trucks and cars on Sapulpa's Dewey Avenue wait for the light at Main Street to change. Some at the "old crossroads" will continue on Route 66, and others will take US 75, or maybe just stop and spend some time in "Sapulpa, Crossroads of the Nation."

Four

The Boom Days
Developing a Local Economy with Black Gold

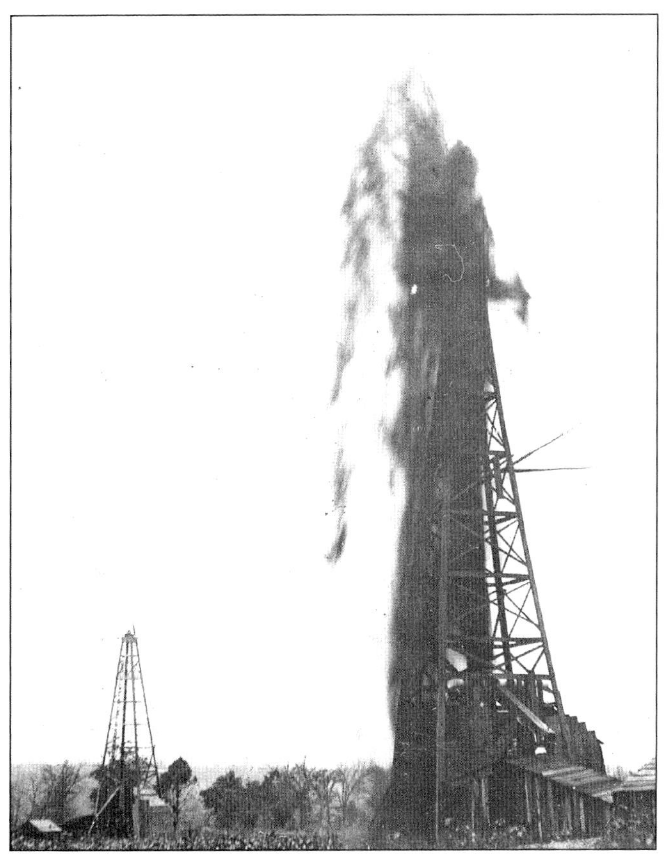

Oil Gusher Deluxe. On November 22, 1905, wildcatters Robert Galbreath and Frank Chesley drilled for oil on farmland owned by Creek Indian Ida E. Glenn and created the first oil gusher in what oilmen meeting in Sapulpa in the spring of 1906 called the Glenn Pool. The well was completed at a depth of 1,481 feet for a production of 75 to 85 barrels per day. Populations of nearby towns grew from hundreds to thousands. The town of Glenpool was born. Oil derricks were erected rapidly after Ida Glenn No. 1 was drilled. The oil boom was on. The town of Kiefer became a boomtown complete with dirt streets, tents, and an influx of workers. Because of its proximity, Sapulpa soon grew into a thriving oil city.

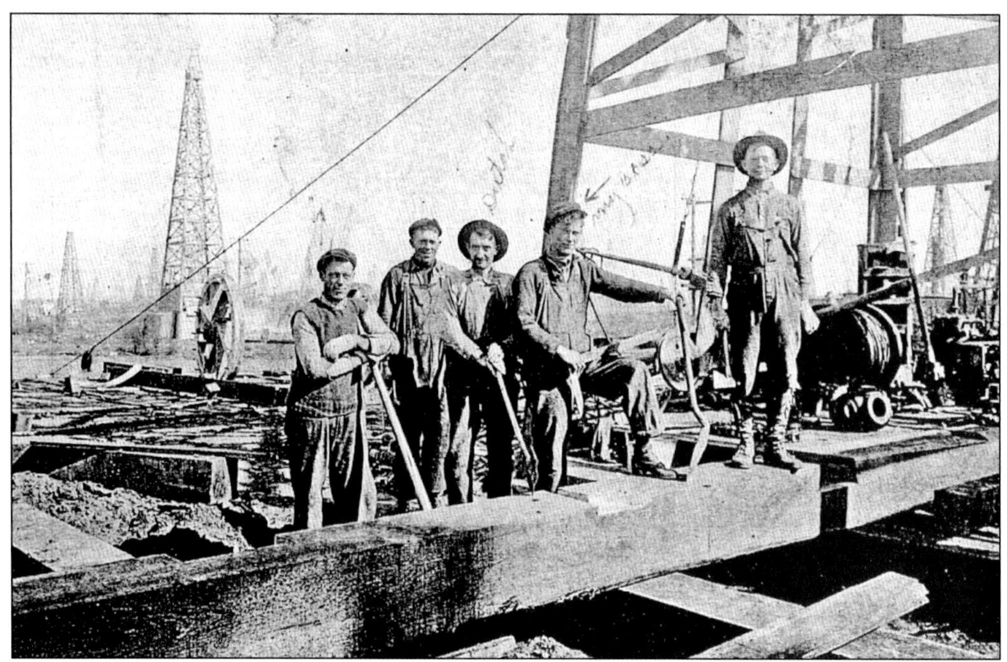

Roughnecks and Roustabouts. They came from all over when they heard drillers had hit oil near Sapulpa. Oil field workers had steel-hard muscle and backbone and with their willingness to work hard for a good day's wages, they brought their families and tents. Here, it appears one of the men (probably Dutch) prepared a keepsake picture of the experience.

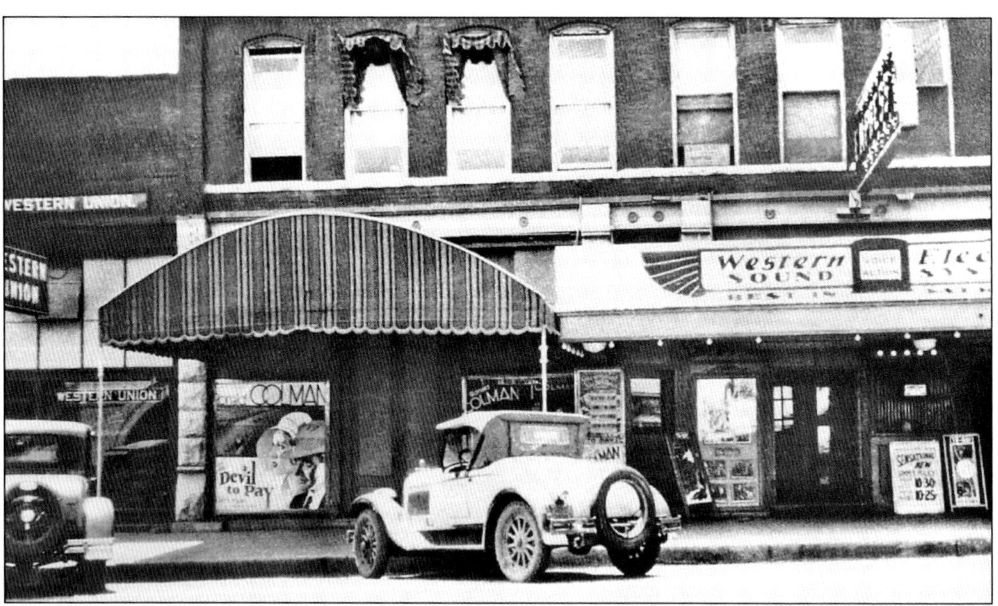

Talkies in Town. It had been 25 years since oil was discovered in the Sapulpa field. The Roaring Twenties had come and gone. The Stock Market crashed in 1929, and in 1930, *The Devil to Pay!*, a pre–Hays Code romantic film starring Ronald Coleman, Frederic Kerr, Myrna Loy, and Loretta Young was playing at the old Empress Theater downtown between the Western Union and Western Electric Sound Systems.

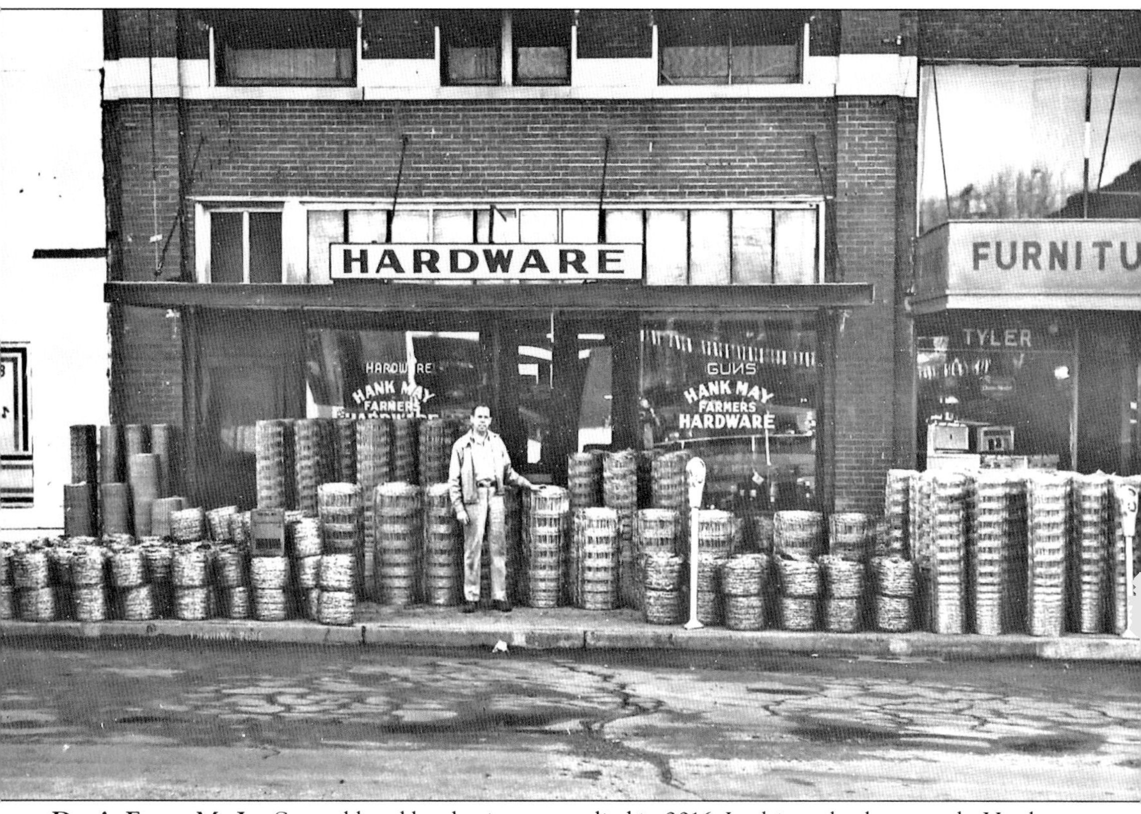

Don't Fence Me In. Several local key businessmen died in 2016. In this early photograph, Hank May is surrounded by wire fence and other products at his popular hardware store on North Main Street in downtown Sapulpa. The lifelong Sapulpa businessman and civic leader was 98. Ed Wells, who ran a furniture store and the Wells Office Building, also died in 2016. He was 90.

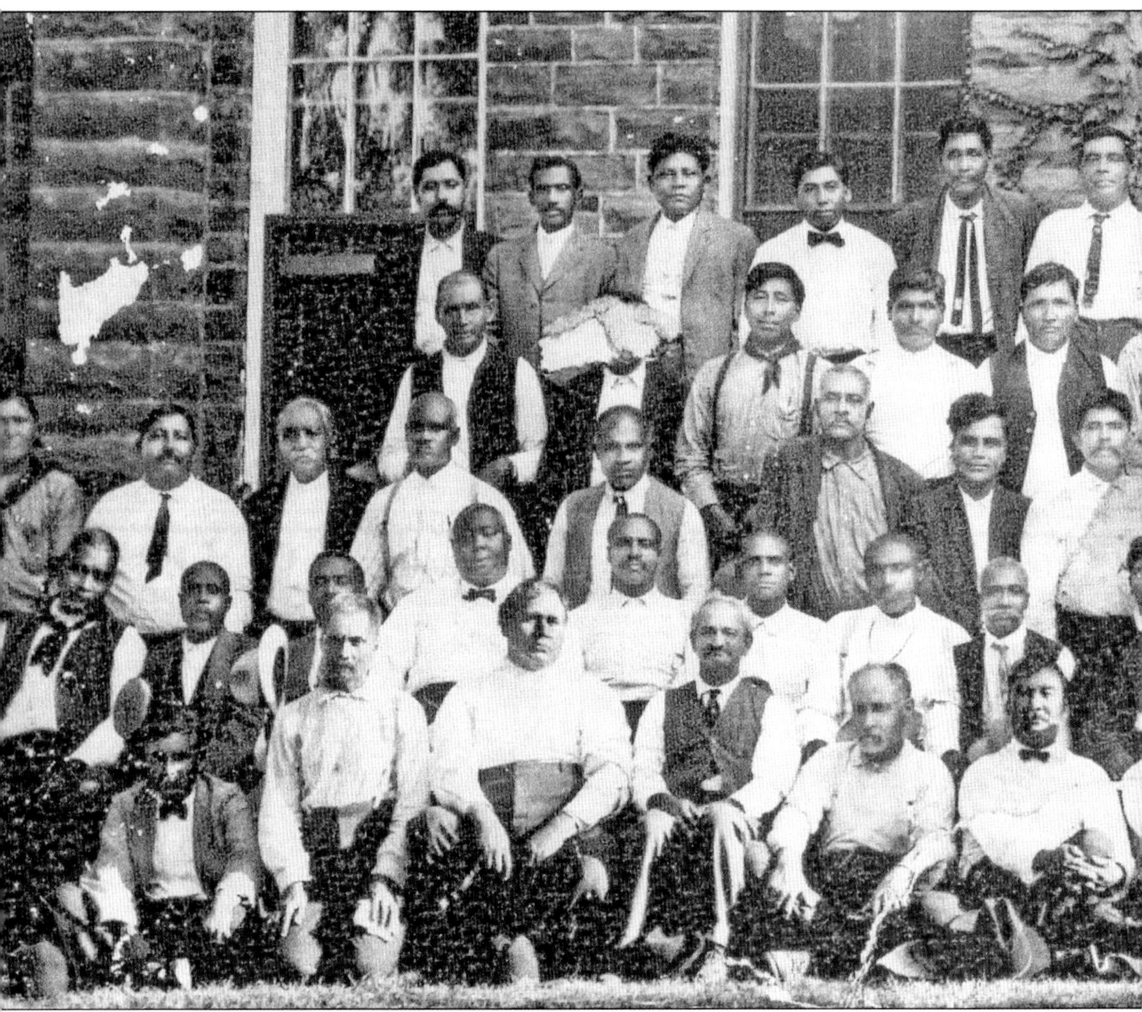

Local Indians Had a Say. Sapulpa is in the Creek Nation, where Indian leaders were part of the guiding force in the town's founding, its early education system, and government. It also had a consulting voice in how the use of natural resources, including oil, would be handled. Its members owned the oil-rich land. Native Americans with Sapulpa ties are shown in this House of Warriors photograph taken at the Creek Council House. Many are unidentified, but in latter times family and tribal members noted those they recognized, from left to right, as follows: (first row) Willie Chisson, Neffie Grant, Dave Fields, Robert Francis, Peter Ewing, Sam Checote, and Isaac

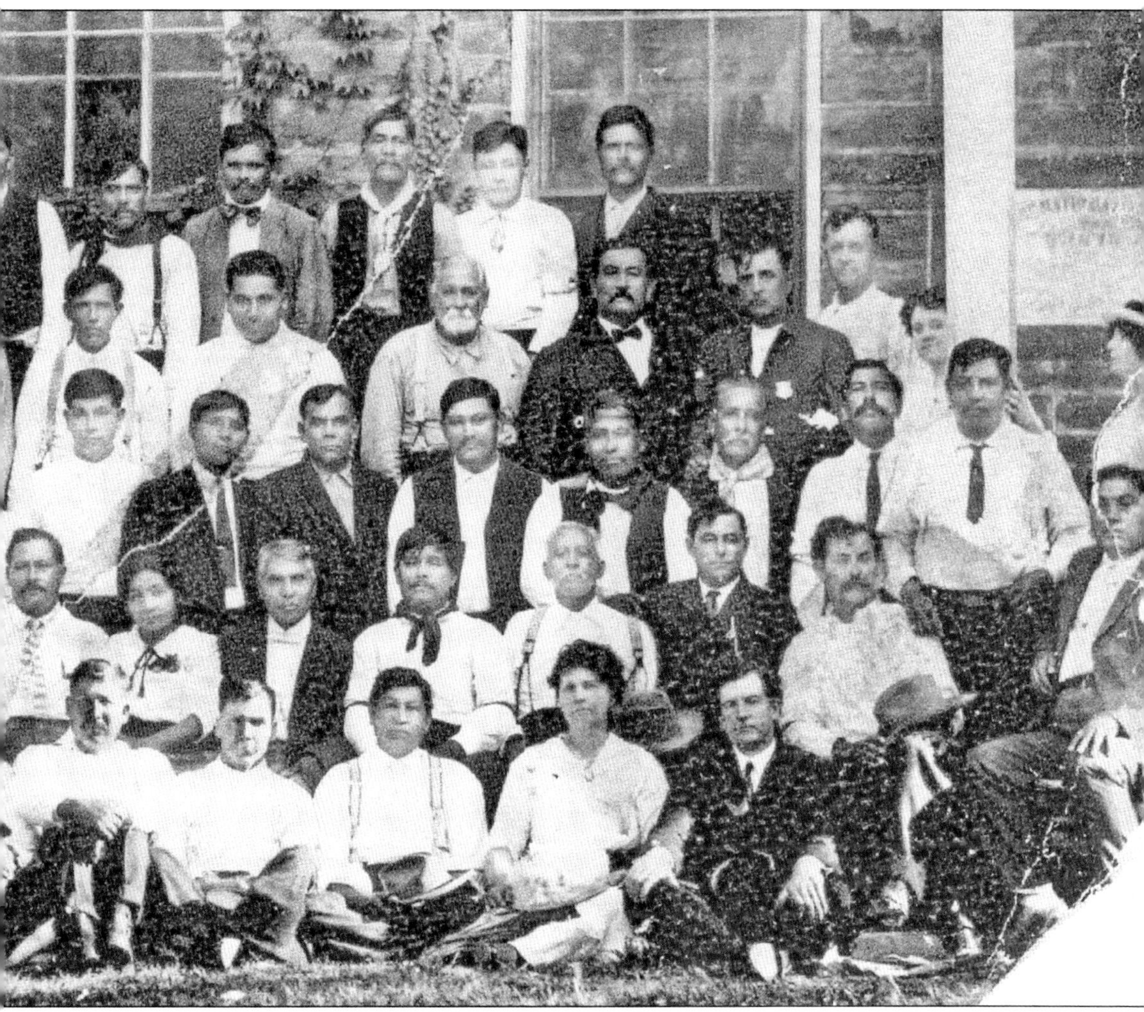

Miller; (second row) Martin Checote, John Lowe, Louis Scott, Issac Manley, James Tiger, Leser Williams, George W. Hill, Willie Brown, and George Stidham; (third row) Peter McNac, Marsey Harjo, Soloman Bullett, Sam Davis, Mitchell Davis, Joe Grayson, Jeff Canard, Alex Thompson, Albert Burgess, and Lee Nevins; (fourth row) Cody Johnson, E.B. Childers, Mrs. Dan B. Childers, Dan B. Childers, Thomas Riley, James Hill, Euchee chief Sam Brown, Mitchell Wadsworth, and Joe Bruner; (fifth row) William Green, Billy Yahola, Henry Land, William McCombs, Bunny McIntosh, Jerry Morrison, and Johnson Tiger.

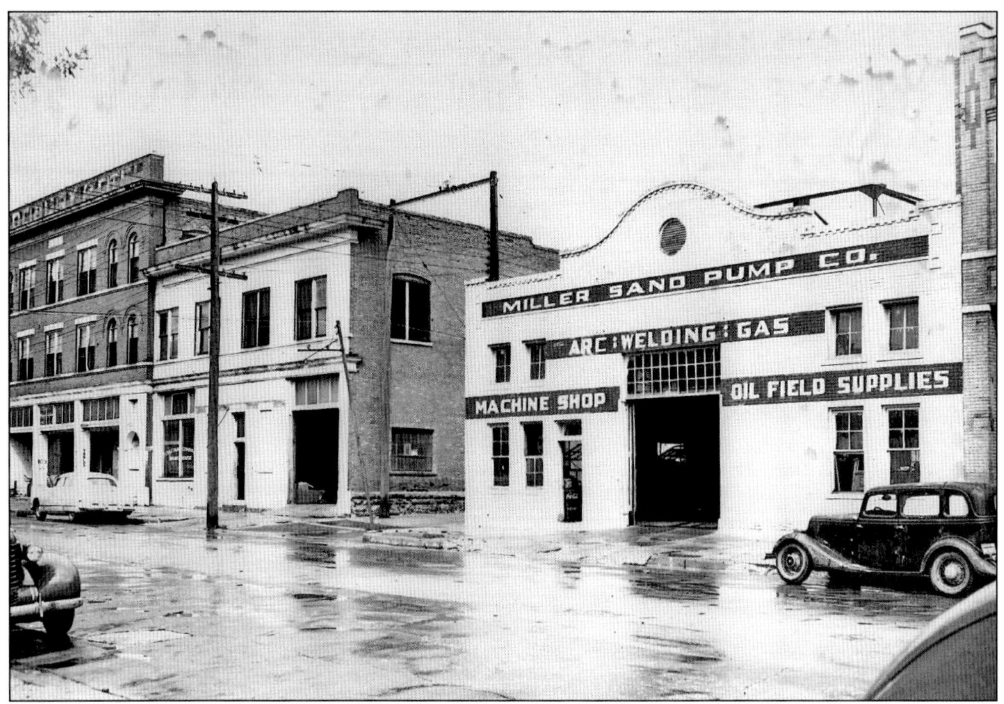

Related Businesses. With the development of the oil and energy sector in the Sapulpa area came all kinds of oil supply companies, from machine and sheet-metal shops like these on East Hobson Avenue to lumberyards and hardware stores to the large manufacturers of oilfield and delivery equipment.

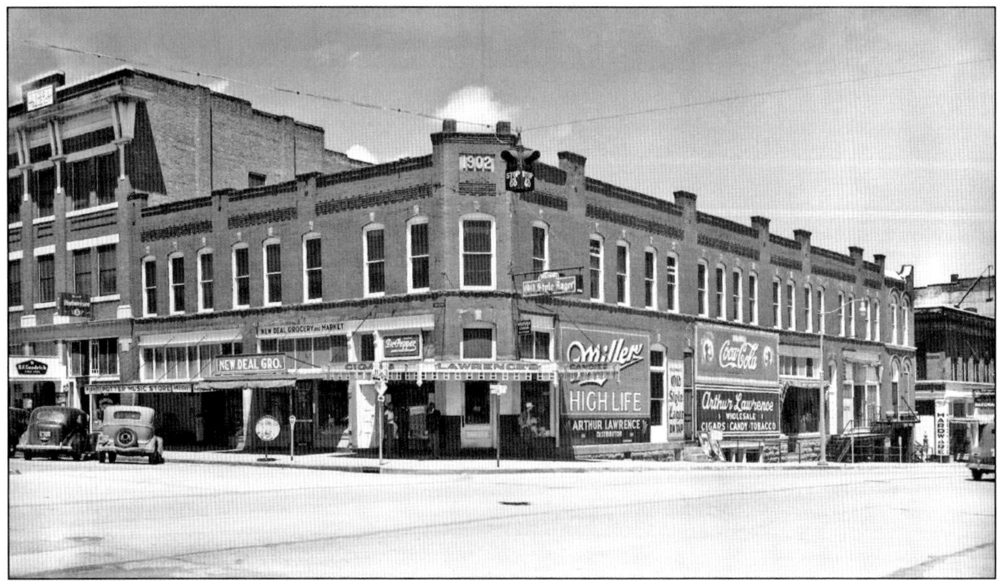

Cigars and More. Arthur Lawrence was an early Sapulpa businessman with a sense of good timing and location. His cigar store at the corner of Main Street and Dewey Avenue was a downtown landmark and a favorite place for railroad, oilfield, and glass and brick plant workers to spend some of their paychecks. A *Tulsa Tribune* writer at the time described the store as "a stop where a man could get a vest pocket full of cigars to last the day."

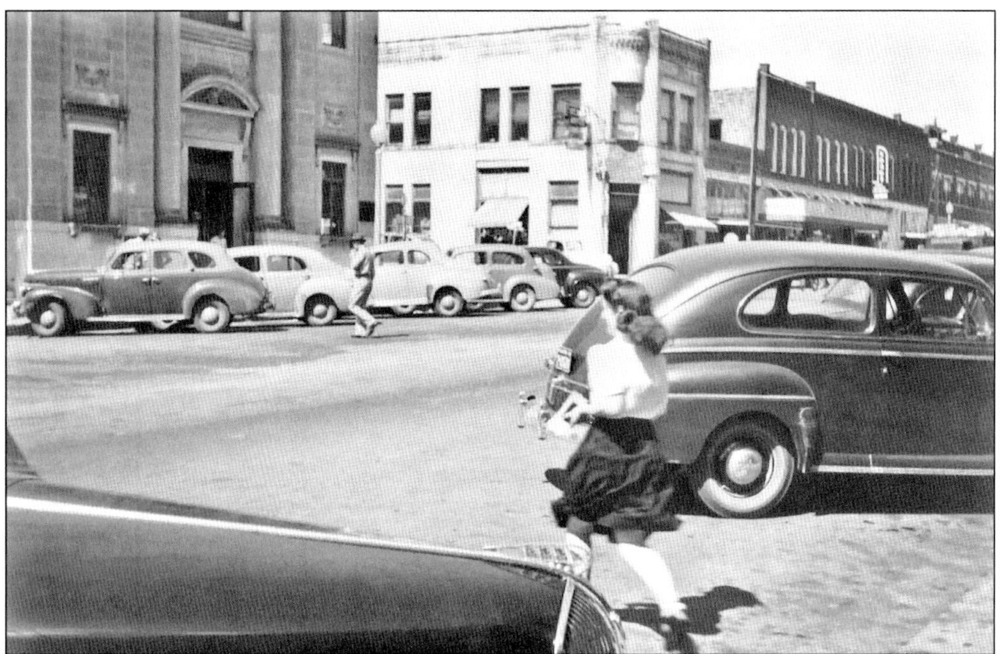

Pretty Woman Walking. Lunchtime in the 1940s was a busy time in downtown Sapulpa. A young woman, perhaps a telephone operator, grabs lunch and visits her bank before returning to work. A lot of women worked in shops, department stores, offices, and service businesses all over downtown. Some were business owners.

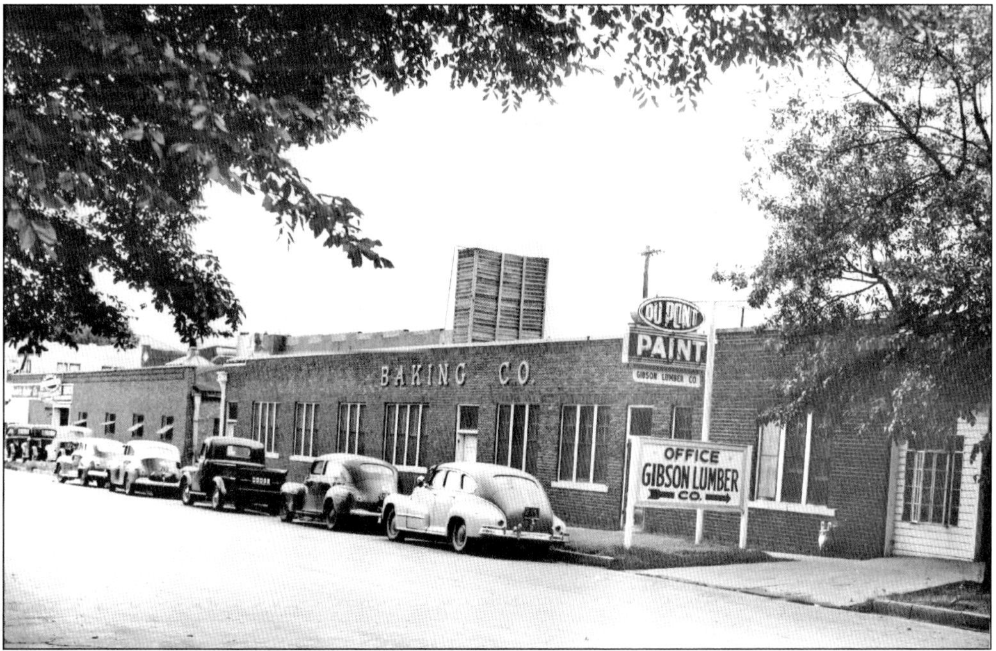

Sapulpa's Home Depot. Before the days of the big-box store by that name, stores like home-grown Gibson's Lumber Company on East Hobson Avenue was Sapulpa's "build it and fix it" depot. The building and business are gone today, as are other locally owned and operated lumber and hardware outlets.

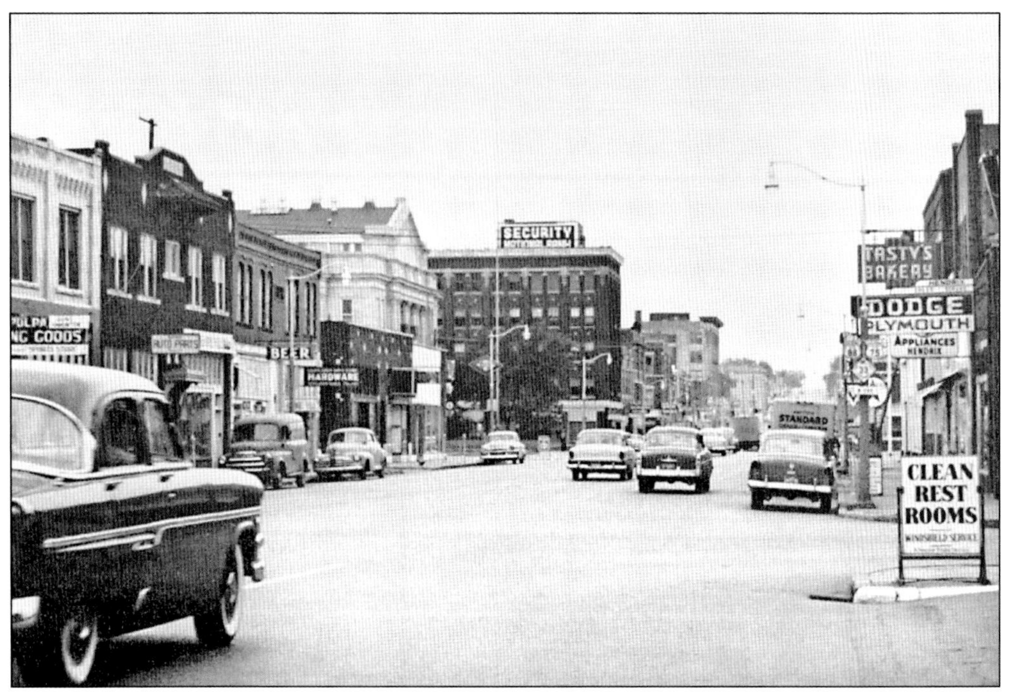

EVERYTHING DOWNTOWN. In the 1950s, there was not much one could not find downtown. Businesses on the right include a service station, a car dealership, a bakery, and an appliance store; to the left, heading west are a sporting goods store, an auto parts shop, a beer shop, and a hardware store. There is also the courthouse and then a DX station; next is Security Bank in the Clayton (later Wells) Building, and just beyond that is the Berryhill. The multistoried structures were built with oil money.

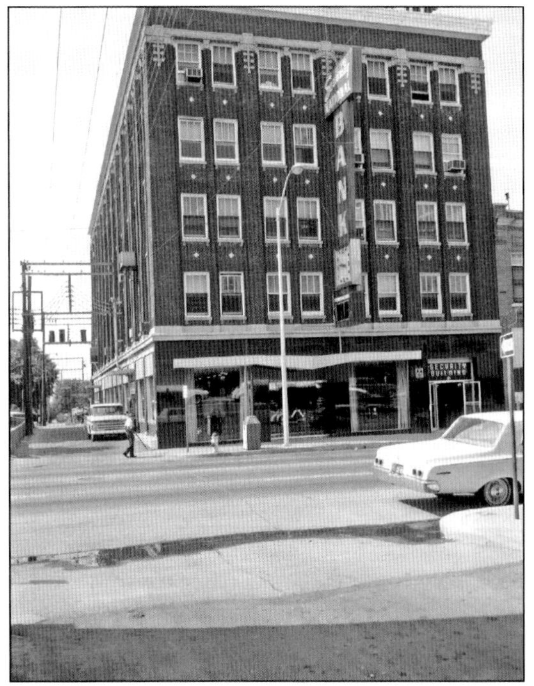

EARLY DRIVE-THROUGH. The Security Bank, located on the ground floor of the Wells Building, offered a drive-through window in the alley next to the Creek County Courthouse. Originally known as the Clayton Building, this structure was built for Ernest Clayton and sister Bessie, Creek Indians who used royalties from the Glenn Pool allotment. Local prominent black leader Henry Lowrance oversaw the project.

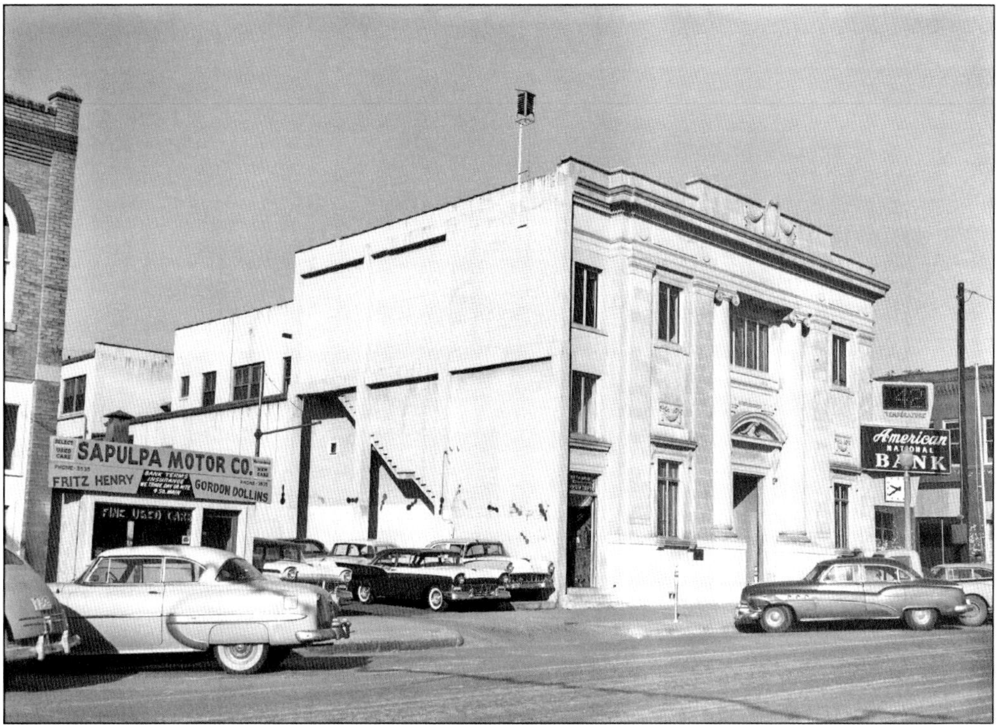

Banks for Oilmen and Car Dealers. Banks came and went in the early days as oil money flowed and business boomed and waned. Several banks were on downtown corners of Main Street and Dewey Avenue. American National today is American Heritage, which also has drive-in banking and parking where the Fritz Henry used car lot once was.

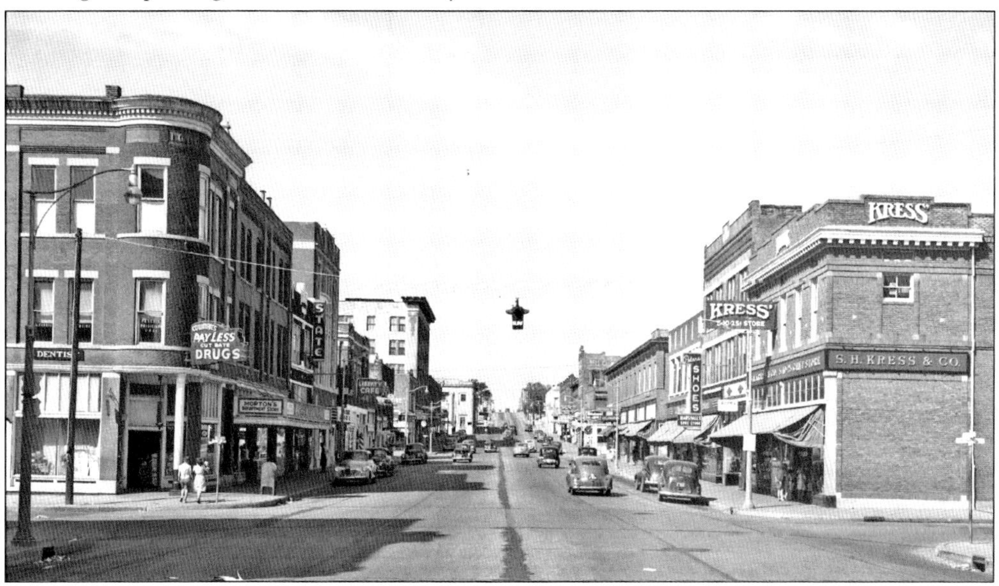

Glory Day Buildings Alive. Today, the Kress' 5-10-25¢ Store is not there, and the shoe store and Newberry's have moved on. One cannot see a movie at the State or eat at Liberty Café, but these three blocks of buildings on East Dewey Avenue and even across Main Street still stand today and are occupied by idea-driven merchants who offer free parking.

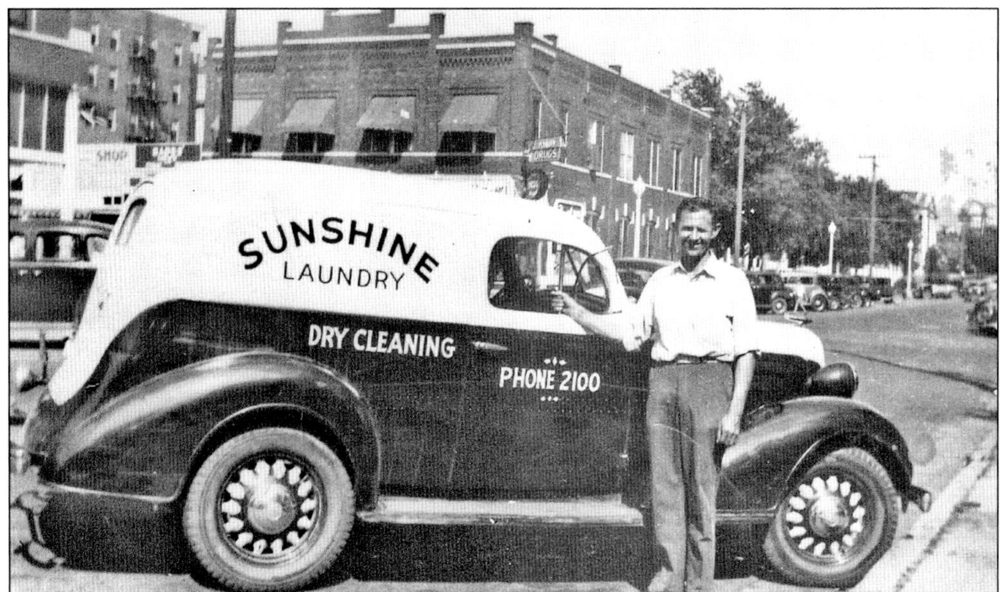

WARM AND FUZZY NAME. If you are going to name your business "Sunshine," it helps to have a cool panel delivery truck and a driver with a smile that matches the branding. The man in the photo is C.I. Mauch, founder of Sunshine Laundry, shown with his c. 1939 Chevrolet Panel delivery truck and his "service with a smile" attitude. The Mauch family operated the business for years. Before the days of laundromats, and before washers and dryers were in every home, Sapulpa's laundries competed for the business and offered a better option than hanging the family clothing on the clothesline and dragging out the ironing boards.

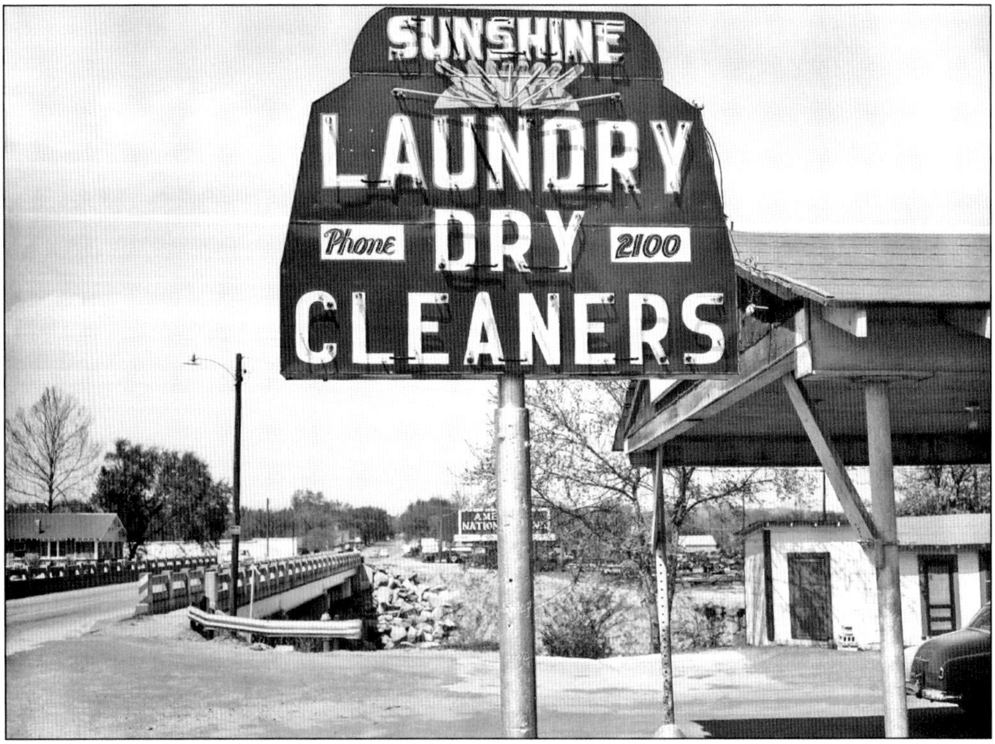

Five

Industry to Infamy
Reputation Built with Bricks, Glass, and Pottery

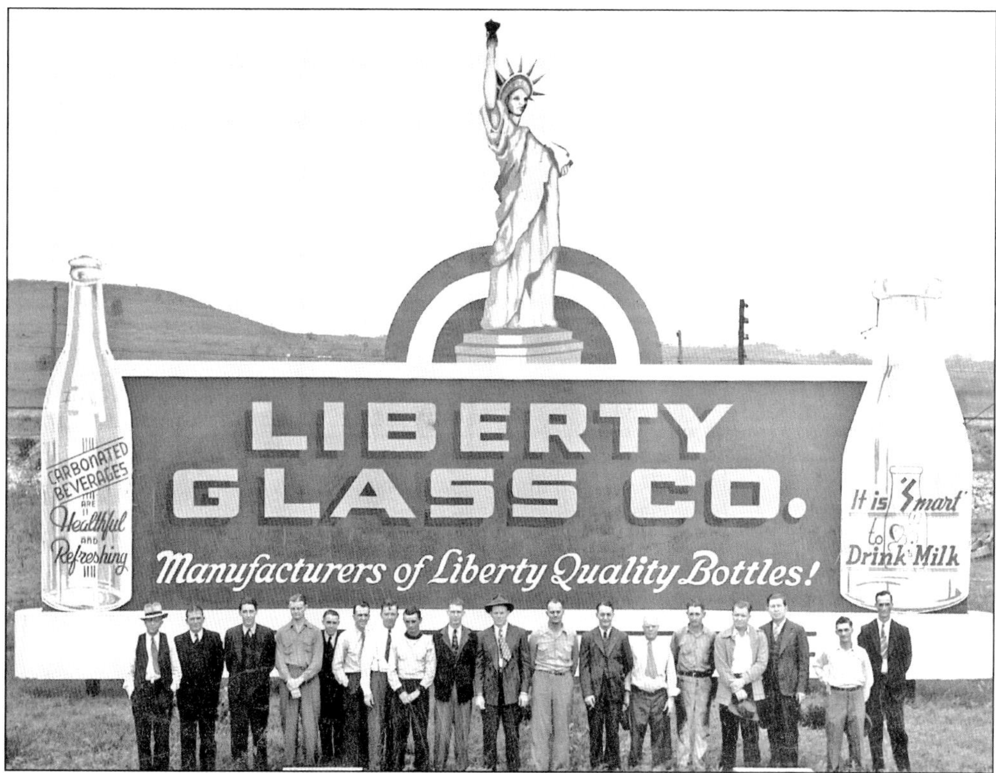

Liberty Glass Plant Billboard. Liberty Glass Company advertised with this early-day billboard. The company began in 1912 as Premium Glass. George F. Collins and H.U. Bartlett became partners and built the Bartlett-Collins Glass plant in the central part of town. The partnership dissolved. Collins became owner of Premium Glass and renamed it Liberty. Bartlett became owner of Bartlett-Collins, which excelled in the making of tableware. Liberty continued making milk and beverage bottles.

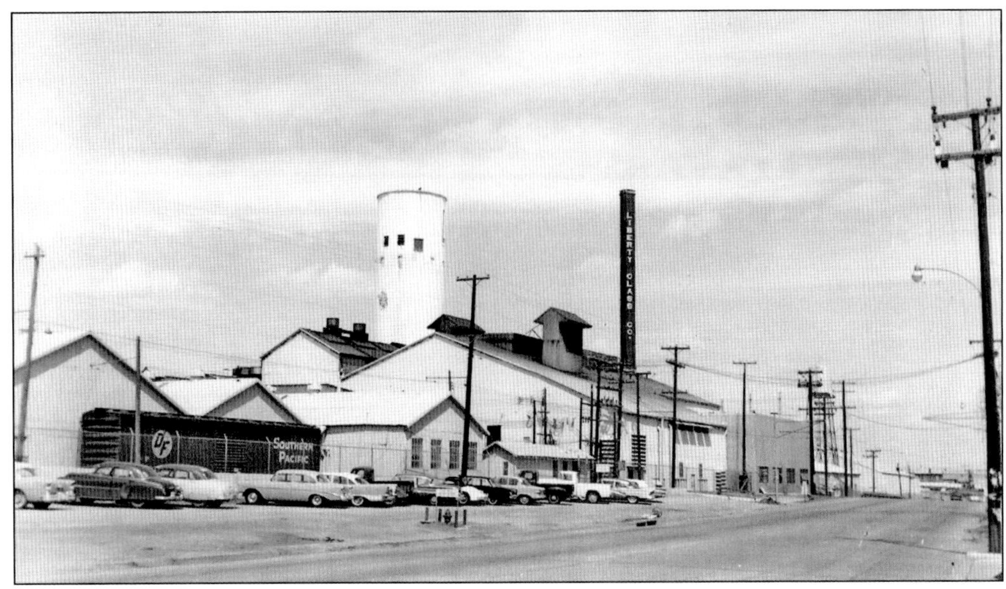

First Glass Plant. Premium Glass built a plant at Mission Street and Haskell Avenue and was Sapulpa's first glass plant. It became Liberty Glass in 1918. It was owned and operated by the local Collins family until the 1990s, when it was acquired by Foster-Forbes of Marion, Indiana. Today, the Ardagh Group is part of the French company Saint-Gobain. Besides bottles and jars, Sapulpa's first glass plants made things like lamp chimneys, lantern globes, door and drawer pullers, jelly glasses, tumblers, and goblets. Schram Glass made fruit jars. Sunflower made window glass panes. Sapulpa was called "Crystal City of the Southwest."

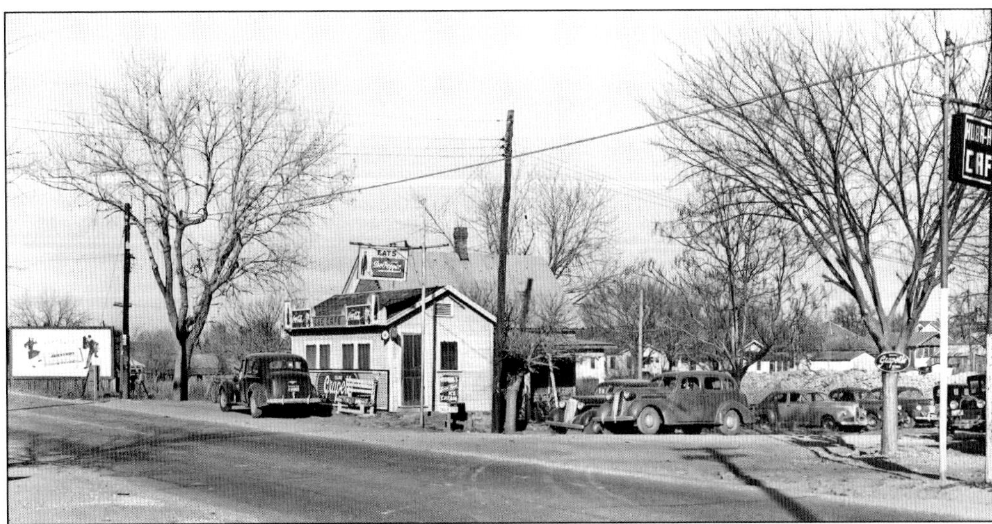

Grapette Soda Pop. A couple of Sapulpa's competing eateries in the early 1940s knew one thing: they had best offer the new soft drink rage of the time, Grapette, as reflected in the signage. The local connection went further. Grapette syrups were sold across the country to be bottled and distributed locally, but Sapulpa's Liberty Glass made some of the popular grape-flavored soft drink bottles between 1940 and 1970. Advertisements for Coca-Cola, Dr. Pepper, and, on the highway billboard, Juicy Fruit chewing gum are also seen here.

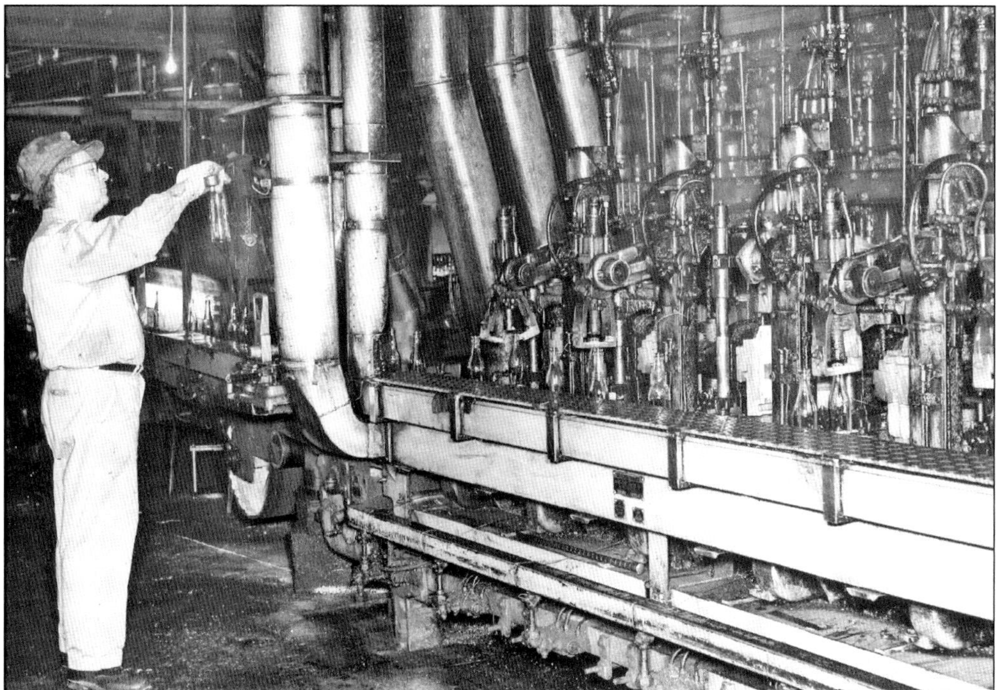

Pop Bottle Making. Liberty Glass Company's Owen Hill is shown here as an operator in the forming department, better known as the "Hot End." This was the department where the machines formed the bottles in the molds. Hill is visually inspecting a bottle that has just been formed—perhaps a Grapette bottle. The operators were required to do a sample inspection hourly.

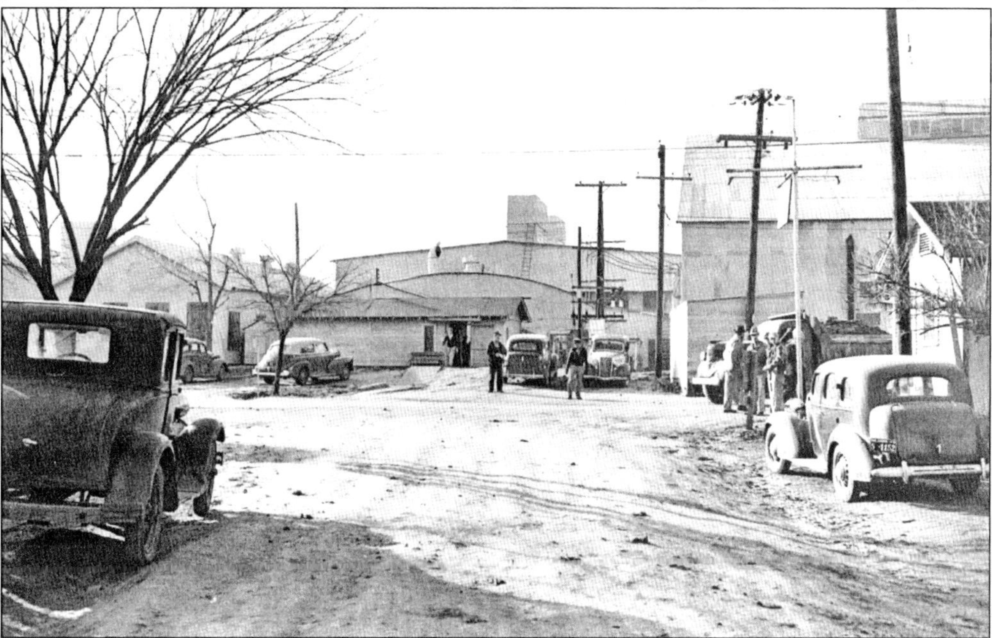

Street Talk at Shift Change. The work is hard and hot in the furnace rooms of a glass plant—as well as noisy. However, factory workers at Liberty Glass in the 1940s were like family and would catch up with the latest news during shift changes on North Mission Street.

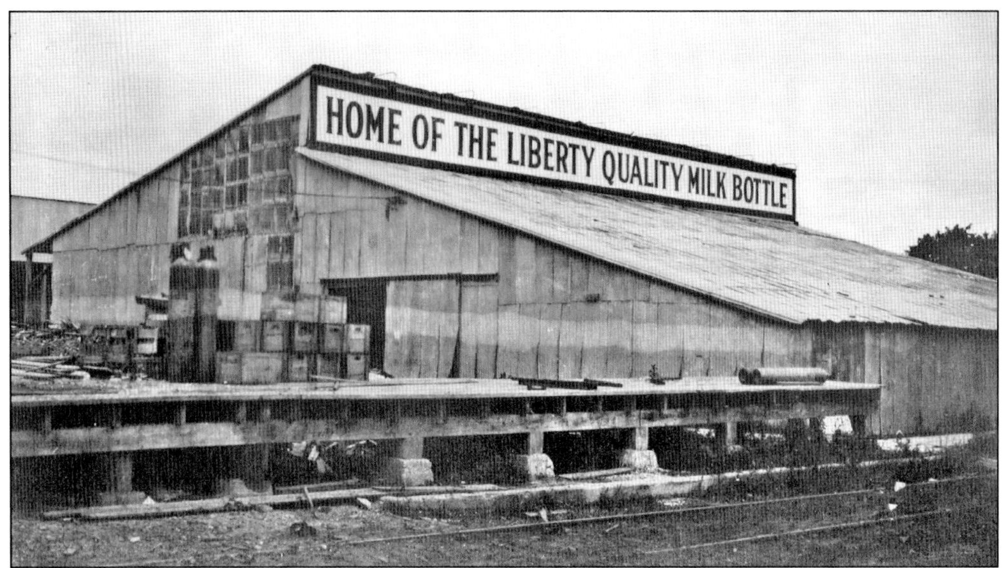

Liberty Milk Bottles. This c. 1920s photograph of Liberty Glass Plant shows its main line of bottles. By 1919, the plant was stamping its glass containers with "LG," something bottle collectors still look for in flea markets and antique shows across the nation. Today, as part of the Saint-Gobain Company, its furnaces, machinery, and 300 employees work virtually around the clock still producing bottles, mostly for beer.

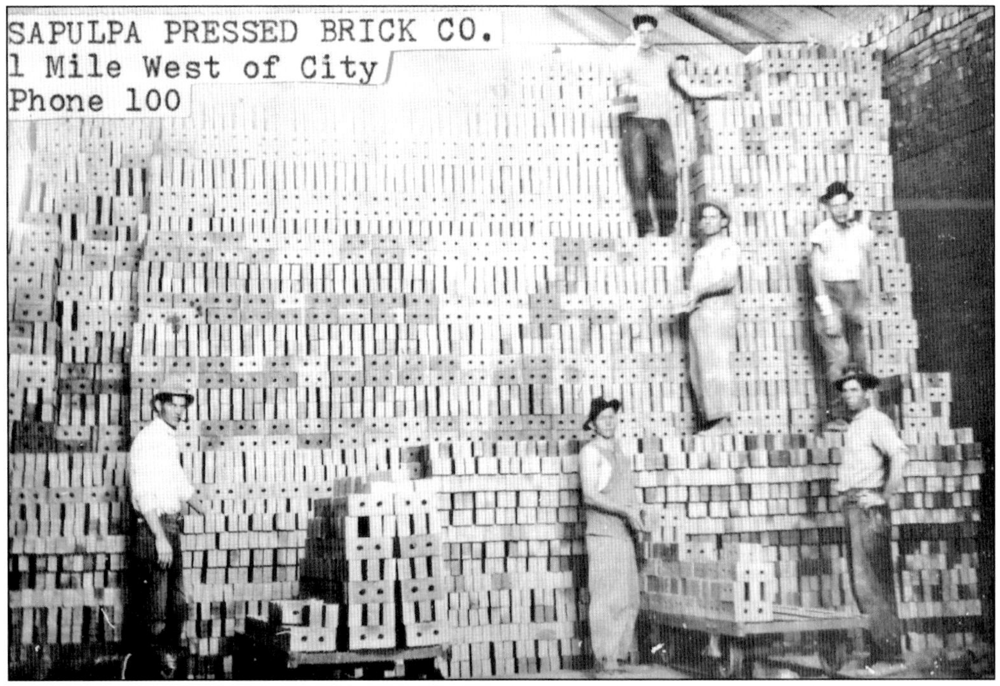

All Those Bricks Local? Bricks are produced and stacked at early brick plants just west of downtown Sapulpa and shipped everywhere. Many of them were used right here. The Sapulpa Pressed Brick Company was incorporated in 1898, with J. Boyd, Fred Pfendler, and Webster Wilder as owners. The company had 55 acres of land with ample shale reserve located at the west side of town just past Independence Street, on the south side of the Frisco Railroad tracks.

Sapulpa Brick and Tile Company. The Sapulpa Pressed Brick plant was sold in 1902 and became the Sapulpa Brick and Tile Company, owned by the Hermes family for many years. Dick Hermes, one of its final managers, is shown here with one of the famous Sapulpa bricks.

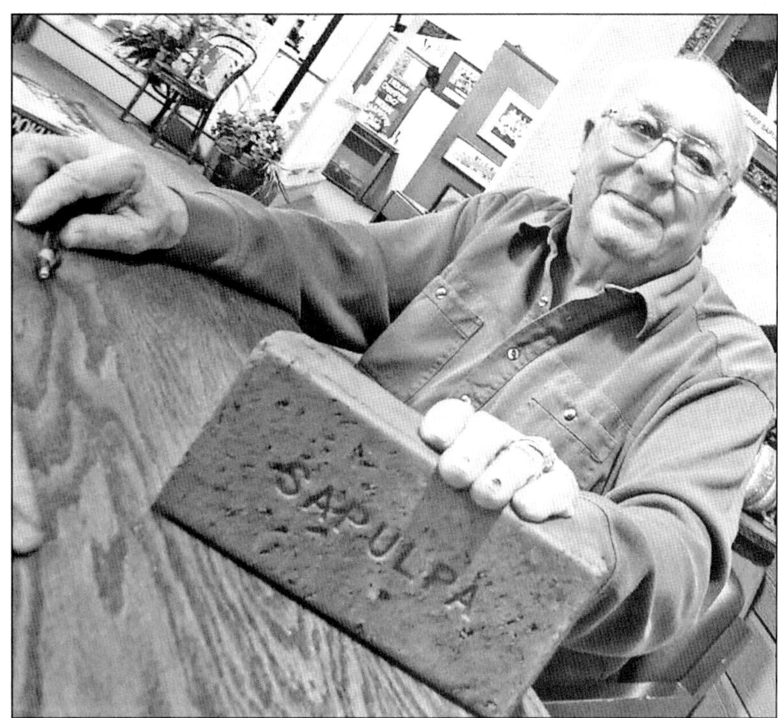

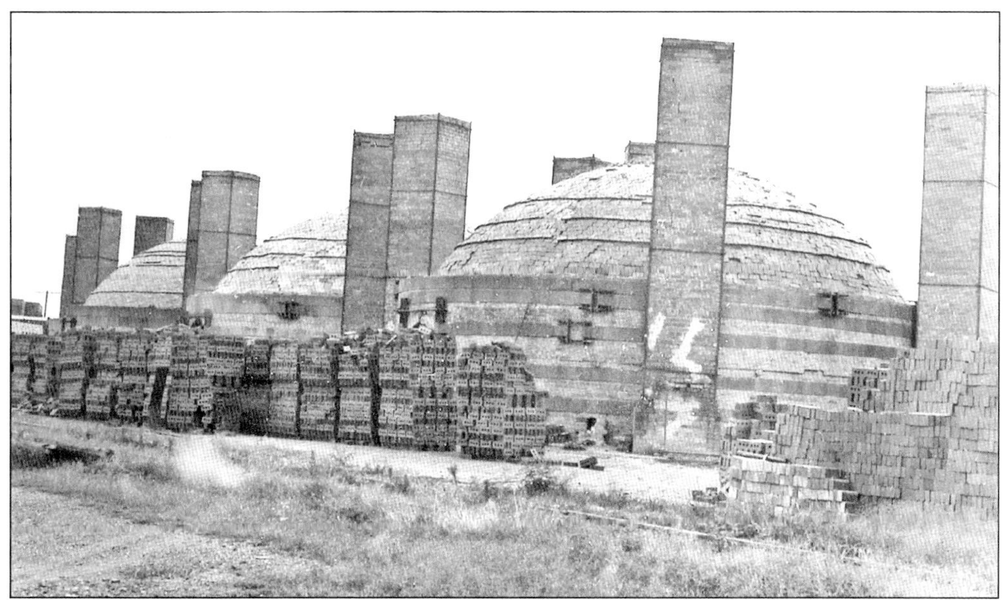

Sapulpa's Brick Plants. After livestock, walnut trees, farm crops, and the rail industry itself, brick-making (or rather, brick-baking) was the big industry during Sapulpa's formative years. Buildings, streets, and parking lots utilized massive amounts of locally produced bricks.

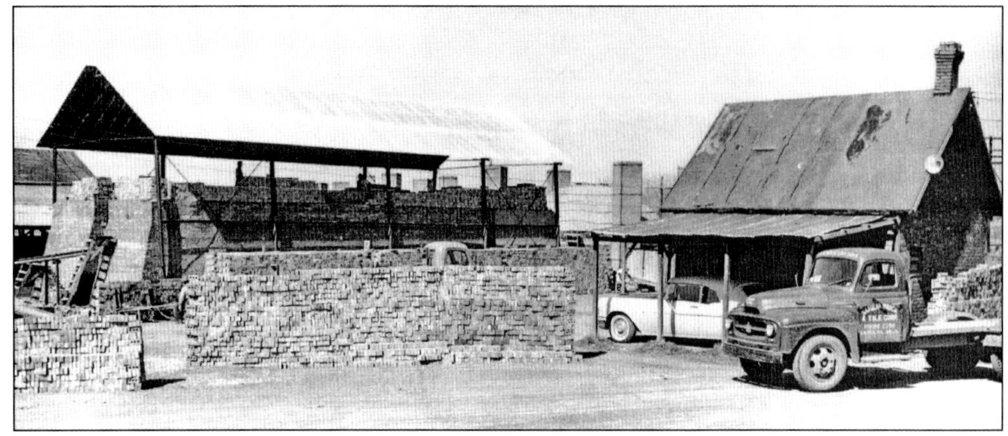

Paving the Way. There were two plants west of town on both sides of Route 66: Sapulpa Pressed Brick Company, and a few years later, Sapulpa Brick. The needed clay for the bricks and gas for the ovens was nearby. Because it was fire retardant, brick became the preferred construction material in the late 19th and early 20th centuries. Local brick was red or dark buff in color, thereby giving character to the main streets of many towns.

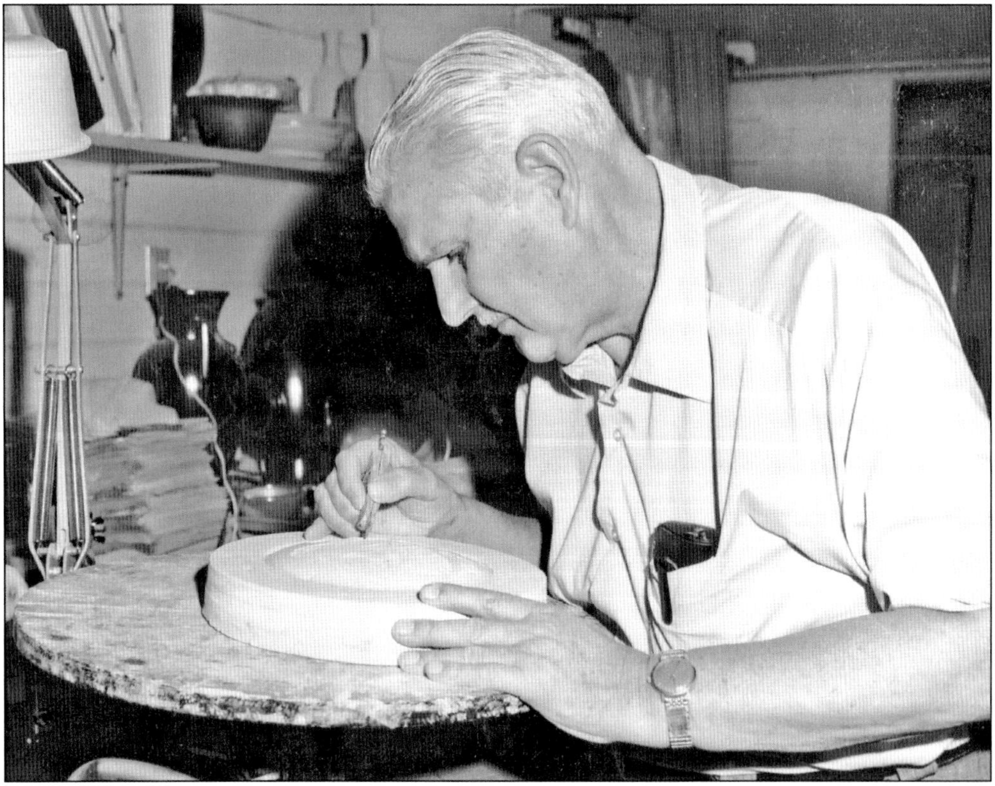

Potter and His Clay. There were a host of things that put Sapulpa on the map, not the least of which was Frankoma Pottery. The story is as well known locally as the pottery is well known around the world. University of Oklahoma ceramics professor and artisan John Frank was looking for and found the right combination of location and the right clay at Sapulpa. He founded Frankoma in 1933 at Norman and came to Sapulpa in 1938. Shown here at the potter's wheel, Frank also became a community leader and storyteller. Using his wheel, he enjoyed sharing the Biblical narrative.

Sculpting the Future. Frank operated the company with his wife, Grace Lee Frank, until his death in 1973. Their daughter Joniece took over the company for a time, and another daughter, Donna, authored a book about Frankoma.

World-Renowned Frankoma. A row of Ford products in front of Frankoma Pottery on old Route 66 reflects the success of the company in 1950. John Frank is on the right with a Mercury and a sales staff supporting new Fords. The name "Frankoma" was created from Frank's last name and the last three letters of the state of Oklahoma.

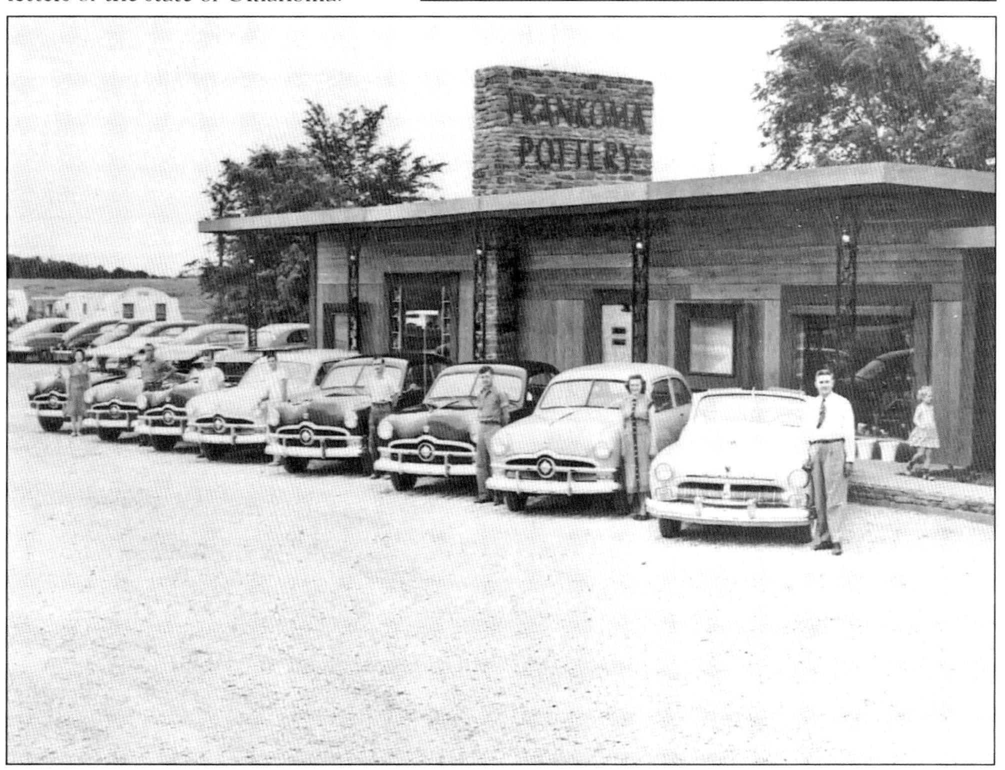

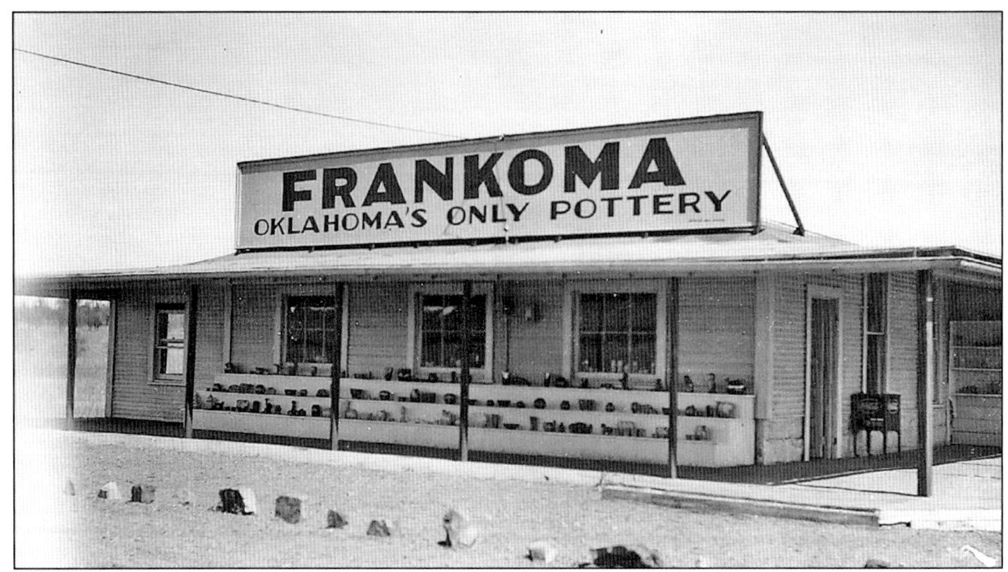

Frankoma Pottery for Sale. Frankoma Pottery was displayed and sold across the country, including at this side building on Old Route 66 at Sapulpa. The nearby plant also was a longtime tourist stop. Out front, Old 66 took the name Frankoma Road. Only the building remains today, but the unique Frank home and Frankoma collectors' gatherings still get written up regularly.

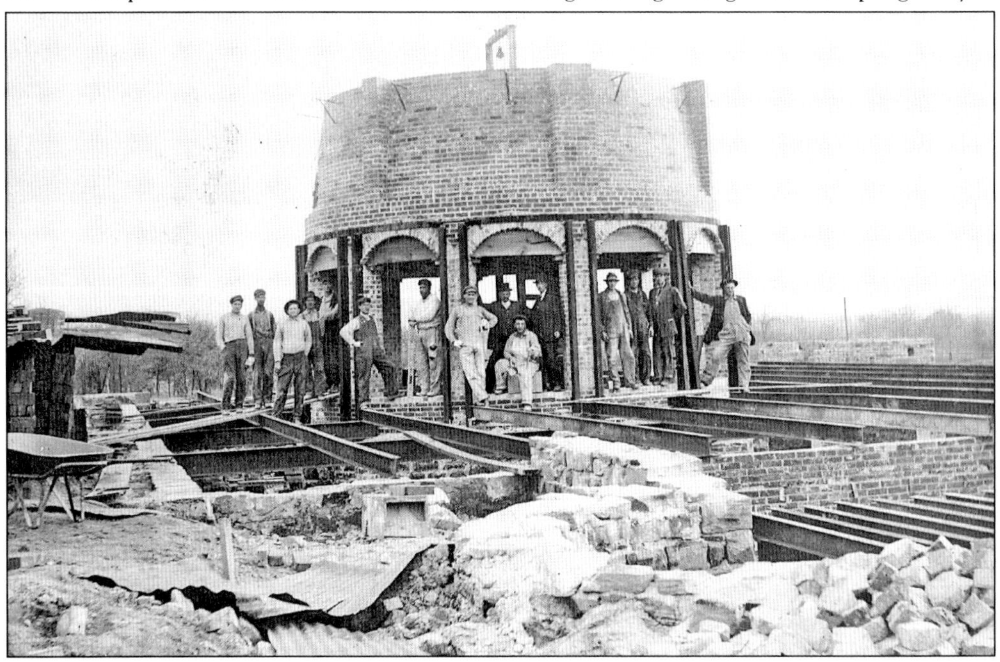

Bartlett-Collins Furnace. Standing inside the Bartlett-Collins Glass Company's original pot furnace in 1915 are (from left, the two men in center wearing business suits) H.U. Bartlett and H.E. Whitehead. The company would ultimately focus on tableware. Other glass producers in Sapulpa included Premium Glass (which became Liberty), Schram Glass, and Sunflower Glass Company. Sapulpa is also home of world-famous Frankoma Pottery. A sculpture featuring a bottle, plate, and drinking glass at the town's northeast gateway on Route 66 marks the legacy, but only the former Liberty Glass remains.

Six

Life Quality
Getting Educated, Eating Out, and Being Entertained

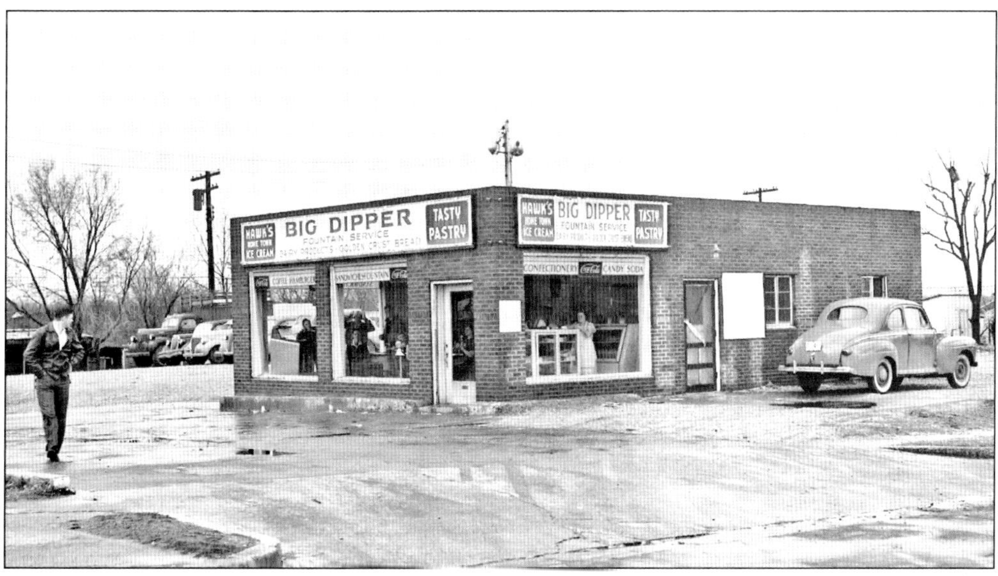

Big Dipper Remembered. Those who cruised Route 66 along Sapulpa's main drag remember their favorite stops. Doc and Vernie Tharp operated the Big Dipper drive-in restaurant at Dewey Avenue and Maple Street into the late 1950s. Today, the lot is occupied by what was the Sonic Drive-In, which recently moved to another Historic Route 66 corner across from the high school at Mission and Dewey. The man pictured walking outside is not identified, but he or the photographer apparently had the attention of the diners.

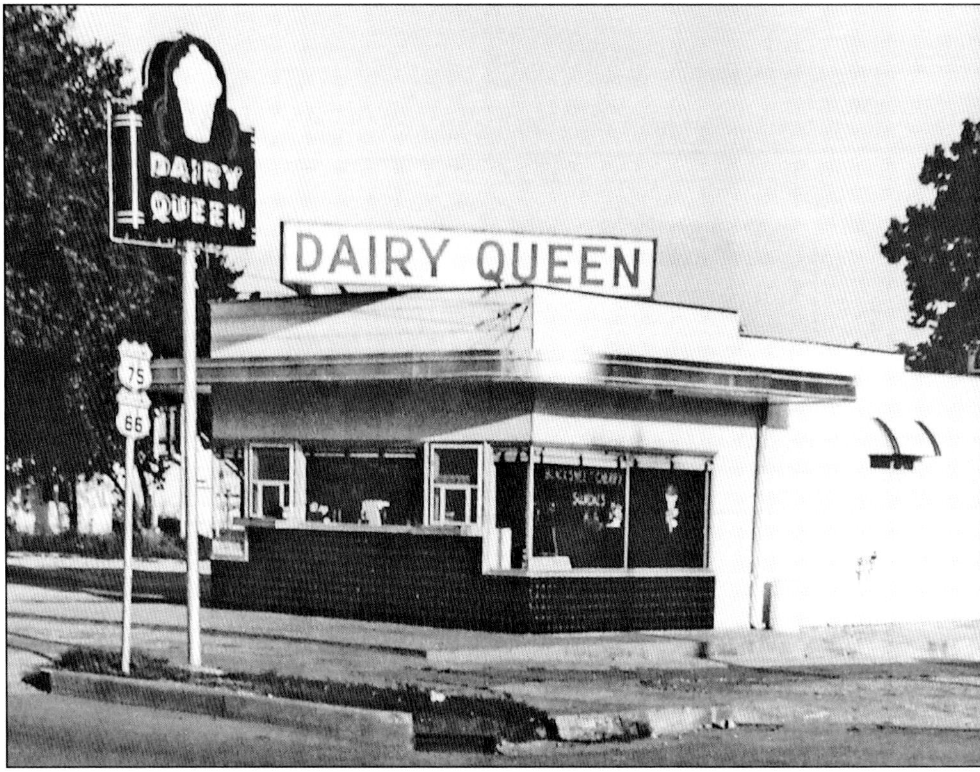

Early Dairy Queen. By 1950, franchising like that of Dairy Queen soft-serve ice cream was spreading across the country. The "DQ" in Sapulpa on Route 66 (where Sapulpa's main fire station on Dewey Avenue is today) was among more than 2,500 in 1955 and was one of several popular malt and burger places on the famous road and local cruise route.

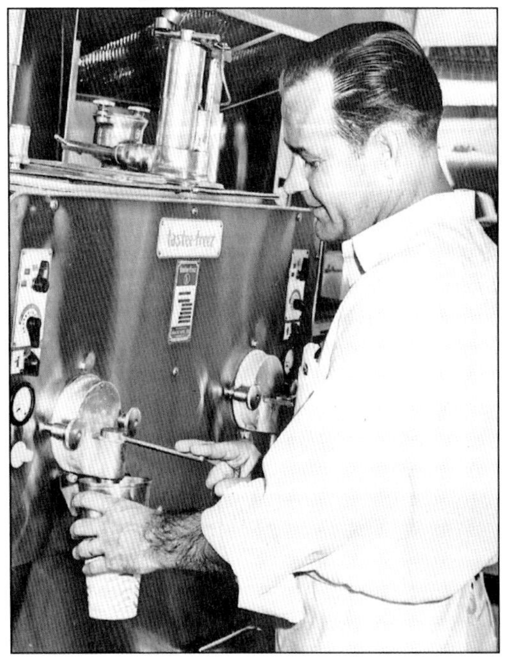

Cruising Sapulpa's Main Drag. Another soft serve, Tastee Freez (today, Happy Burger), also was on the local cruise route. Shown here, Bob Nabozney draws ice cream to make a chocolate malt. McDonald's was built right next-door, but local owners outlasted the big chain with burgers, fries, and shakes more preferred by the locals. Depending on who you talk to, the Friday and Saturday night cruise route on Route 66 and Main Street began at the Beacon Drive-In or Carl's Pig Stand on North Mission Street and ended at Cornwell's on South Main Street. Along the way were other root beer stands.

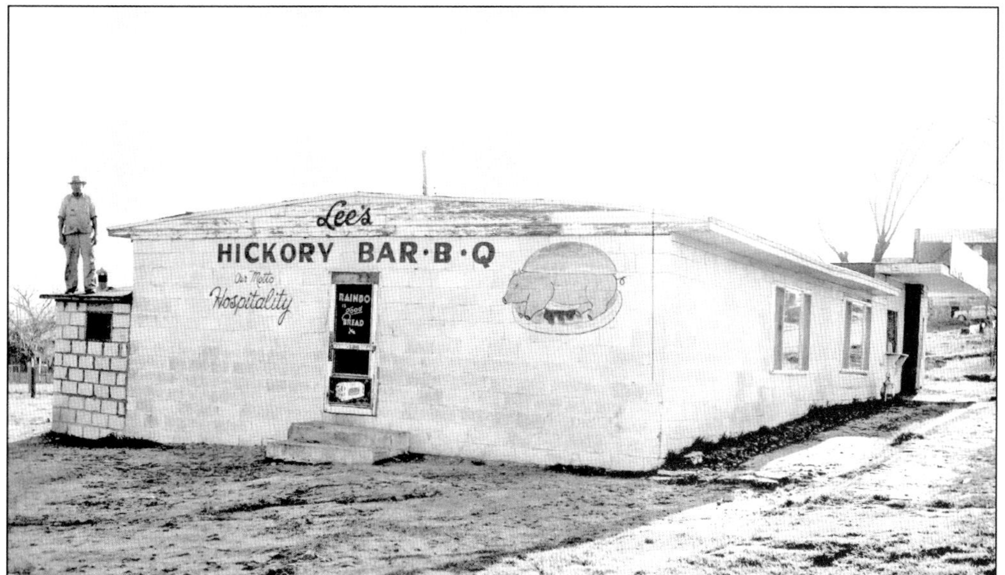

Barbecue and Hospitality. It is unknown if Lee Birmingham is fixing his roof or if he just finished smoking up another batch of ribs to serve at Lee's Hickory Bar-B-Q, situated at 411 East Hobson Avenue near Walnut Street. At any rate, he pauses for a photograph here. A block south is another diner, an old revamped street car known as Wimpy's.

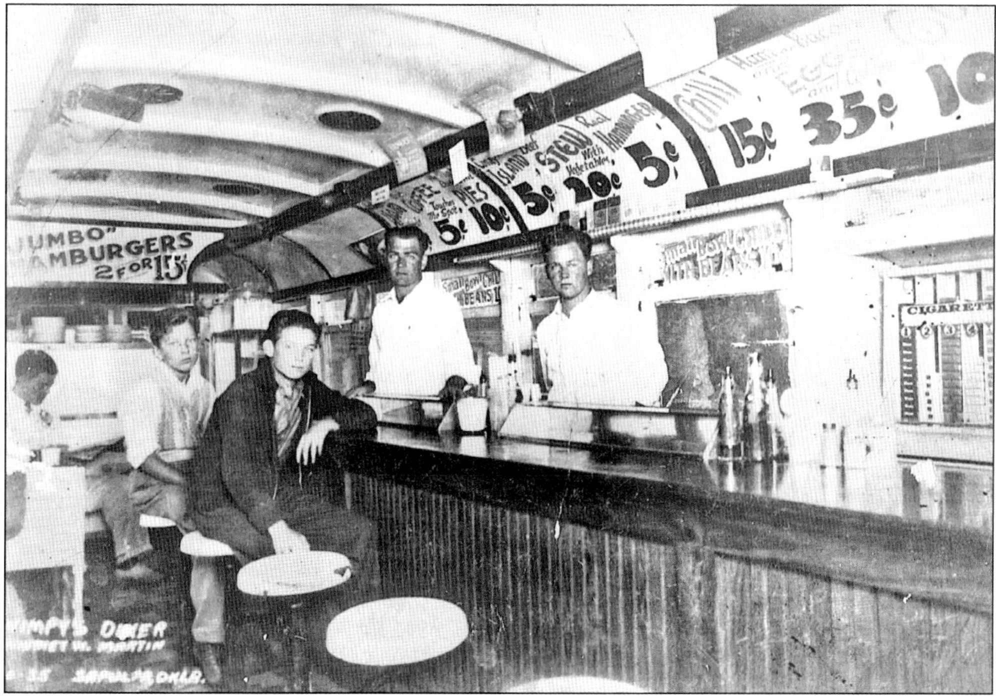

Old Streetcar Diner. It has been suggested that the two unidentified boys on the stools at Wimpy's Diner in downtown Sapulpa look like the two grown-ups serving up hamburgers and Coney hot dogs behind the counter. In 1932, Whitney "Wimpy" Martin bought one of the old trolley cars from the interurban and turned it into a diner at 515 East Dewey Avenue. It became an icon before it closed in 1973.

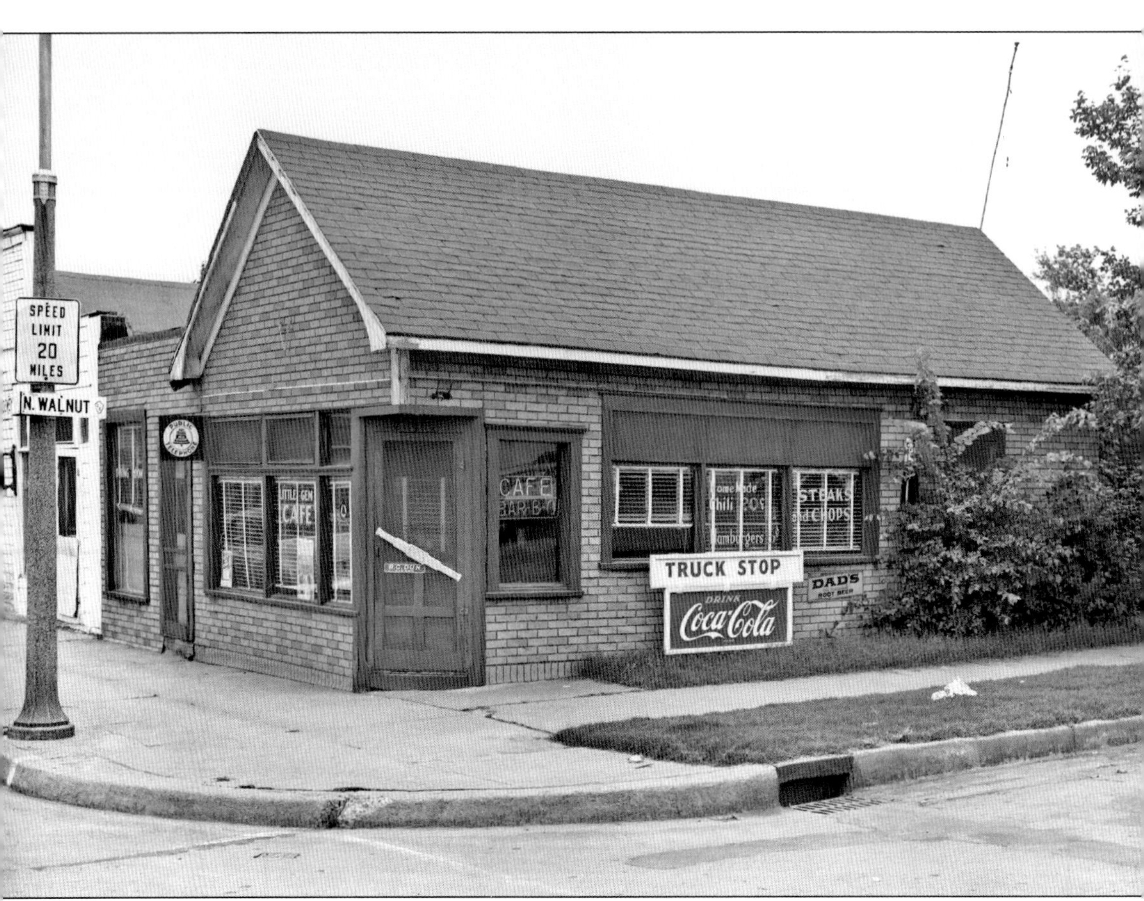

Where Truckers Eat. It was no secret: for a hearty meal that pleased the taste buds of the ordinary man, one should eat where the truckers eat. This café at the corner of North Walnut Street and East Dewey Avenue served homemade chili, hamburgers, steaks, chops, and Dad's Root Beer—surely winners for any hungry trucker or local diner.

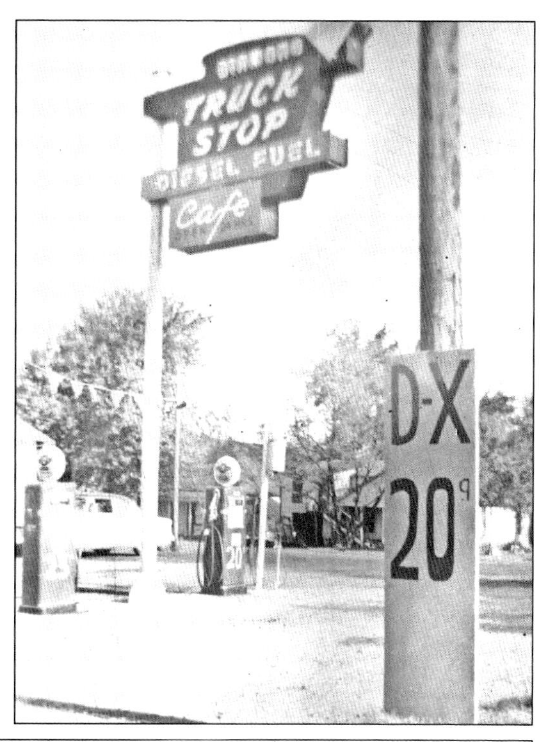

EVEN ELVIS LIKED DIAMOND. Listed among the famous travelers along Route 66 who stopped for a burger and fries at Diamond Truck Stop and Café at 408 North Mission Street is Elvis Presley. According to various newspaper accounts, "the King" and other celebrities driving down Route 66 were attracted to the iconic restaurant because of its widespread reputation. Indeed, bikers, old-car buffs, and Old Route 66 fans made the Diamond Café an icon that lasted into the 1990s. Menus and advertisements like this one became souvenirs.

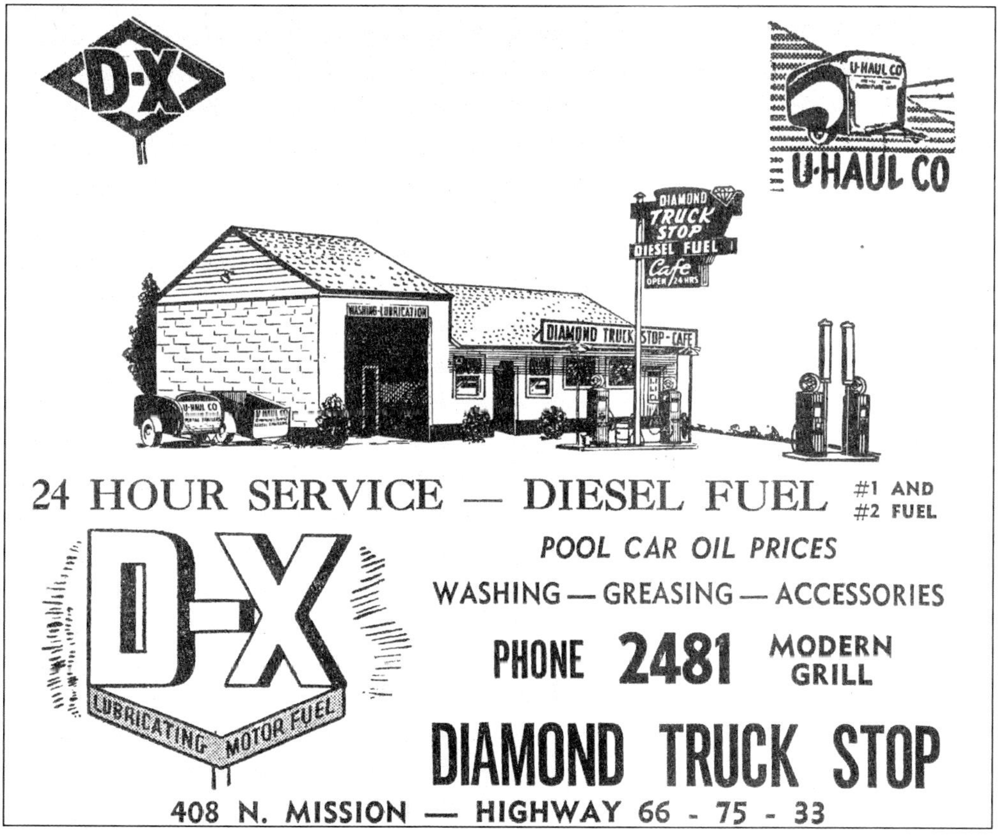

D-X

U-HAUL CO

DIAMOND TRUCK STOP DIESEL FUEL Cafe OPEN 24 HRS

WASHING-LUBRICATION

DIAMOND TRUCK STOP-CAFE

24 HOUR SERVICE — DIESEL FUEL #1 AND #2 FUEL

D-X LUBRICATING MOTOR FUEL

POOL CAR OIL PRICES

WASHING — GREASING — ACCESSORIES

PHONE 2481 MODERN GRILL

DIAMOND TRUCK STOP

408 N. MISSION — HIGHWAY 66 - 75 - 33

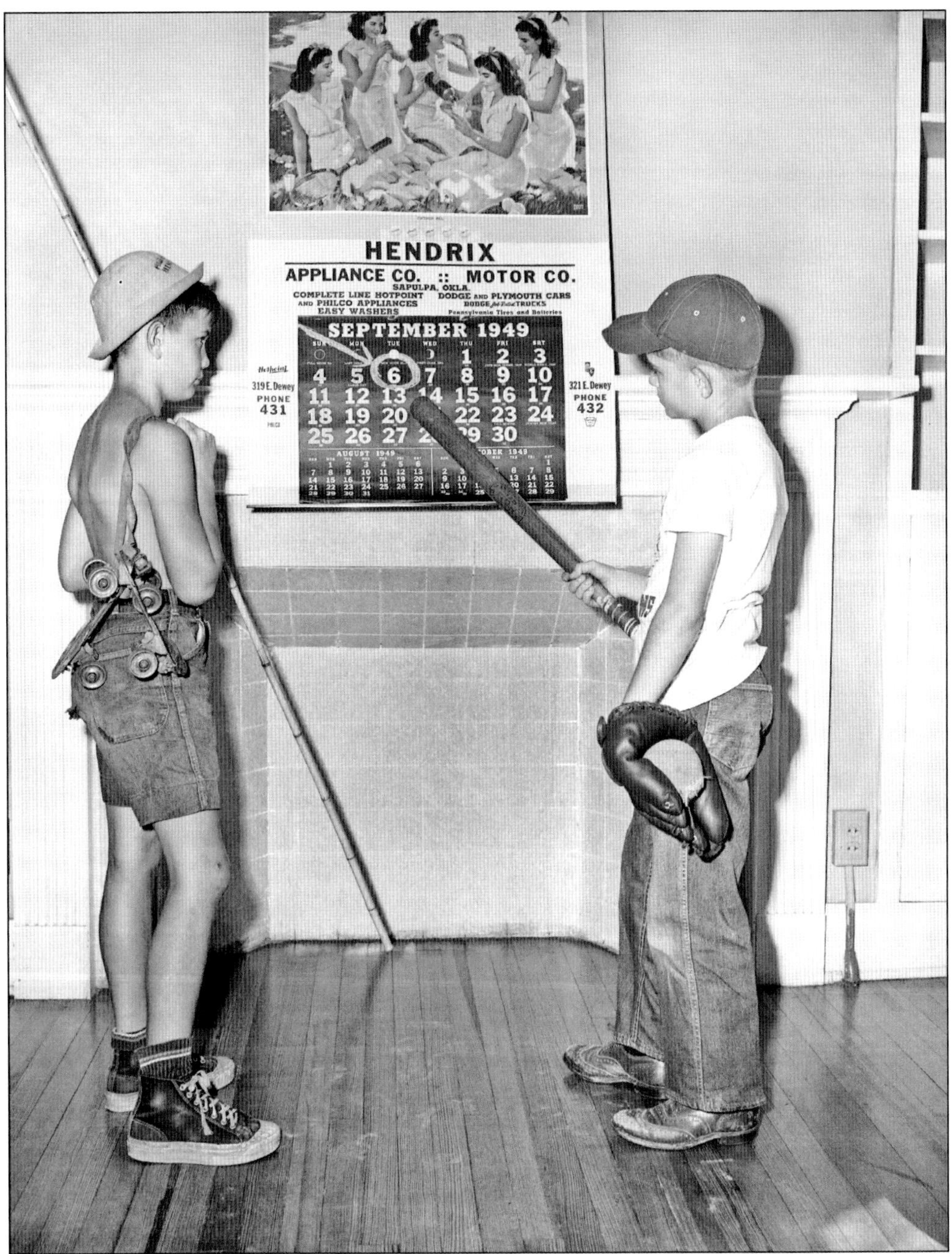

All Good Things Come to an End. On September 6, 1949, it was time to go back to school. No doubt modeling for a back-to-school ad of some sort, two Sapulpa lads bemoan that their summer filled with fishing, skating, and baseball is over and it is time to enroll for school.

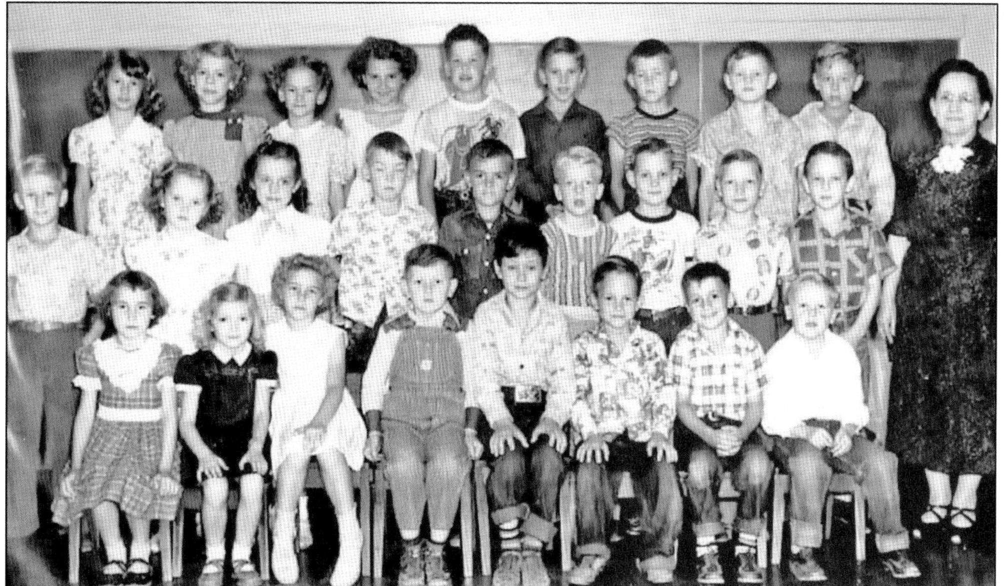

Disc Jockey's Classmates. This is Tulsa's rock 'n' roll–era disc jockey Rockin' John Henry's second-grade class picture from Liberty School. From left to right are (first row) Patsy Dunback, Linda Standifer, Sharon Pritchett, Jewel Hardy, James Peck, David Gibson, Richard Hughes, and Richard Doe; (second row) Doyal Evans, Linda Evans, Peggy Rhodes, Danny Lynn, Eugene Doe, Charles Groff, Ray Enlow, Millard Clark, and Johnny Henry; (third row) Hazel Stevens, Pamela Crisp, Barbara Sloan, Faye Matthews, Randy Scott, "Clif" Clifford, Patrick Engles, Jerry Sivadon, and Jerry Cockrell; the teacher is Laura Gaddy. (Courtesy of Jill Henry Riley.)

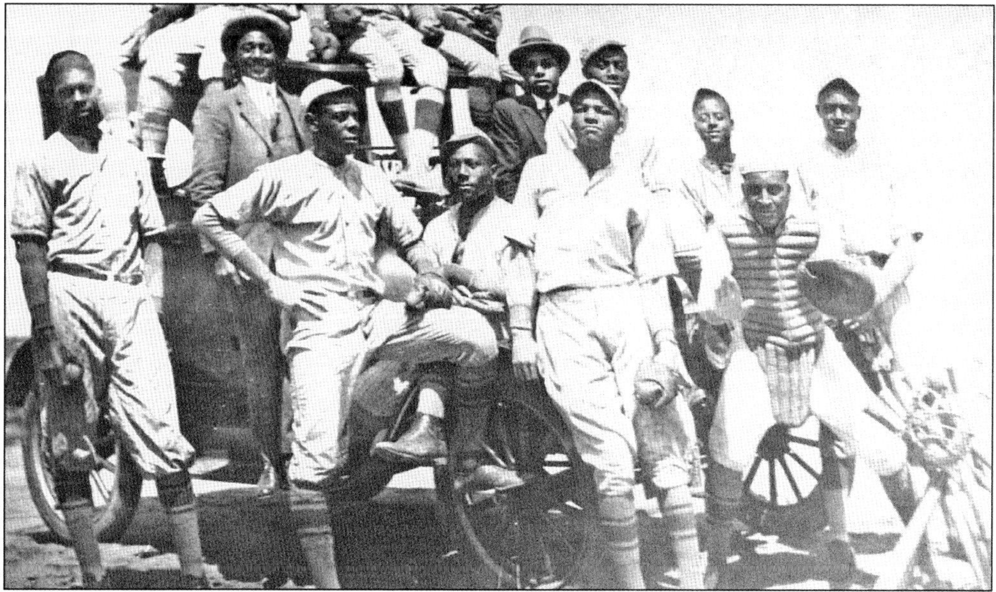

Negro Baseball Thrilling. Despite segregation and Jim Crow laws, Sapulpa's African Americans excelled in baseball in the 1920s, much to the delight of their community and anyone who wanted to come out and watch. From Booker T. Washington (BTW) High School to the Negro National League, black baseball brought thrills wherever the teams played, whether at urban centers or in the rural countryside.

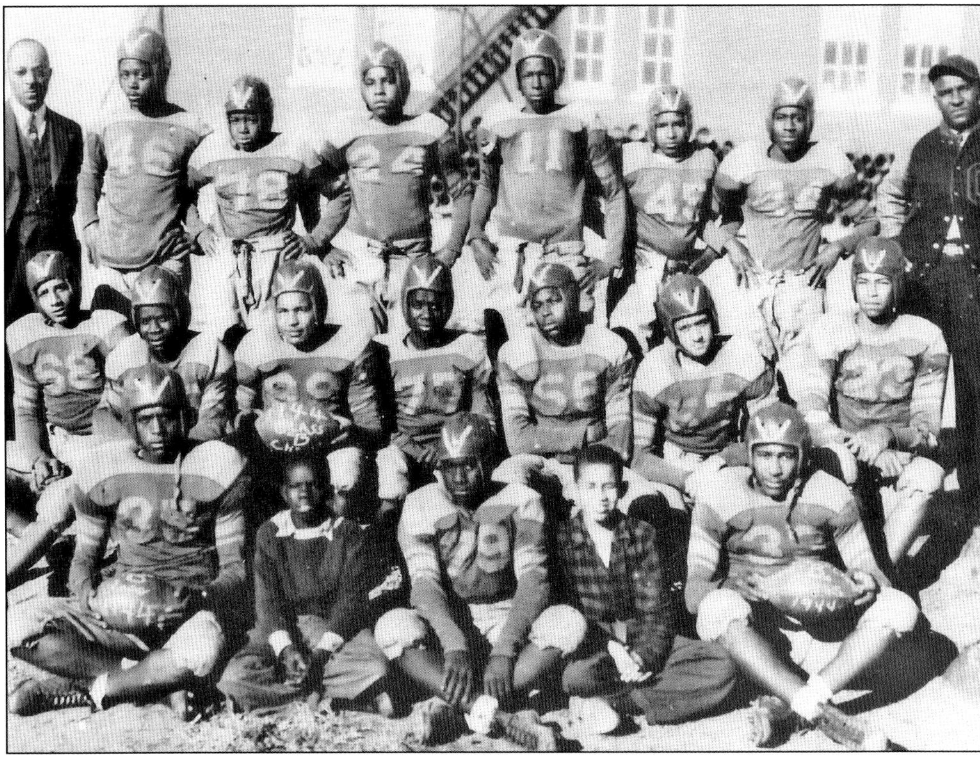

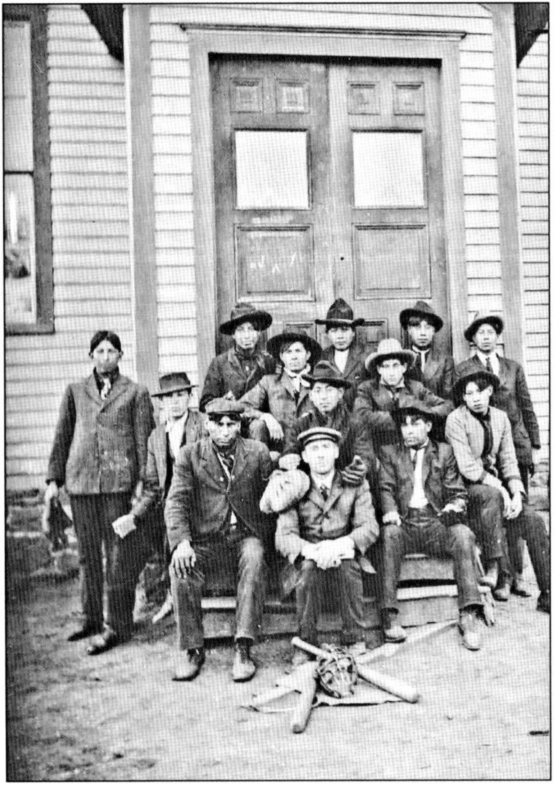

BOOKER T. FOOTBALL. Besides academia, music, and art, there was athletic education at Booker T. Washington School in Sapulpa. After integration in 1960, Sapulpa High School benefitted greatly in all areas to help the Chieftains gain statewide titles and notoriety. Sapulpa High School graduate Tom Colbert became the first black chief justice of the Oklahoma State Supreme Court in 2013.

INDIAN BALL, ANYONE? Granted the uniforms may not have been traditional in any sense of the word when it comes to baseball, but the Native American boys at Euchee Mission Boarding School could hold their own against any team. Before eventually integrating into Sapulpa Public Schools, the school offered a variety of sports to its students.

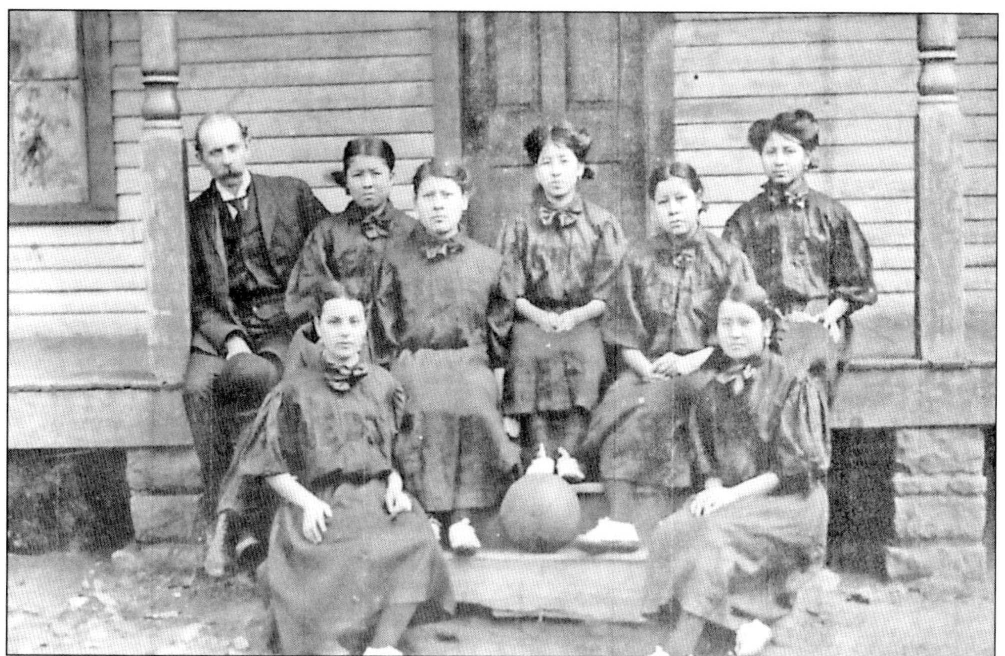

MAGNIFICENT SEVEN. The coach at Euchee Mission Boarding School and his girls' basketball team pose for a photograph. The school enrolled Creek, Euchee, and members of other Indian tribes in its program. The students lived in dorms on campus where today's Sapulpa High School stands. Native Americans continued to excel in athletics after integrating into public schools.

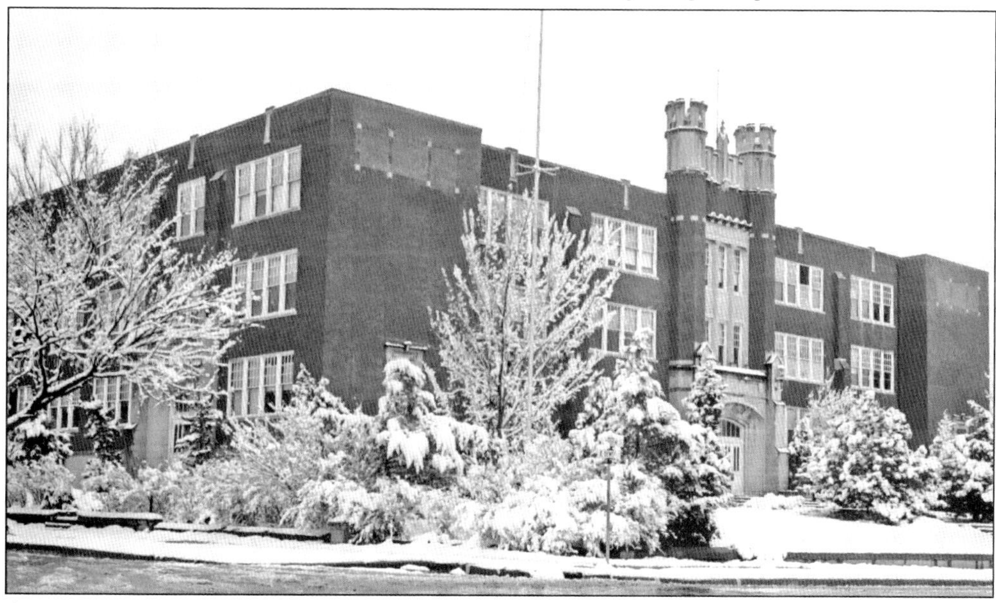

OLD SAPULPA HIGH SCHOOL. The multistory high school building on Dewey Avenue and Maple Street, shown here during a typical once- or twice-a-year Sapulpa winter snowstorm, was constructed in 1918. After serving for a time as home to Sapulpa Junior High, the building was razed in 1969 because it was deemed not "safe or sound." Its walls would not budge at the first strikes of the wrecking ball. The contractor who won the bid to demolish the structure is said to have gone bankrupt trying to accomplish the task.

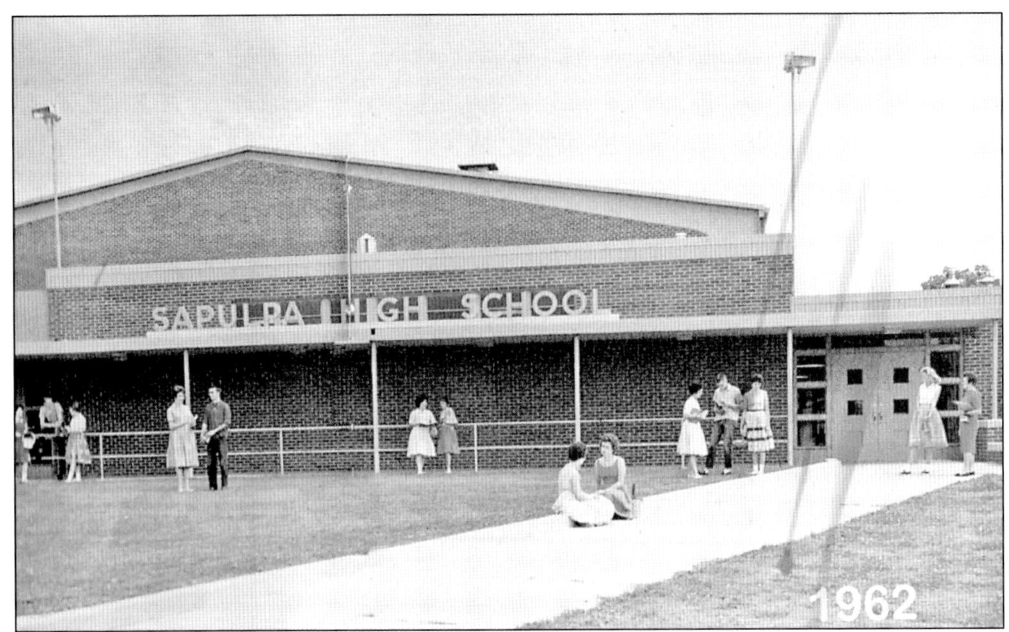

New Building on Old Campus. When the new Sapulpa High School was built in 1960 it was on land formerly utilized for the education of Native Americans, primarily members of the Creek and Euchee tribes. The boarding school campus had dormitories for boys, girls, and staff, as well as school buildings. The land was sold to the Sapulpa School District. Changing laws required Indians to attend public schools.

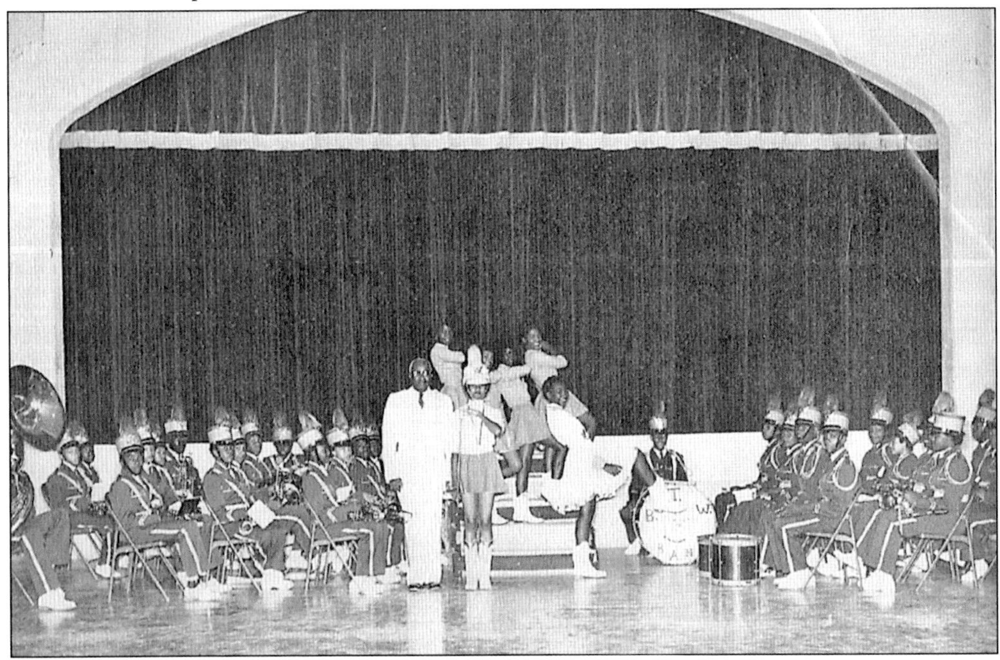

Presenting the BTW Band. Among the model programs for African American students at Sapulpa's Booker T. Washington School was its music education. Here, its director and 30-plus-member BTW Marching Band ready to present a program to the community as they prepare for a parade performance.

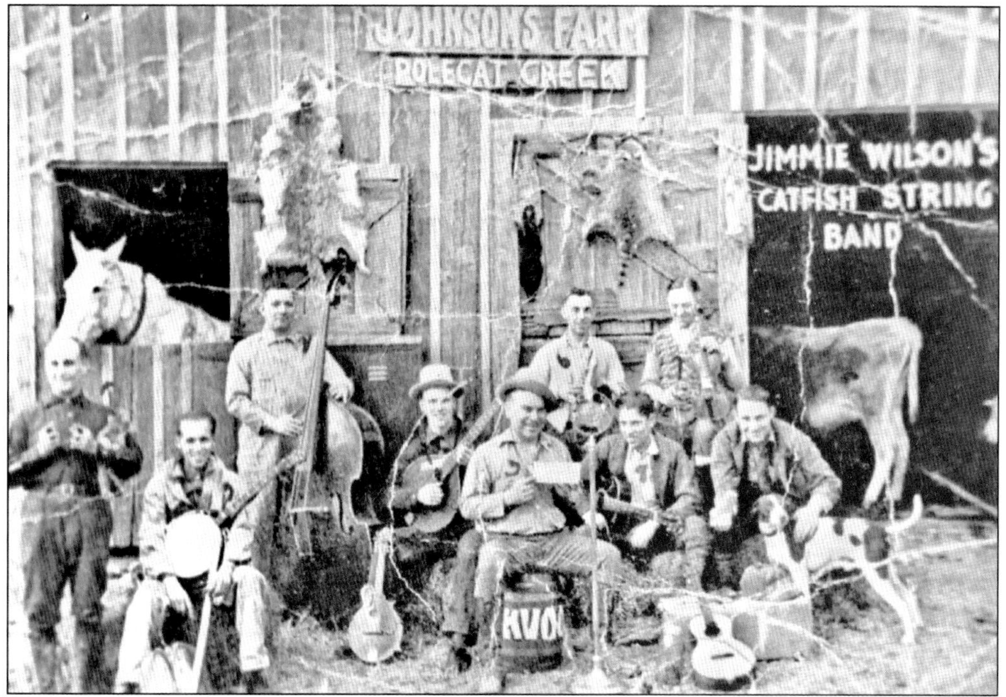

Old-Time Radio Show. When talking about entertainment, it did not get any better than Jimmy Wilson's Catfish String Band, shown here in the 1920s with a check from sponsors that paid for the old-time radio show on KVOO "broadcast from the banks of Polecat Creek." The band actually produced the show from Wilson's home on South Poplar Street. The band recorded for RCA Victor in 1929.

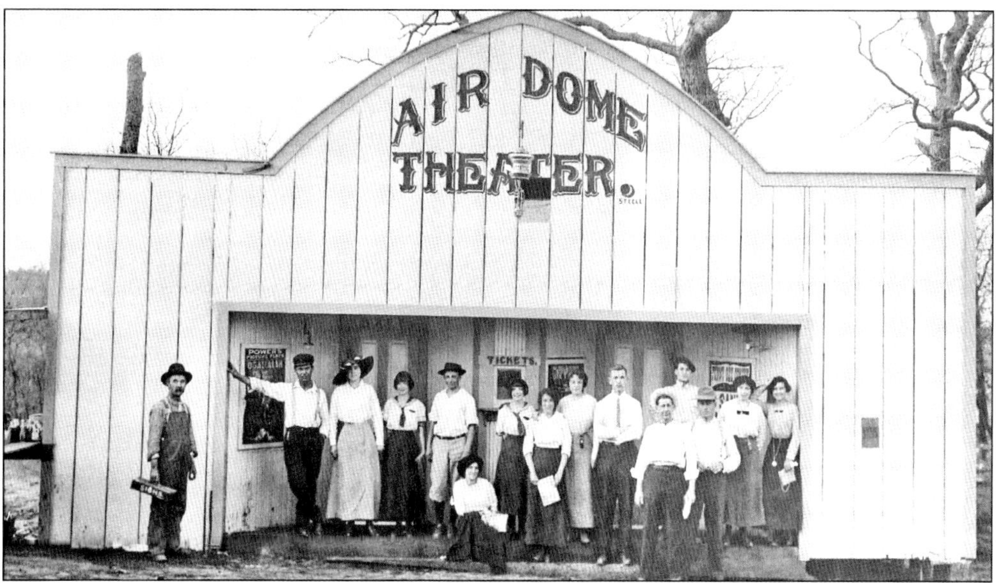

Outdoor Entertainment Venue, 1911. The sign painter (left) and performers take time out for a photograph as another production is readied at Sapulpa's Air Dome. Performing arts always have been a big part of community life in Sapulpa. Its first theaters hosted live performances and, in the case of this theater, shows were presented in the open air.

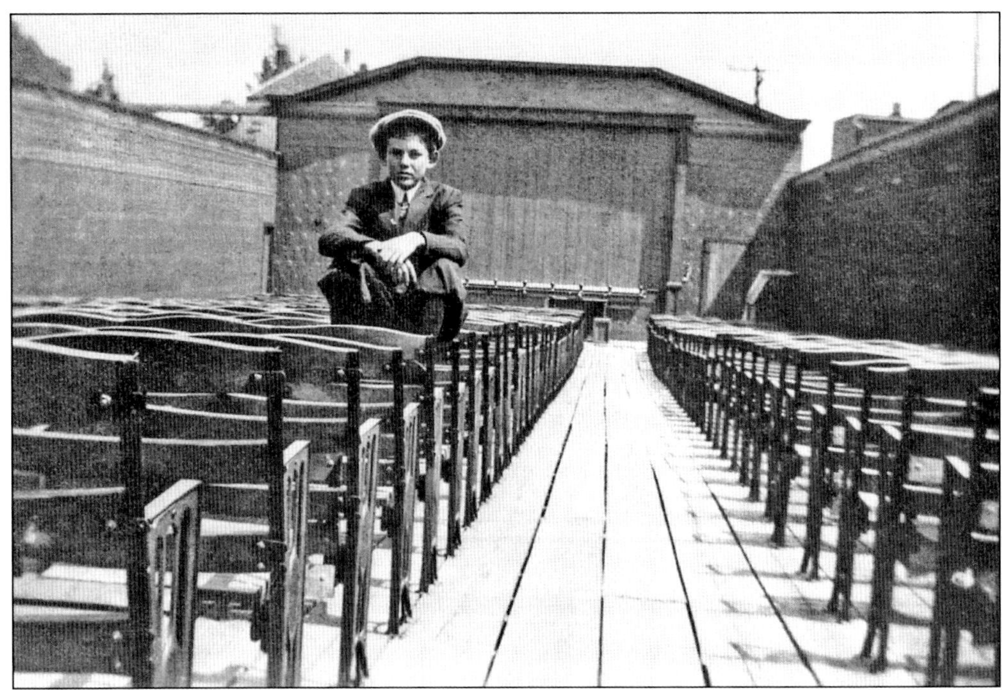

Striking a Theatrical Pose. A young Roy Baxter, seen here around 1910, destined to become an entertainer himself, sits atop the seating at Sapulpa's Air Dome Theatre at 110 South Main Street. Live performances also could be seen at inside venues like the Lucile Opera House. Silent screen movie theaters followed, and then came the talkies.

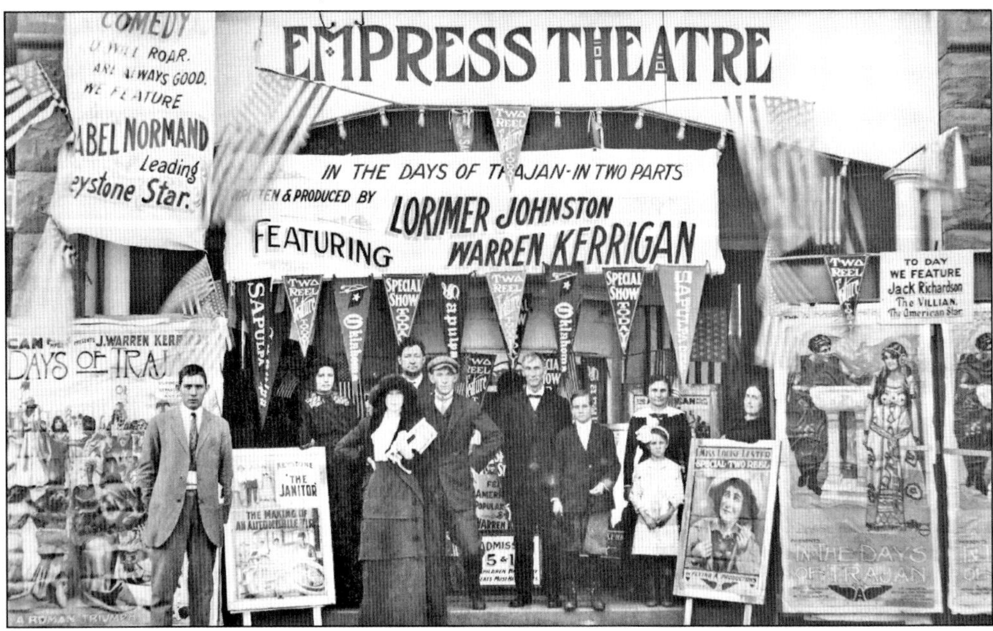

Sapulpa's Silent Screens. Before talkie movies, Sapulpa theaters like the Empress and Grand featured silent movies and stage productions. Pictured here, theater personnel (and vaudeville performers) promote the 1913 silent movie *In the Days of Trajan* starring Warren Kerrigan. Trajan was a Roman emperor who sent his enemies to the dungeons.

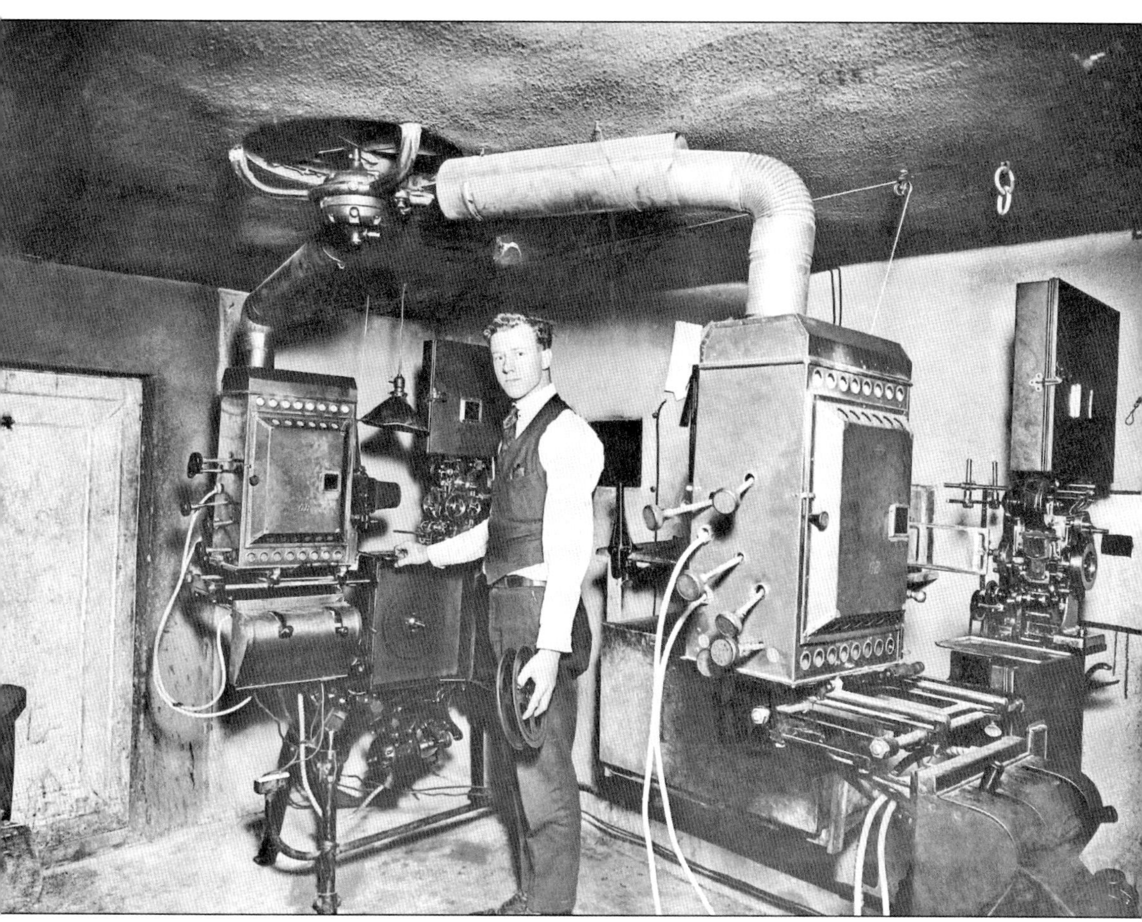

The Projectionist. Before the days of multiscreens, computers, and automation, the skills of a projectionist to keep the reels running at Sapulpa's popular downtown movie theaters—the Criterion, the State, the Yale, and Tee-Pee Drive-In—were crucial. This unidentified projectionist and his equipment were typical.

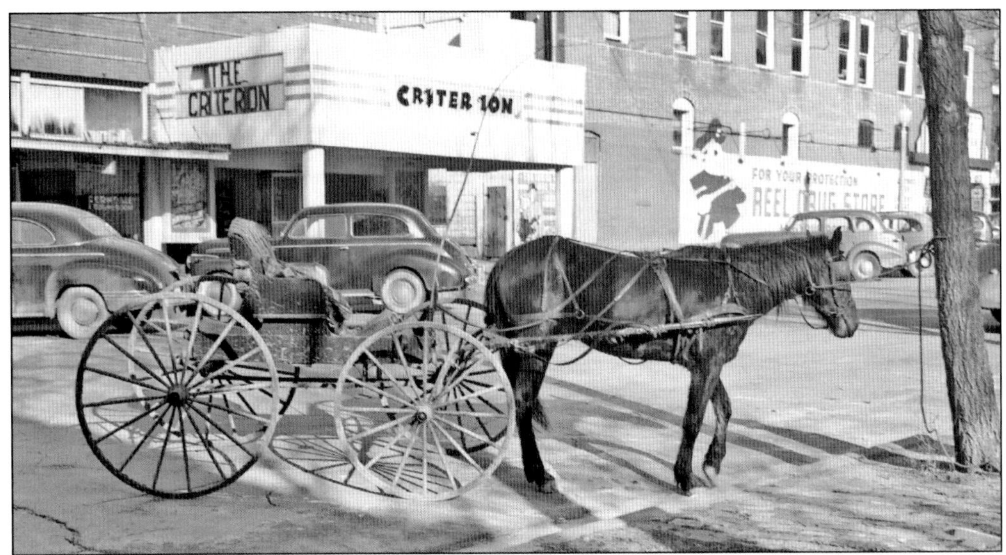

Taking in a Movie? The driver of this horse and buggy tied to a tree across from the Criterion Theater may be taking in a movie or picking up some meds at Reel Drug Store around 1940. It was not uncommon to see horses and buggies into the 1940s, but at least one photographer thought this one picture worthy.

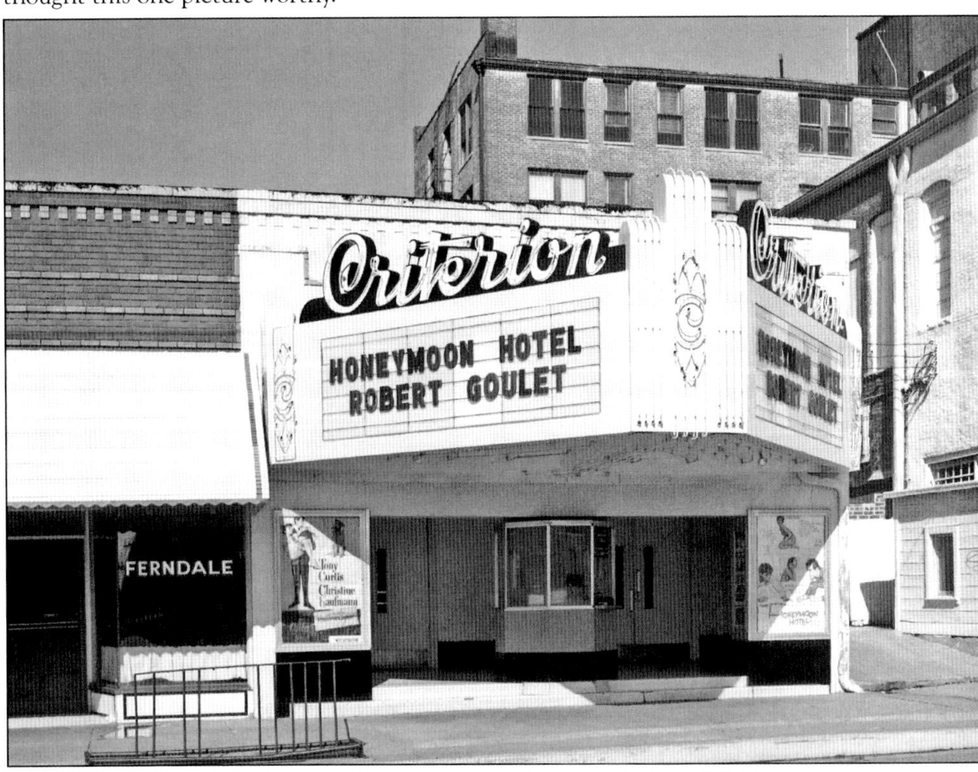

The Latest Movie. The Criterion Theater, situated next to the Ferndale Restaurant in downtown Sapulpa, sports a nice marquee advertising the 1964 film *Honeymoon Hotel.* It starred Robert Goulet, Nancy Kwan, Robert Morse, and Jill St. John. Unusual for its time, the film centered on an interracial romance, but the racial difference is never mentioned.

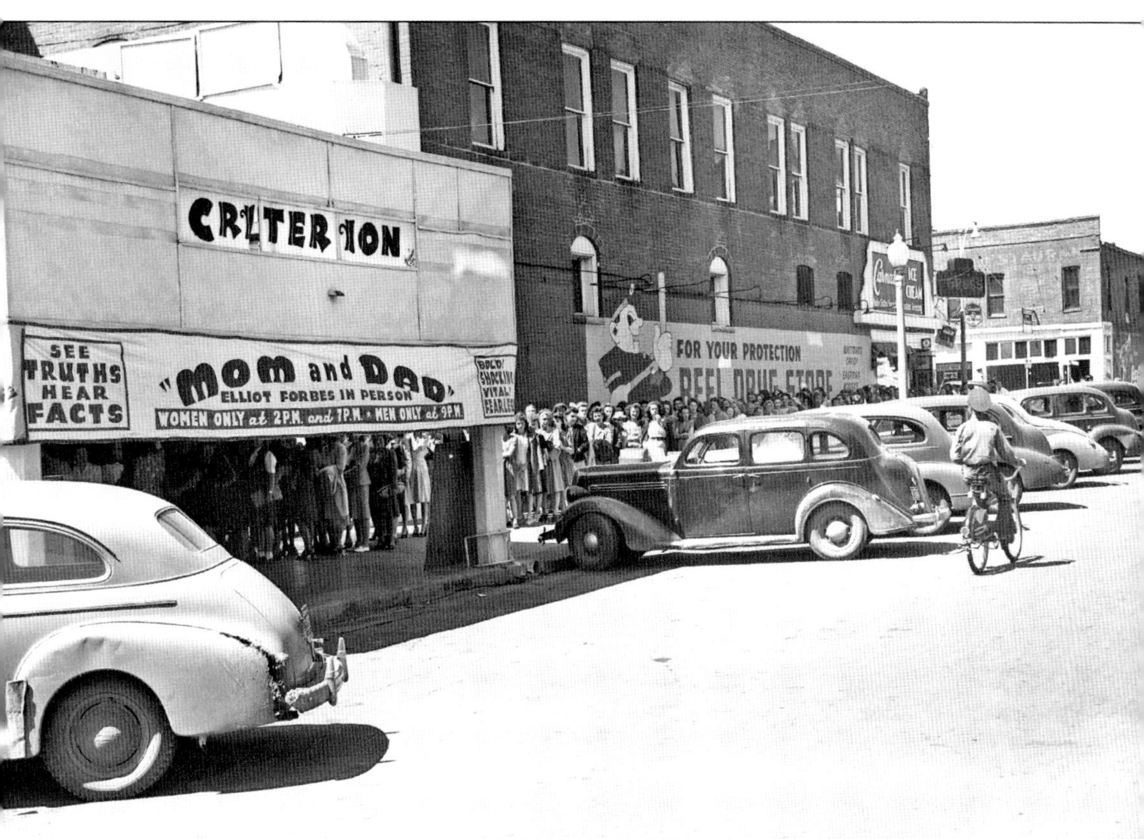

Crowd for "Sex Hygiene" Film. *Mom and Dad* was a feature-length 1945 film largely produced by exploitation filmmaker Kroger Babb. The film carried a lot of hype about "sex hygiene," and maybe because it was condemned by the National Legion of Decency, huge crowds came to see it. In Sapulpa, people wait to buy tickets.

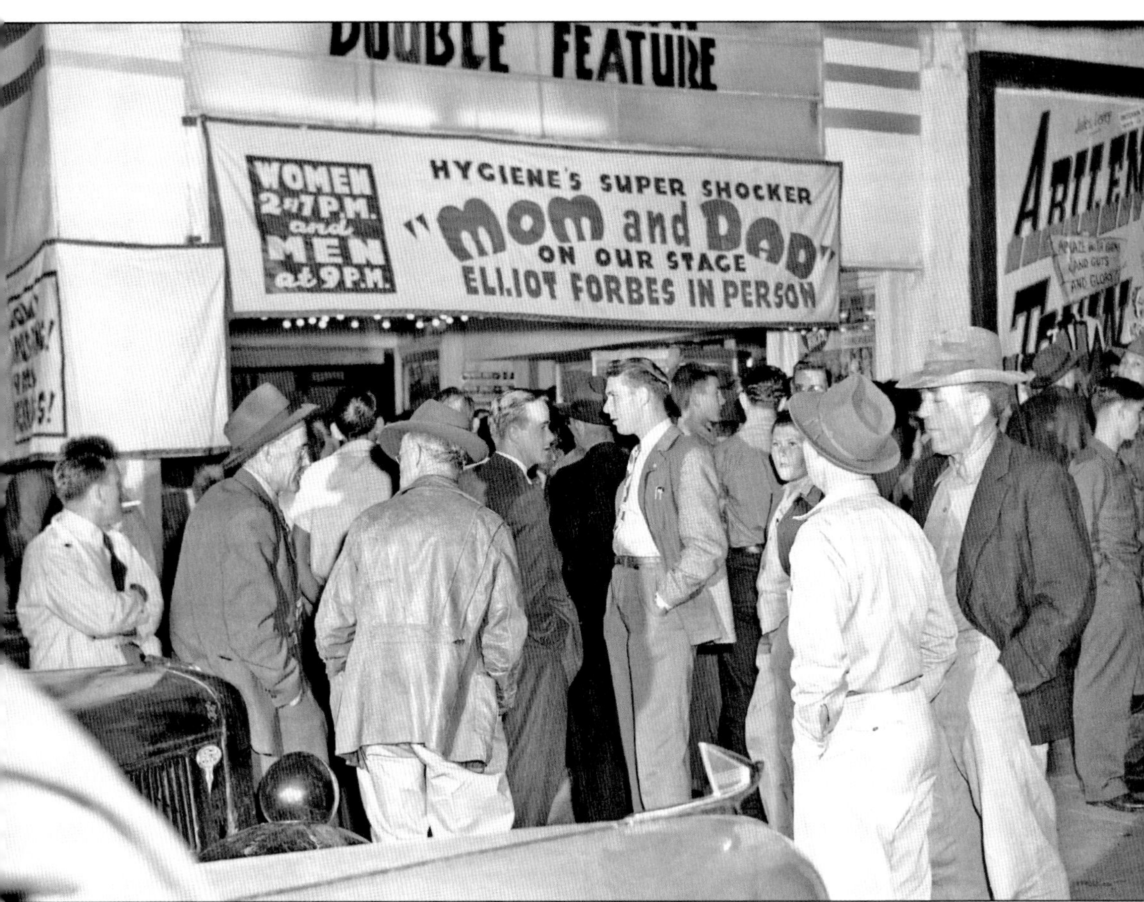

Sex Segregation. The theater that screened *Mom and Dad* offered separate viewing times for males and females. It was one of the highest-grossing films of the 1940s. The film was exploitation repackaged with controversial content to establish "educational value" to circumvent US censorship laws. Babb's marketing of his film incorporated old-style medicine show techniques and used unique promotions to build an audience.

Seven

Our Changing Landscape
People, Places, Politics, and Parades

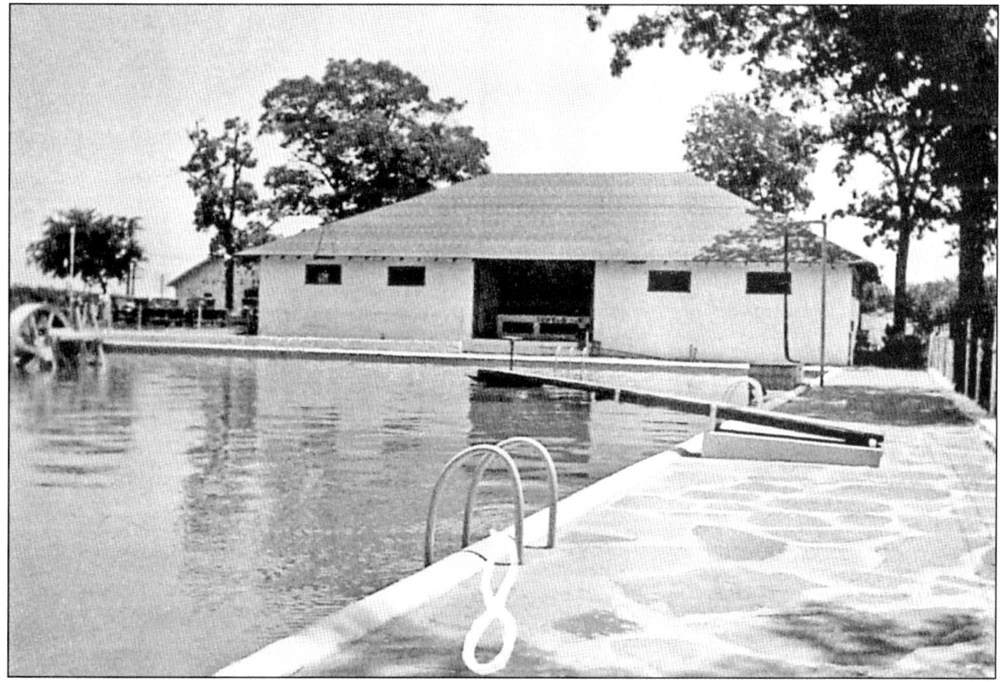

Famous Dixieland Pool. The swimming pool filled with springwater along the Route 66 tourist route was very famous. The pool was not only an attraction for tourists and locals during the heyday of the Mother Road and its motor courts. Gold medalist swimmer (and *Tarzan* star) Johnny Weissmuller, along with other celebrities, are said to have come here to swim because of the pool's water and diving board. The Dixieland Supper Club also was famous.

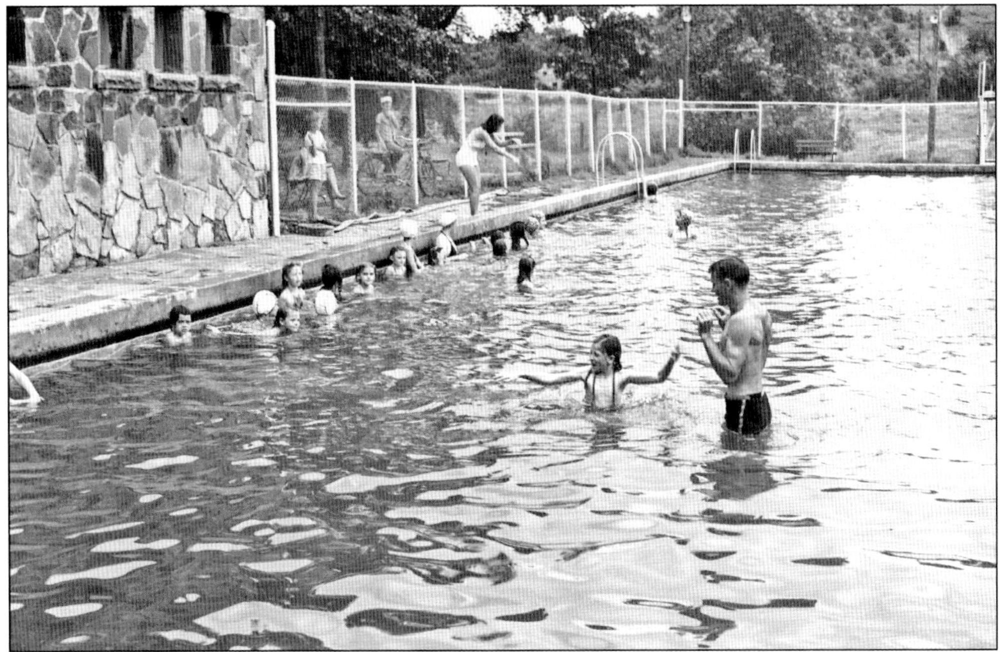

Swimming Holes. Yesteryear's swimming pools and kids' wading pools looked a little different than today's walk-in Aquatic Center and Rotary Splash Pad in Liberty Park, but many stayed cool, and boys and girls learned to swim at Sapulpa's WPA-era municipal pool west of town. Today, the municipal park is Sapulpa Golf Course.

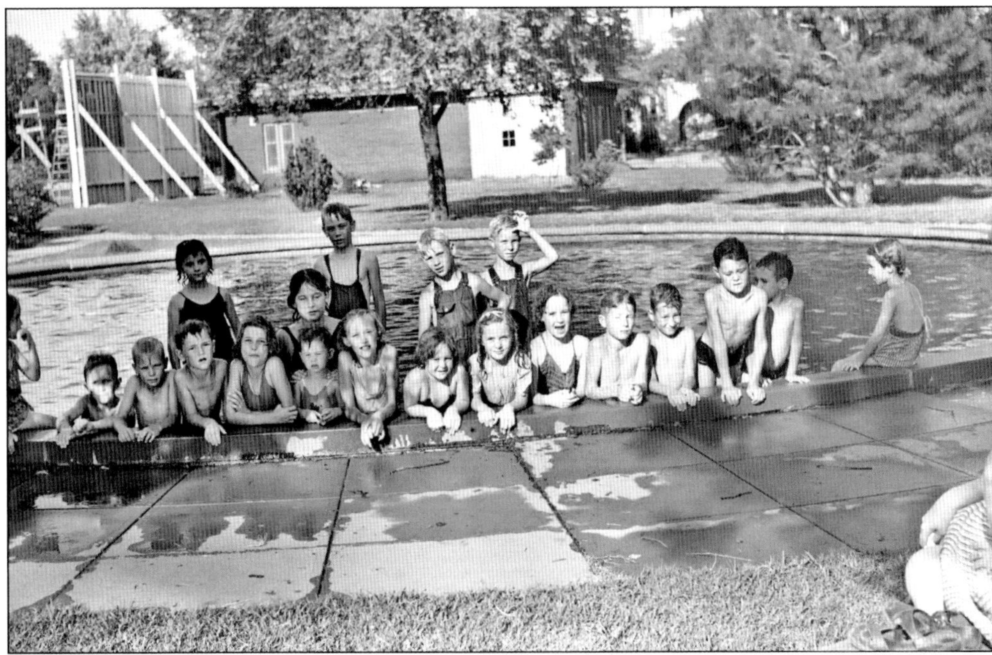

Yesterday's Splash Pad. A group of Sapulpa youngsters take time out from splashing and water fights for a photograph in the 1950s. Near the southwest corner of Mission Street and Dewey Avenue, there was a kids' park and wading pool. During the hot days of summer, parents and grandparents would gather up the kids and find relief from the heat.

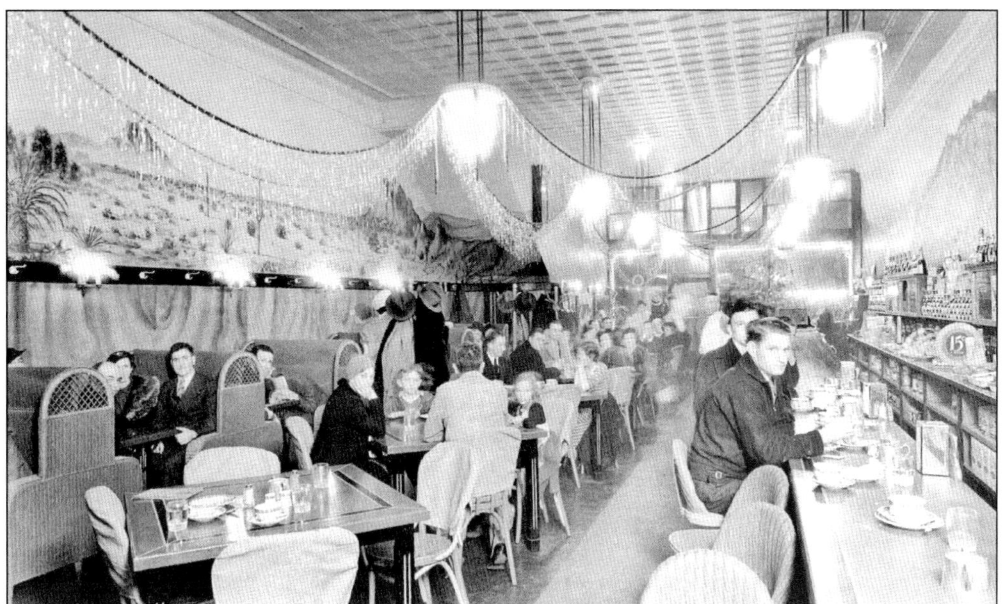

Fine Restaurants Downtown. Restaurants in downtown Sapulpa from the 1920s on were noted for both food and atmosphere. In this c. 1930 photograph, diners pause for snapshot at the Lindberg Café, owned by Steve Theodoris and located on the south side of Dewey Avenue between Water and North Main Streets. Others fine eateries were the Ferndale and Liberty.

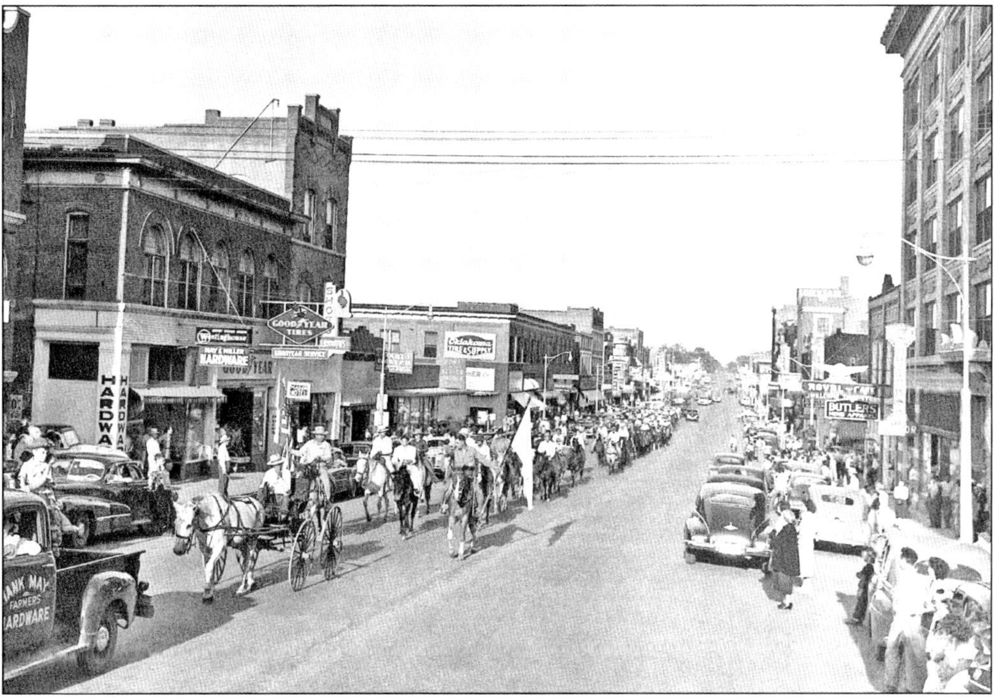

Leading the Parade. Hank May, who has just passed his hardware store on the left, leads a Main Street parade in the late 1940s. Downtown was the stage for Sapulpa High School homecoming parades, the annual nighttime Christmas parade, and the Fourth of July and Labor Day parades, as well as parades honoring returning soldiers, veterans, and hometown heroes.

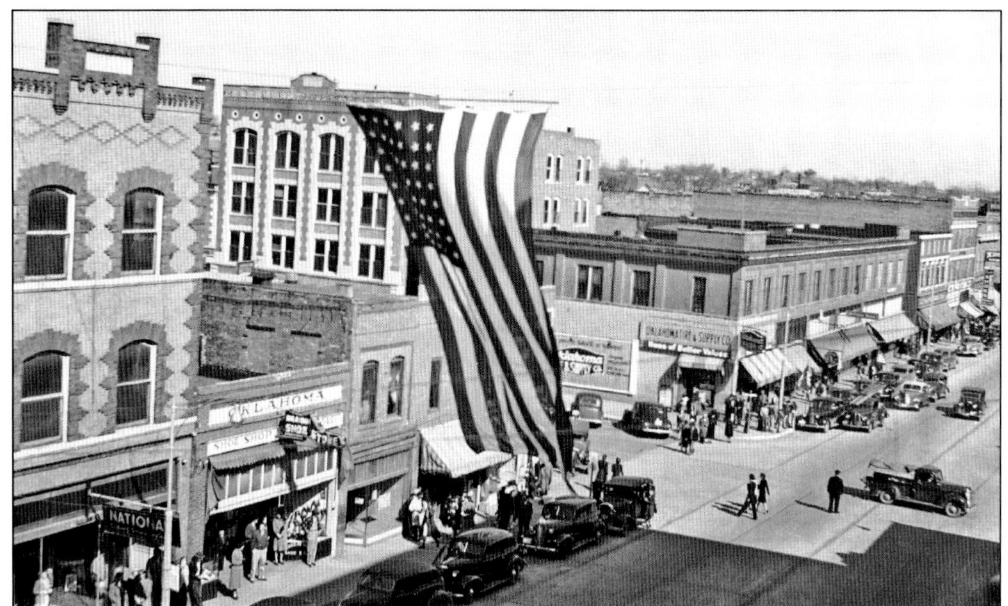

Under the Flag. Sapulpa is proudly patriotic, as demonstrated by this procession beneath the US flag on Dewey Avenue in 1940. Dewey Avenue is also Route 66, where the town's birthdays have been marked by parades and the pomp and pageantry of political rallies played out.

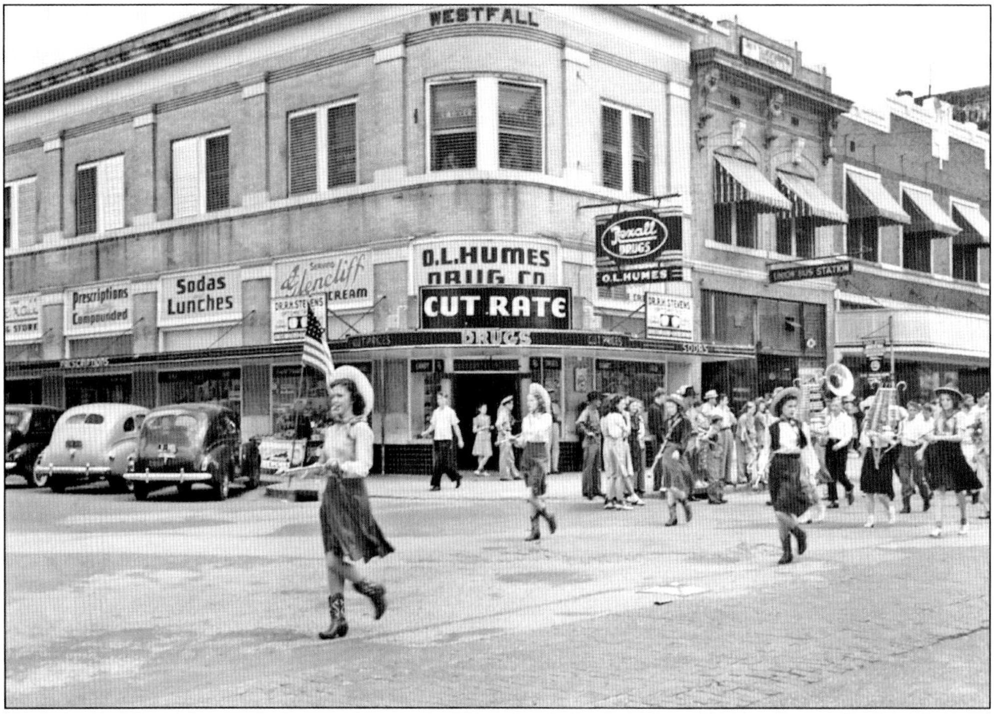

Marching Westward. Young majorette twirlers lead the parade. This may have been a themed homecoming parade in the early 1940s, but it could have taken place in 1948, when Sapulpa marked its 50th birthday. This group is headed west down Dewey Avenue in cowgirl attire, past the Union Bus Station and Humes' Rexall Drug Store.

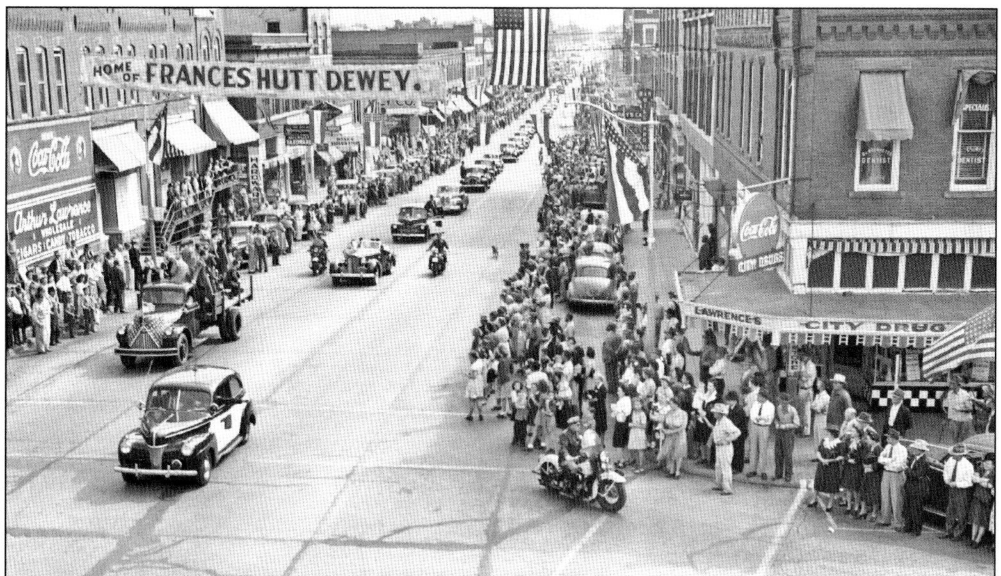

PARADE WELCOMES DEWEY. One of the biggest crowds to ever attend a downtown parade was in 1948, when New York governor Thomas Dewey came to town, but not necessarily to mark the town's birthday. He was running for president of the United States against Harry S. Truman. The star, however, as the banner reveals, may have been his wife, a former Sapulpan. The Dewey automobile is flanked by two motorcycle officers.

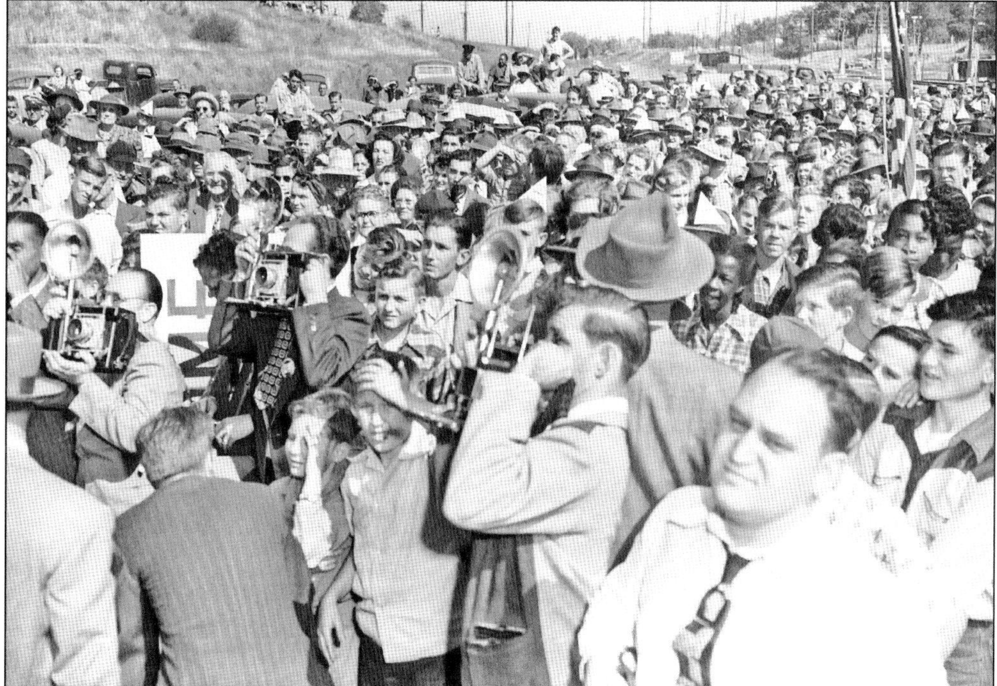

CROWDS WAIT FOR DEWEY. A crowd of local residents, along with reporters, photographers, and the curious from all over, converges at the Sapulpa train depot in September 1948 as a train carrying Republican presidential candidate Thomas Dewey and his wife, Frances Hutt Dewey, arrives. School was let out so students could join family for the momentous visit.

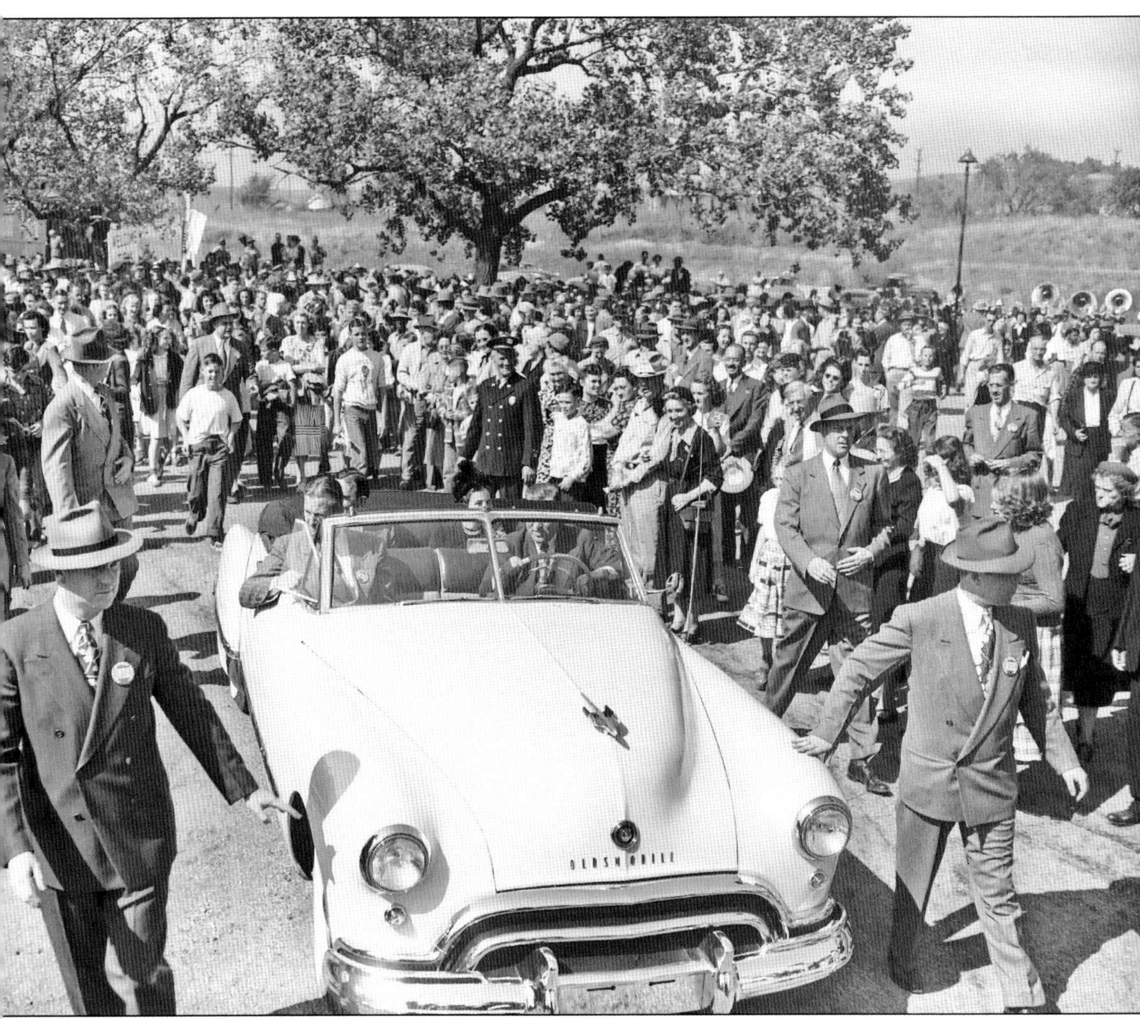

DEWEY DEPARTS. After the train stopped, Dewey spoke from the platform at the back of his car and then rode away in this 1948 Oldsmobile convertible, driven by and surrounded by US Secret Service agents. Enthusiasm was high, and it looked like Dewey would defeat Truman in November. He did not, but Sapulpans were glad to have him visit his wife's hometown.

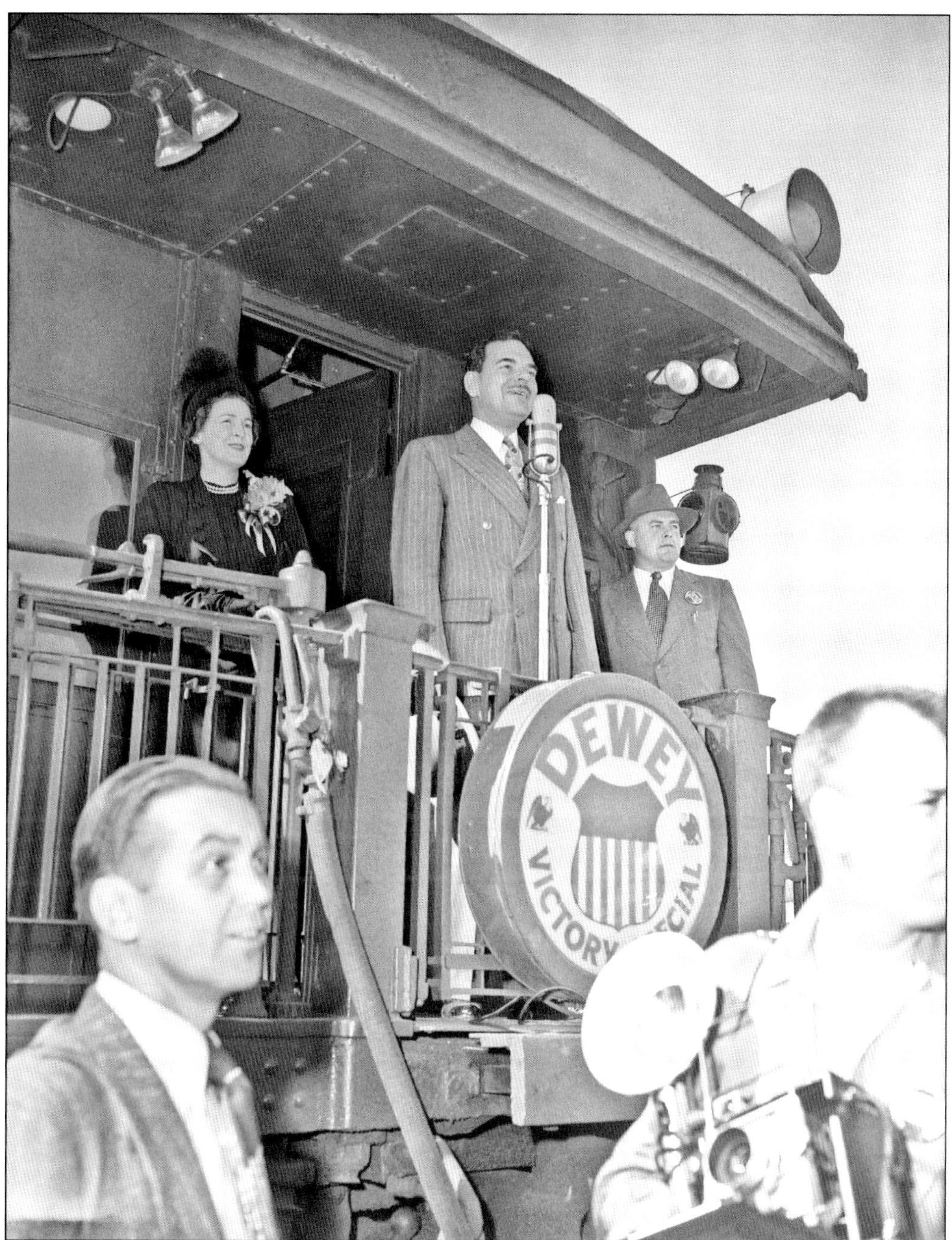

On the Victory Special. Republican candidate Thomas Dewey with his wife, the former Frances Hutt of Sapulpa, addresses a crowd from the back of a train car during a Sapulpa stop. When Pres. Franklin D. Roosevelt died in office, vice president Harry S. Truman became president. Truman was the Democratic nominee in 1948 and many, including the *Chicago Tribune*, were confident Dewey would win.

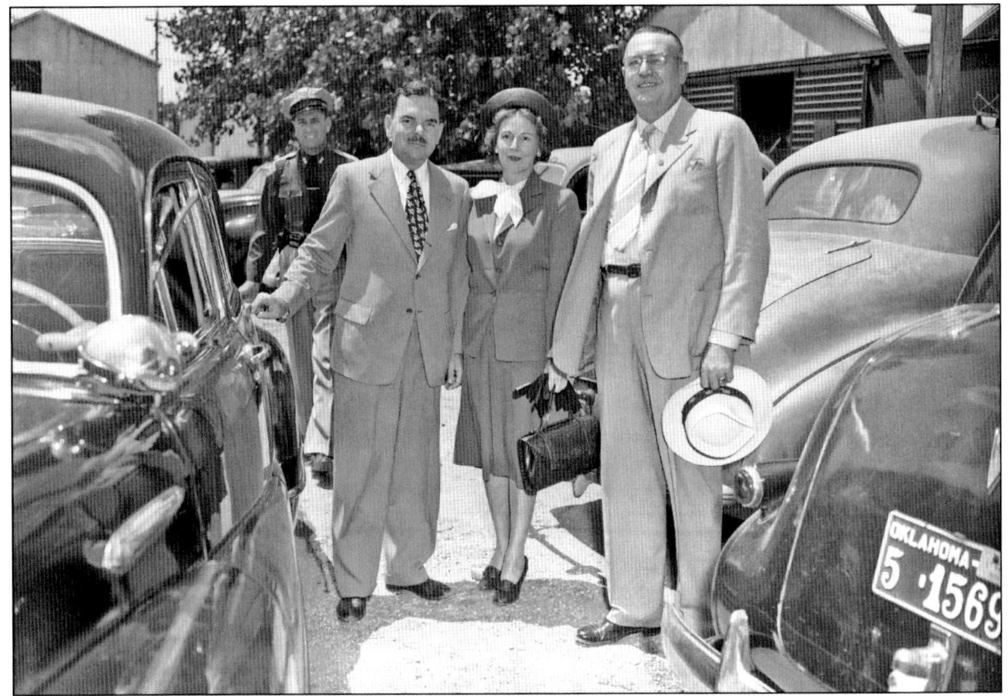

Dewey Visits the Town. Thomas Dewey, who ran a close race against Franklin D. Roosevelt in 1944, came to his wife's hometown of Sapulpa on several occasions. Here, he and Frances Hutt Dewey are shown with an Oklahoma Highway Patrol trooper and an unidentified gentleman. Dewey, the 47th governor of New York, would seek the presidency again in 1948.

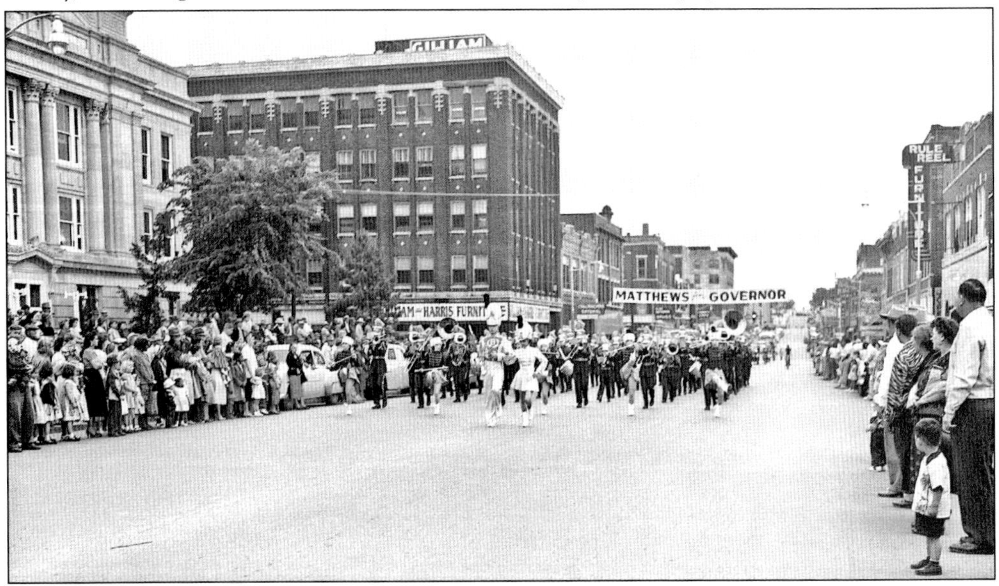

Matthews Runs for Governor. R.P. Matthews, owner of the *Sapulpa Daily Herald*, was named to the turnpike authority after his push and involvement with the development of Turner Turnpike (named for Oklahoma's 13th governor, Roy J. Turner), which runs through Sapulpa. When Matthews sought the governorship on the Democratic ticket in 1954, a parade was held. He was not successful. He sold the *Herald* to Ed Livermore of Claremore in 1958.

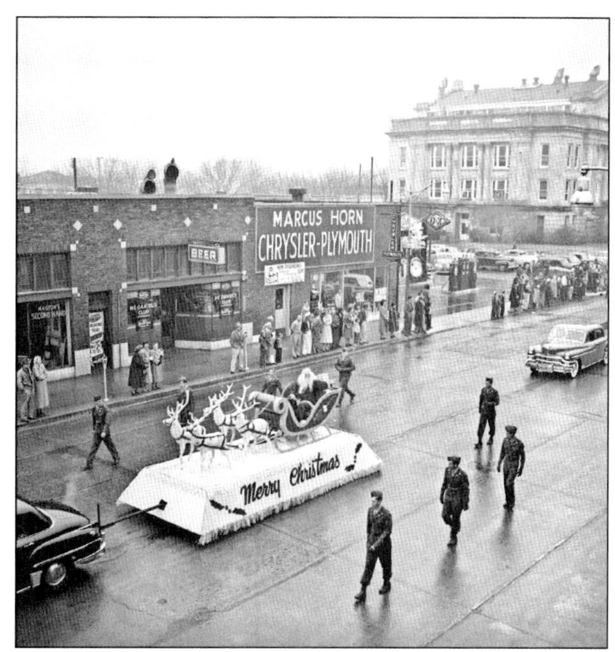

Christmas Parade at Dusk. This picture was taken during an annual nighttime (or at least near dusk) c. 1950s Christmas parade through downtown Sapulpa. Even when it is cold, it is well attended. Prizes are awarded for the best floats. There are police cars, fire engines, horses, marching bands, and at the end, Santa Claus.

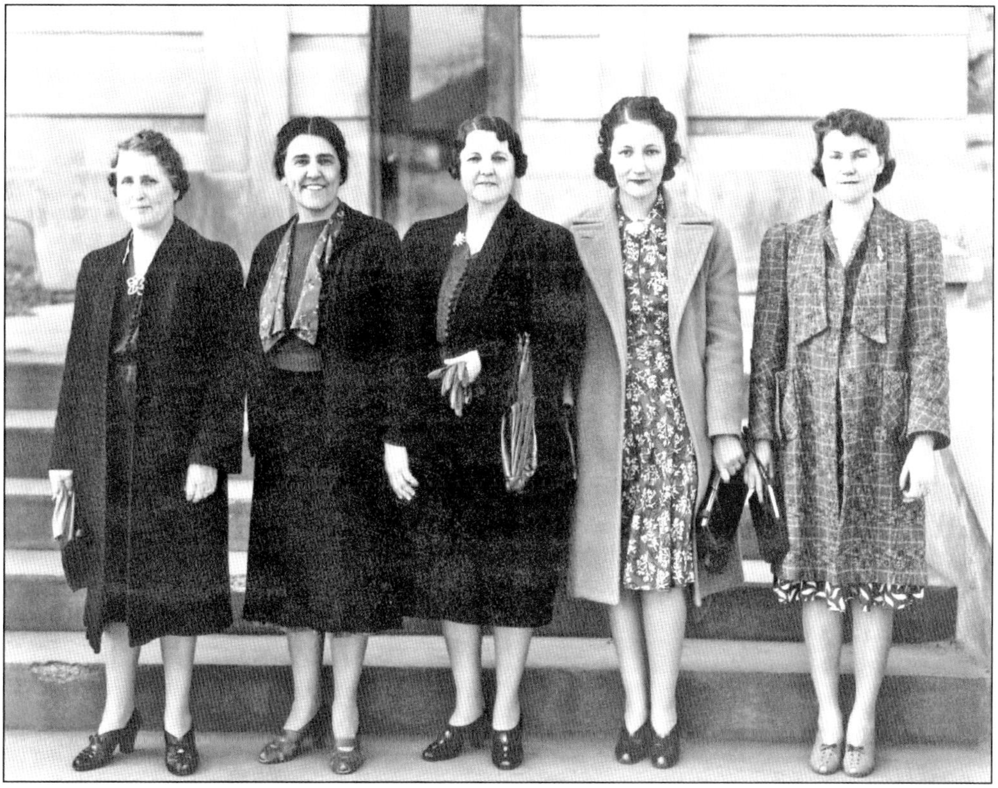

Courthouse Ladies. These unidentified women, probably from the county clerk's or court clerk's office, are pictured on the steps of the Creek County Courthouse. This c. 1950s photograph demonstrates the demeanor and acceptable attire for office holders and their deputies and clerks of the time.

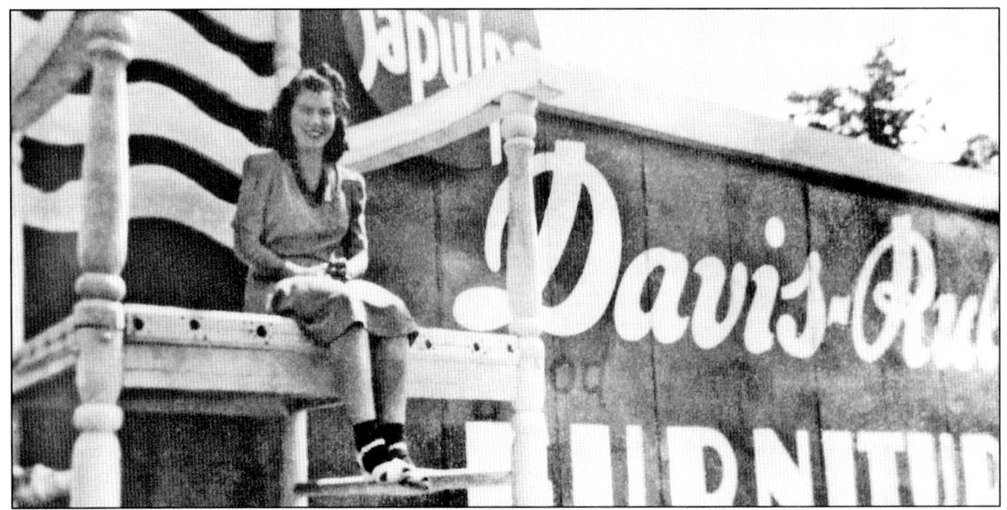

Billboard Becomes Icon. Around 1937, Davis-Rule Furniture hired the Updike Advertising Company to erect some signs along old Route 66 north of town. What the agency came up with became an icon on Route 66, and thousands of people would stop to have their photographs taken with "the Big Chair." In this photograph is Jackie Rule Robertson, daughter of owner Otis Rule. The billboard with its iconic chair are long gone, but there is a plan to bring it back.

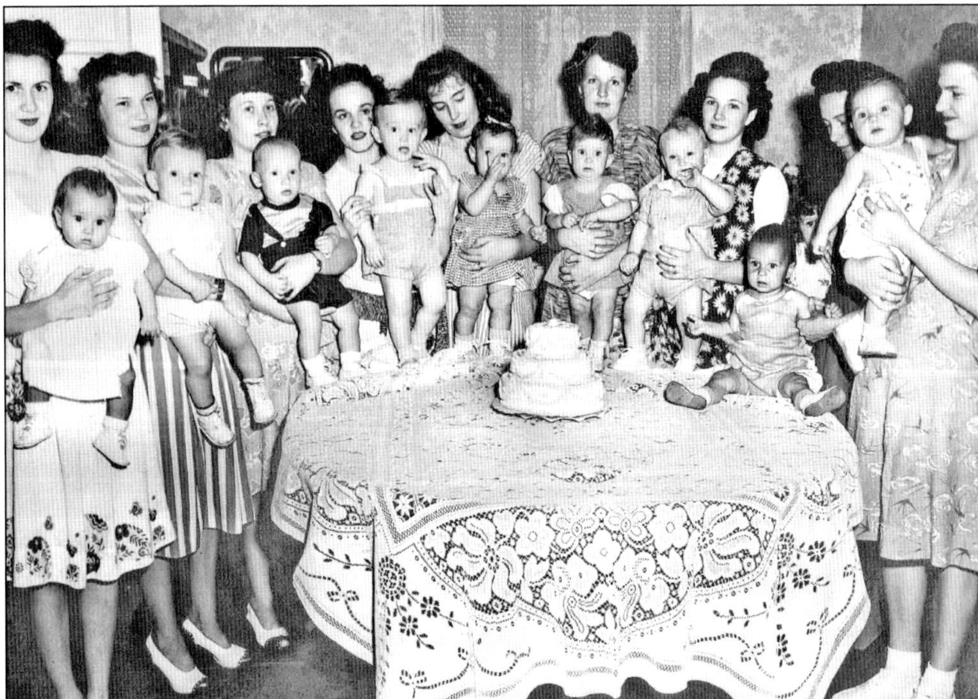

Sapulpa Baby Boomers. When World War II ended in 1945, soldiers came home and started families, creating the baby boom. This 1947 photograph is of a joint birthday party in Sapulpa for one-year-olds. Identities are uncertain, but it is known the mother on the left is Helen Dose Jeffries holding her daughter Ellen. Helen is Sapulpa Historical Museum director Mike Jeffries's mother; Ellen Carol Jeffries (now Graham) is his sister.

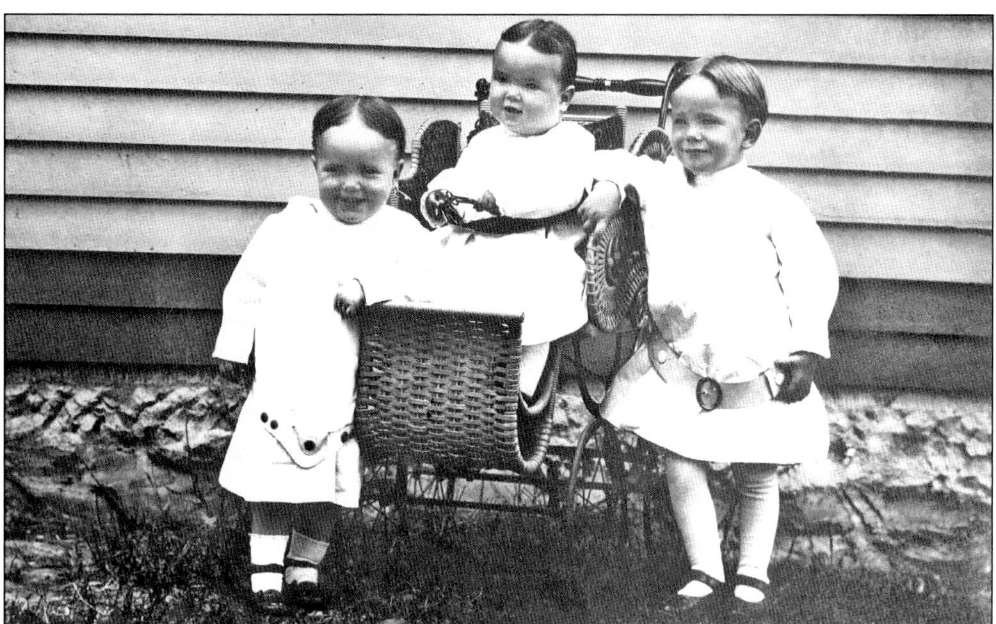

All Dressed Up. Black-and-white photography had come of age by the 1920s. Among the professional businesses downtown were photography studios where high-quality family pictures were made. Even the little boys would get dressed up for the photography sessions. Photographers also shot weddings, anniversaries, parties, and events. Much of their work is reflected in the Sapulpa Historical Museum's collection.

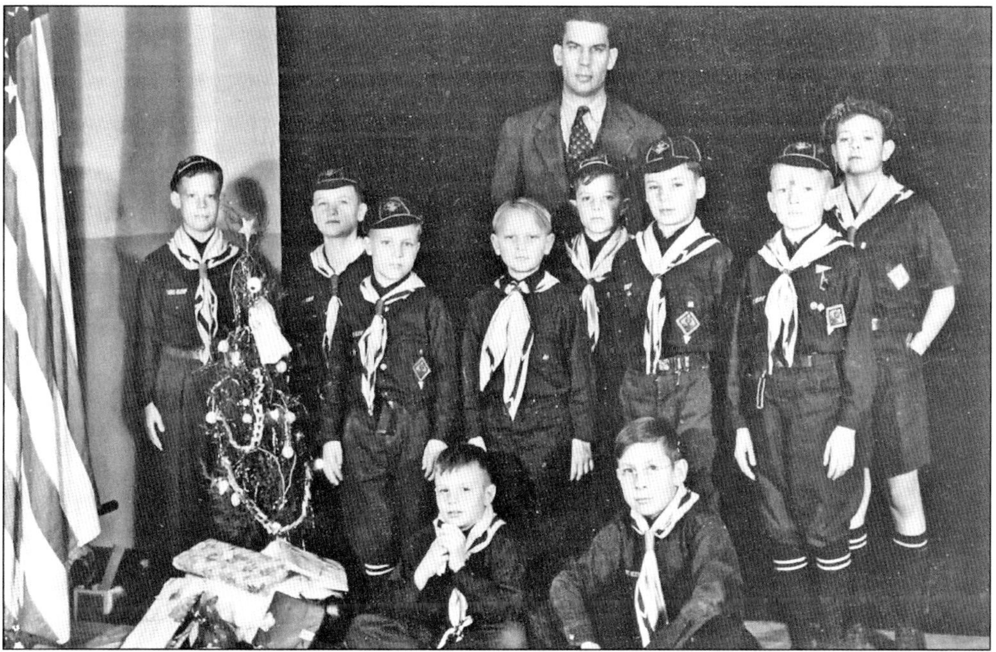

Scouting in 1940s. Boy and Cub Scout programs are integral part of Sapulpa's history. Shown here in the 1940s is Cub Scout leader John Doremus. His son John is second from right on second row, next to Wesley Vineyard, far right. Jim Sherman is the boy on the left behind the Christmas tree, and James Patterson is third from left. Next to him is Charles Carson, fourth from left.

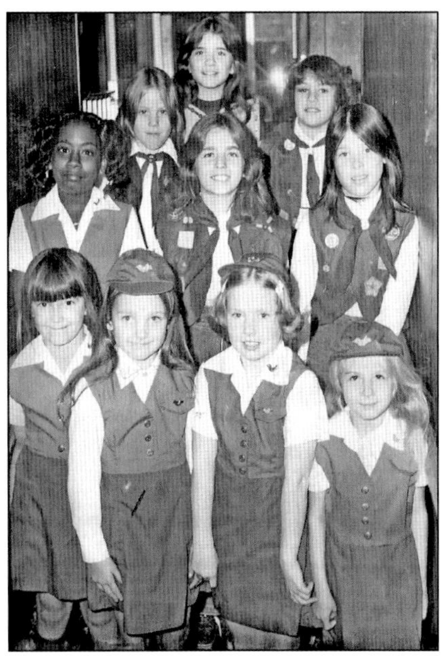

Camp Fire Remembered. Sapulpa always has supported Scouting for its boys and girls. This 1970s Camp Fire photograph includes, from left to right in the first row, unidentified, Stacy Jones DiMarco, Jeanne Hamilton Pitman, and Christina Freeman Upton. Carlotta Carnes, at the top of the image, started out as a Bluebird and went through all levels, earning every badge, bead, and charm available. Tracie Ross Calvin is pictured in the second row at far right.

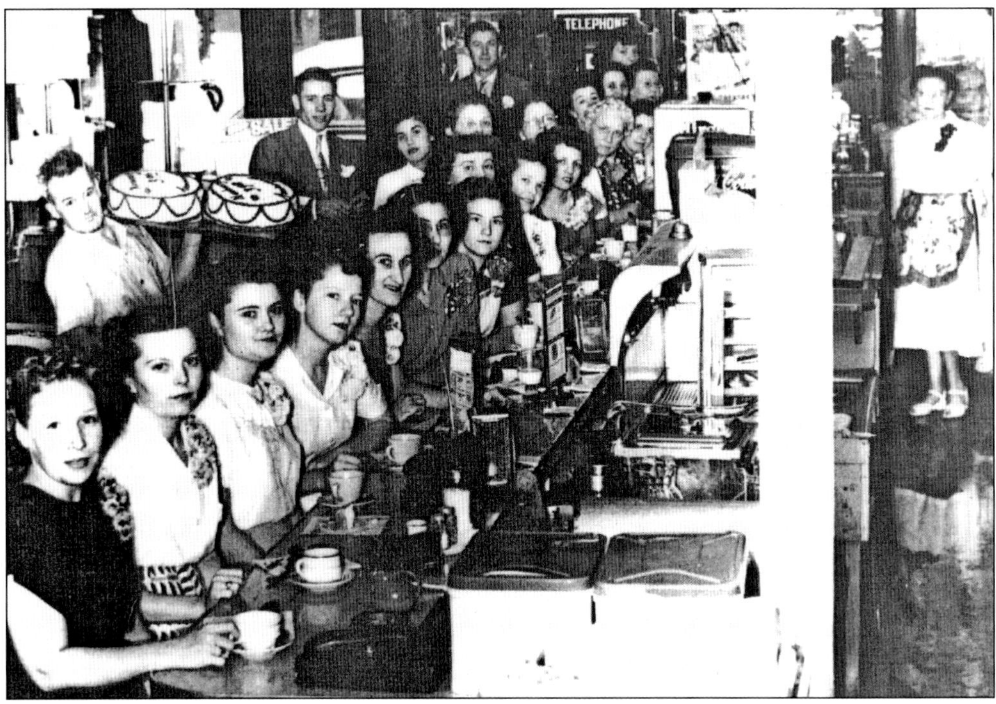

The Famed Lunch Counter. Nearly everyone at least 50 and older remembers lunch counters like this one at Newberry's in downtown Sapulpa. This gathering seems to be a midday birthday party, with cakes being delivered. Kress' and other five-and-dime department stores, as well as many of the downtown drugstores, sported lunch counters. Patrons sat on stools on the outside of the counter while those behind it served up items such as Cokes, malts, sundaes, club sandwiches, and chips. The intent of the lunch counter was to both profit the store by taking care of hungry shoppers and attract people in the hopes they might buy some merchandise or cross two errands off their list in one location. It also was convenient for those working downtown to grab lunch.

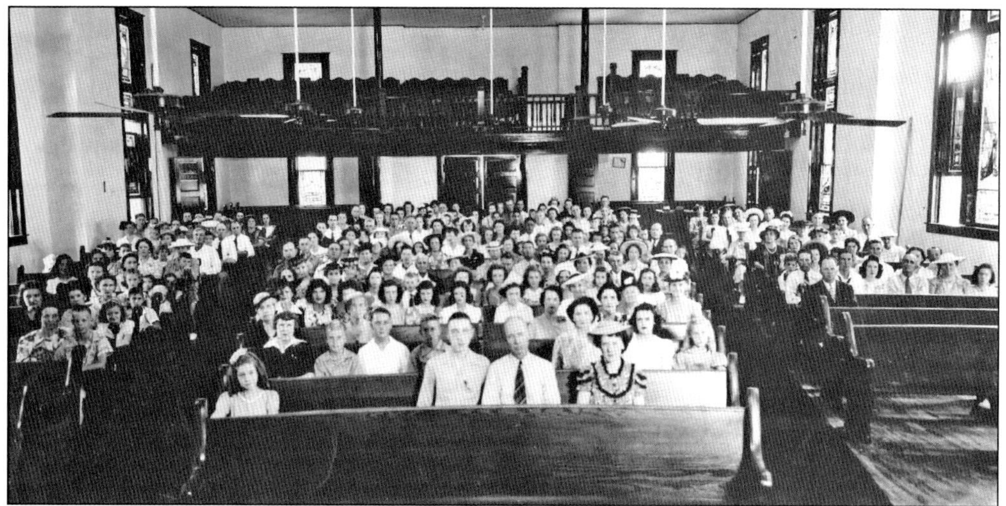

PHOTOGRAPH FROM PULPIT. A lot of yesterday's photographs of church congregations were outside shots, with people usually gathered around the front door or on the steps. Such photographs are numerous at the Sapulpa Historical Museum. The photographer here apparently was in the pulpit at Sapulpa's First Baptist Church on a Sunday morning in the 1950s when he captured nearly every face in attendance.

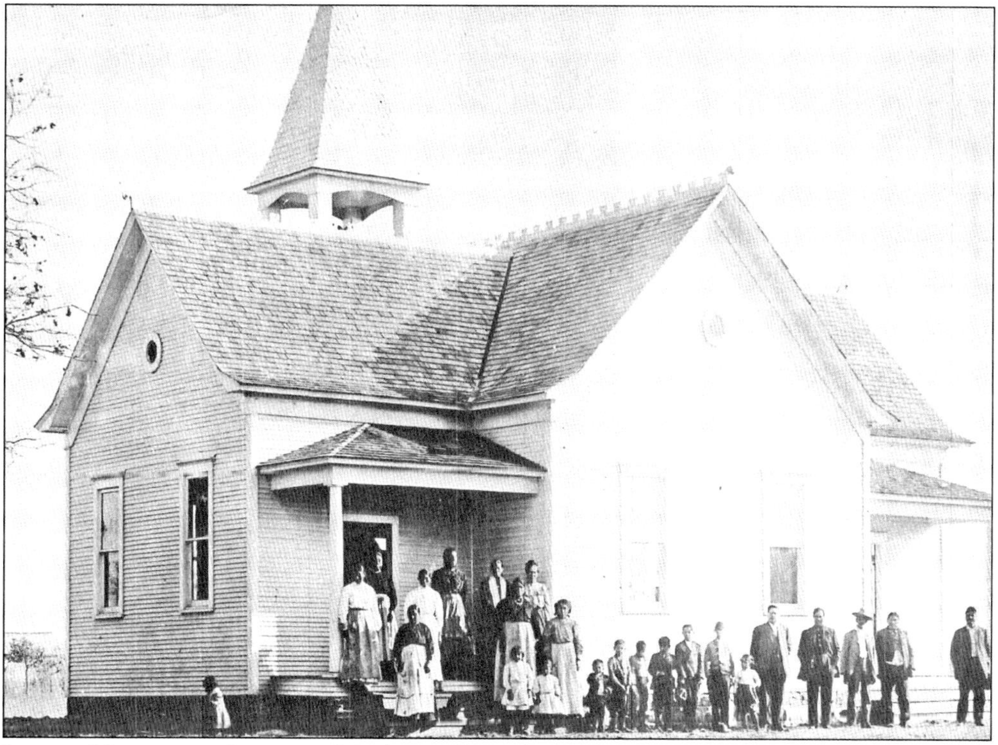

INDIAN METHODIST CHURCH. Sapulpa early on had a diverse religious community—Jewish, Catholic, mainline Protestants, and offshoots. One could fill a separate book with pictures of grand buildings and church activities from baptisms to fellowship suppers. The 1907 Rock Creek Indian Methodist Church building on Hickory Street is gone, but the museum displays several artifacts given by the Sapulpa family.

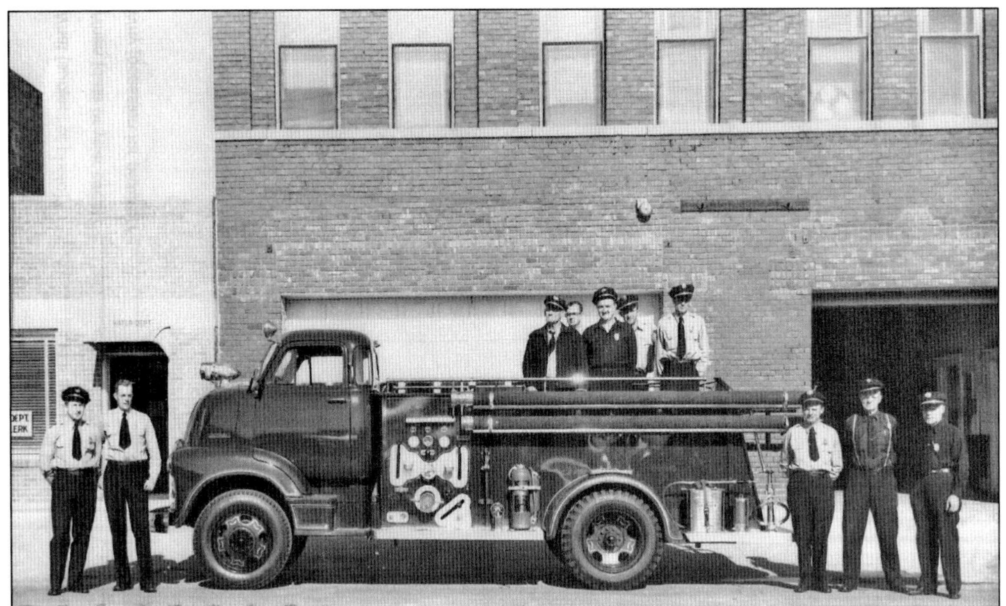

Fifties Firefighters. From the days of horse-drawn equipment housed at city hall to today's four fully manned and equipped stations, the Sapulpa Fire Department has been an integral part of the town's history. Among the firefighters shown in this 1950s photograph are, from left to right, (front of truck) Lloyd Boyd and Lemuel Rhodes; (top of truck) John Brixey, Charlie Ham, Dolph Hull, Kenny Chapman, and Cecil Welcher; (back of truck) George Robertson, Chief Collier, and Jack Wilson.

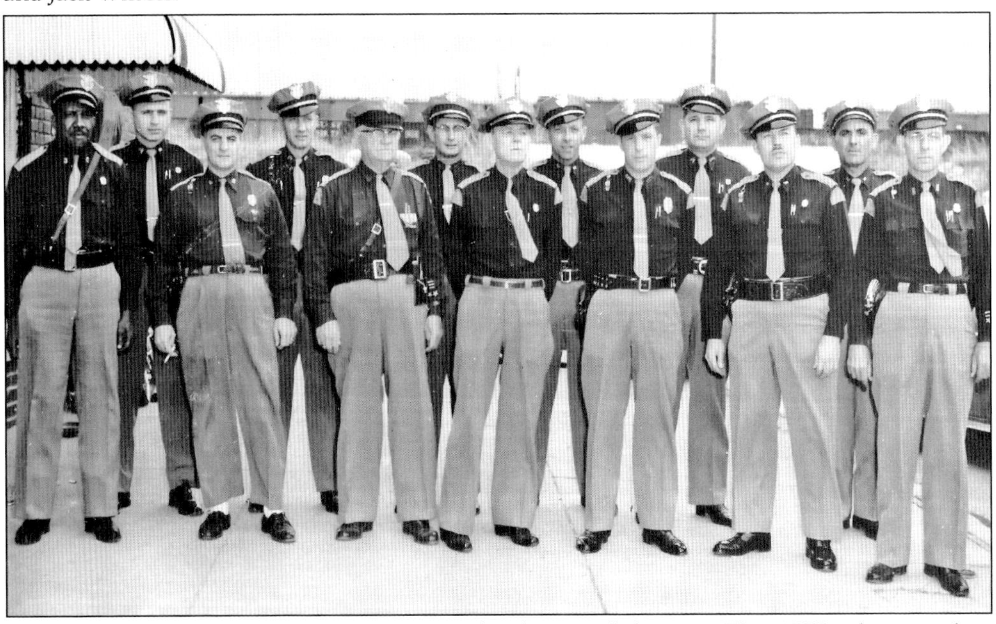

Sapulpa's Finest. Law enforcement in Sapulpa has a rich history. This 1950s photograph is representative of those taken annually of Sapulpa's police department. Shown here are (first row) Burt Randolph, O.B. Knight, Van Nelson, A.B. Holderby, Junior Shelton, Howard Jones, and Ray Sutton; (second row) Elmer Warren, Darrell Vanhorn, Paul Snider, Frank Goins, Bob Vaughn, and Chester Price.

Eight

Overcoming Adversity
Natural Disasters, Wrecks, Issues, and Wars

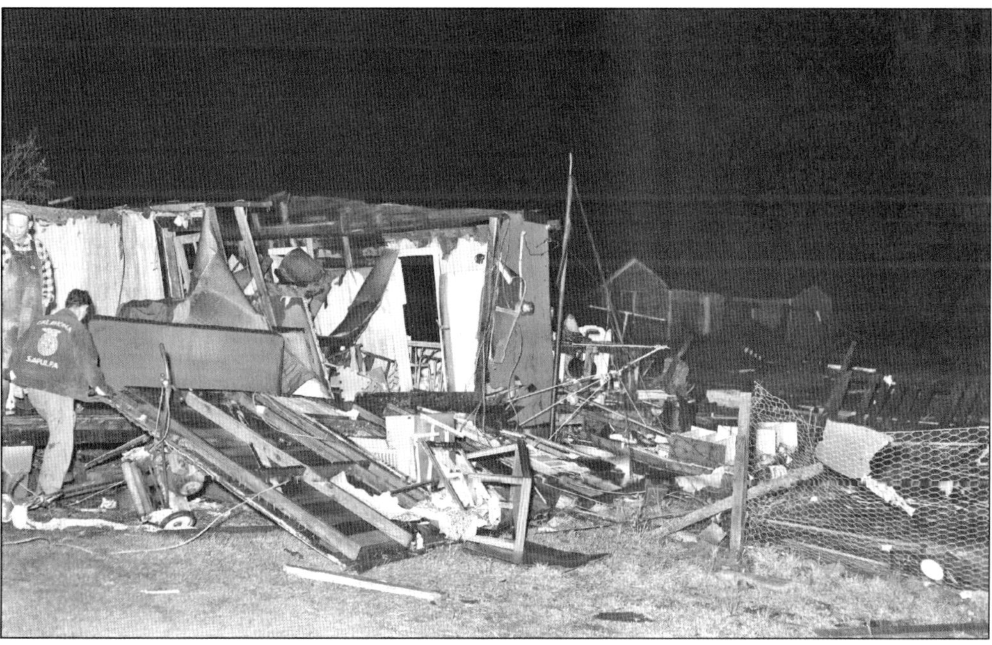

Destructive Tornadoes. As Californians live with earthquakes and Floridians with hurricanes, Oklahomans live with tornadoes. Sapulpa has been more fortunate than some towns along the twister corridor through Oklahoma, but in May 1960, a killer tornado took lives, property, and Booker T. Washington High School. Five people were killed, others were injured, and there were thousands of dollars in damages to residences, schools, churches, and businesses when an F5 tornado hit the northwest part of Sapulpa. This photograph, showing damage at the Lee Birmingham property, is typical. More than 100 homes were obliterated in the northern and western sections of Sapulpa. Mount Olive Baptist Church, a good-sized predominantly black congregation, had to rebuild its large brick building.

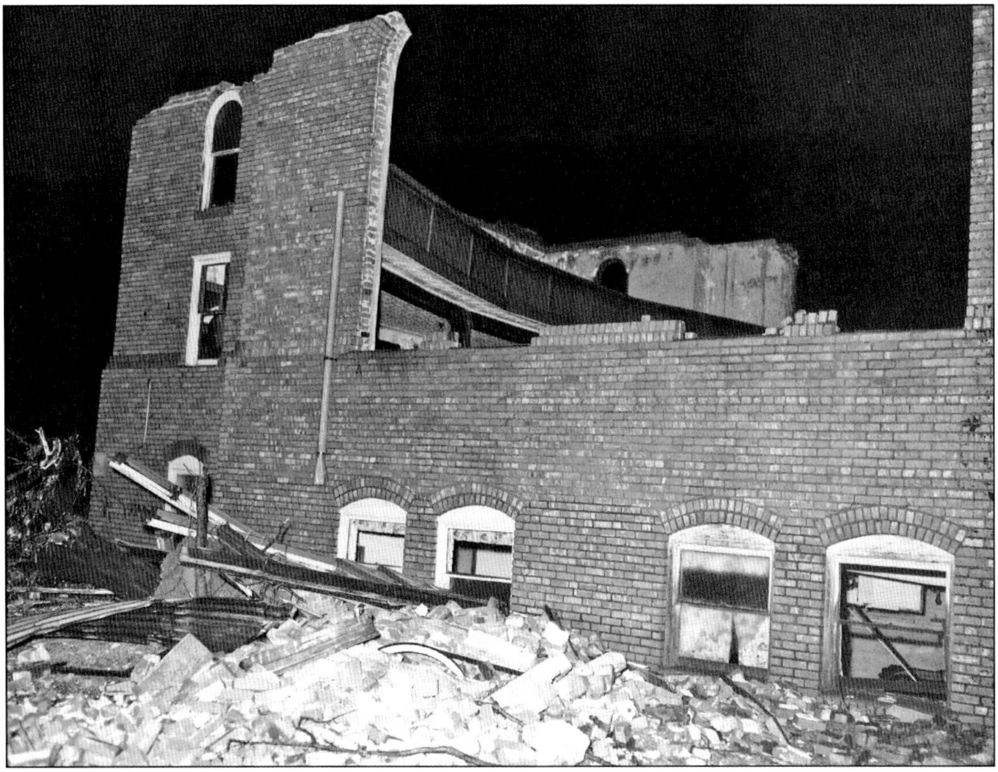

Tornado Hastens Integration. The last graduating class of Booker T. Washington High School was preparing for graduation in May 1960, when a tornado hit the north side of Sapulpa, destroying the high school building and heavily damaging the other structures. Ceremonies for the black seniors were moved to the new Sapulpa High School. The BTW seniors were the first students to use the new high school. The next year, a smooth transition began. The twister in effect began the integration three months before planned, and by the time football and band practice began in the fall, local black students already were involved in their new school. Earlier laws also required Native Americans to attend public schools. In fact, the new campus occupied the old Euchee Boarding School property.

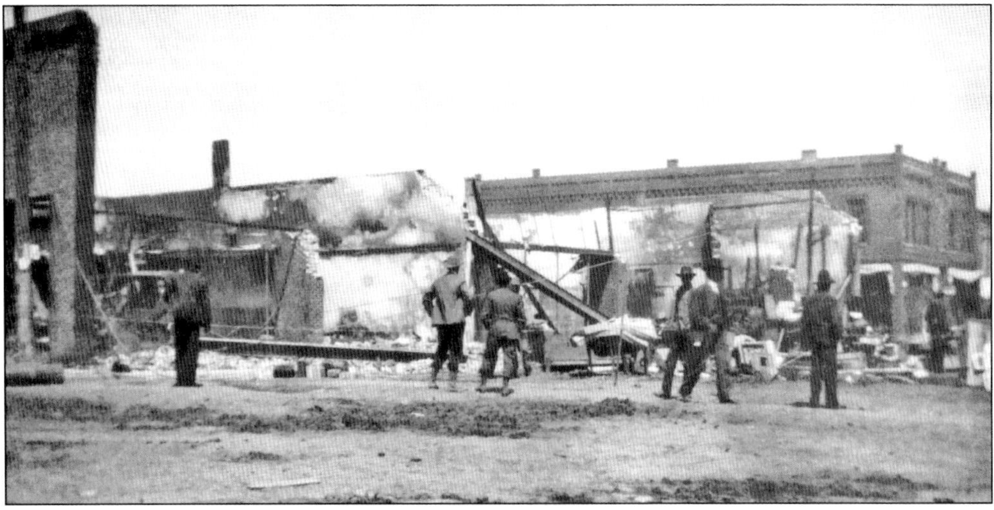

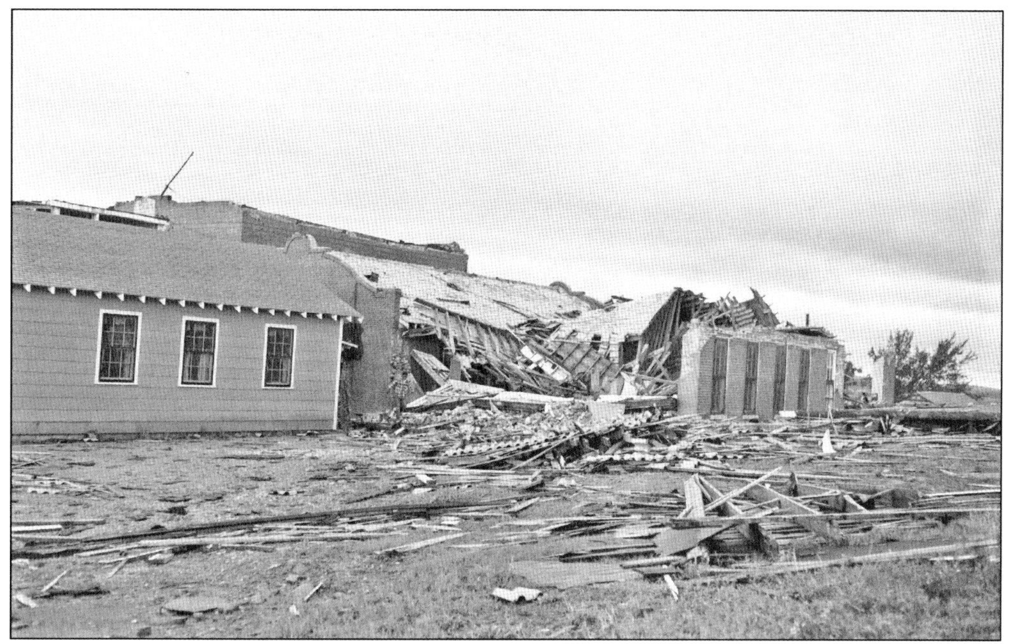

Tornadoes Hit Heights. When the Indian Sapulpa settled in the Pole Cat and Rock Creek bottoms, he reasoned that since the area was like a "saucer," it would be protected from tornadoes. Even today, history marks serious tornadoes, hitting only the heights (north and south) parts of the town. Sapulpa still remains well within Tornado Alley and can incur F4 and F5 tornadoes, as evidenced in these old newspaper photographs. There may be something to the saucer theory, but the rim can take a beating.

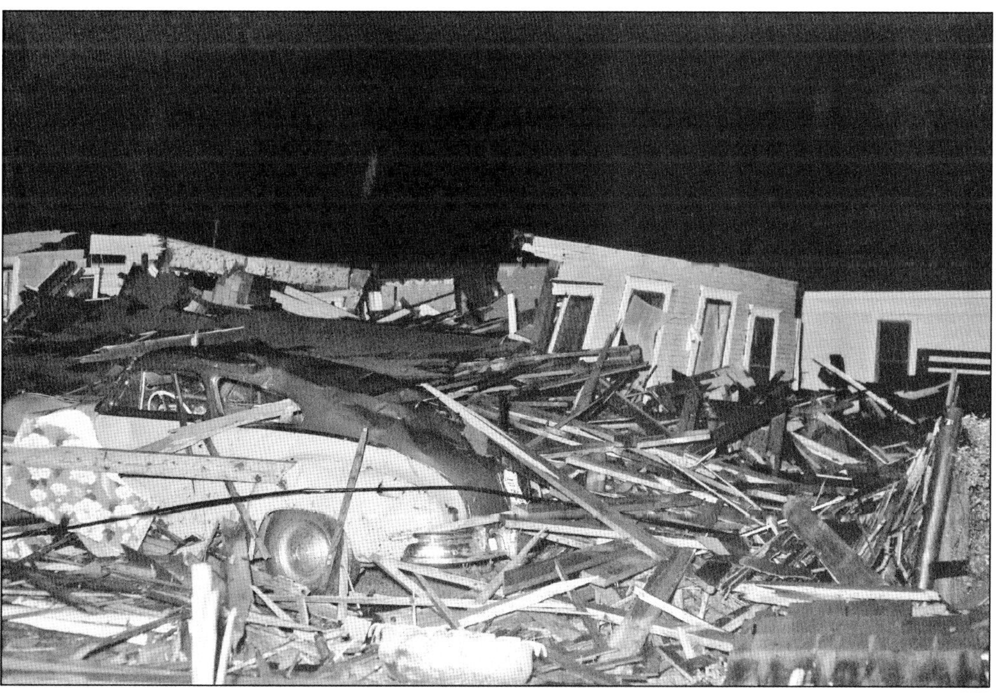

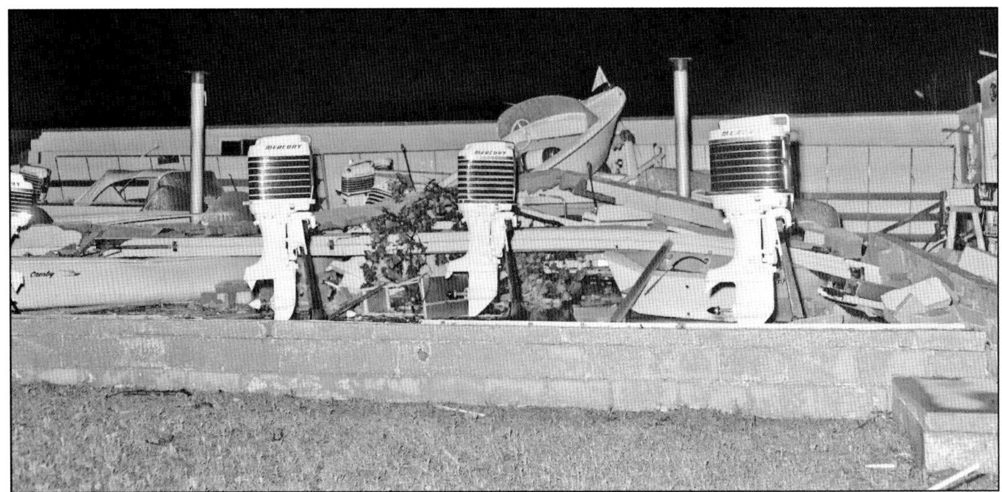

BOATS BLOWN AWAY. Damage to a boat dealership on West Dewey Avenue in 1960 included the roof being torn away and boats sucked up from the showroom floor. Several outboard motors are shown still attached to a display frame. Businesses on hills and homes on the north ridge were hit hardest.

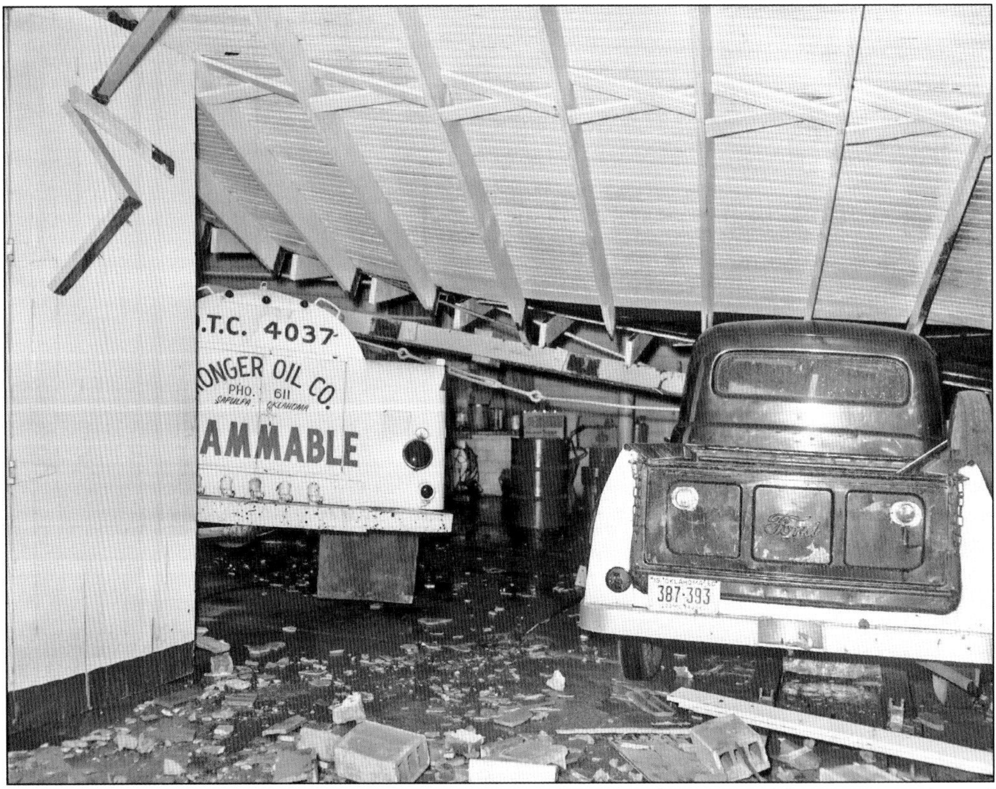

ILL WINDS RIP ROOFS. Sometimes, the straight winds do an equal amount of damage, as evidenced in this 1950s news photograph taken the morning after at the local Chevrolet garage. Other weather events in Sapulpa include periodic ice and snowstorms that can cripple the community and close school for days. As of late, there has been an increase in earthquakes. To paraphrase Will Rogers, "If you don't like our weather, wait five minutes."

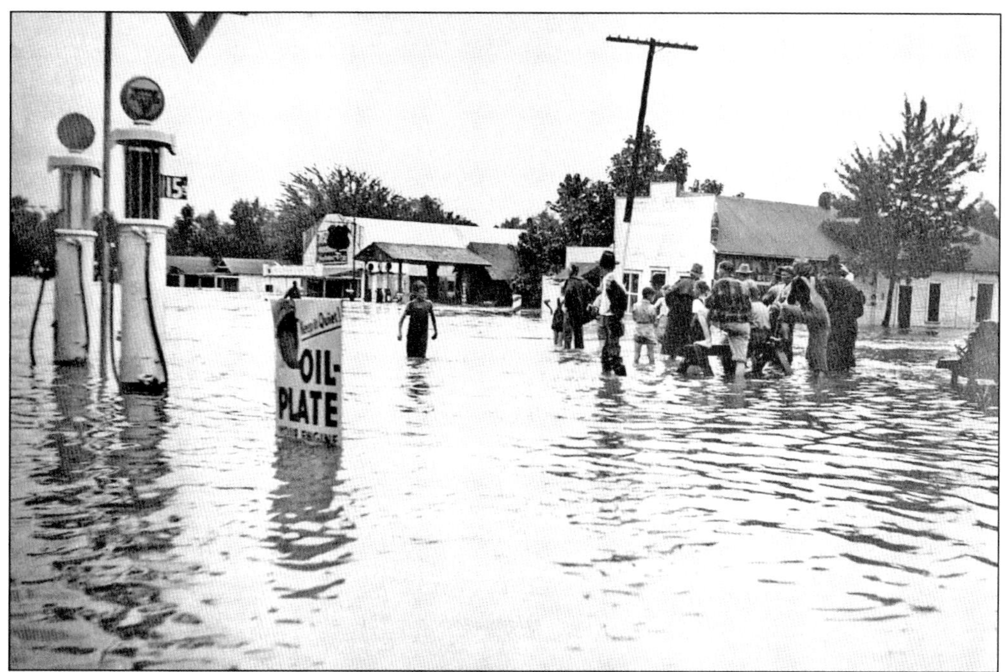

Historic Floods Happen. Living in Tornado Alley is not the only weather negative. Sometimes, it is hot and dry; other times, it is wet—very wet. Despite modern flood control efforts, dams, retention pools, and reservoirs, flooding still occurs along the Arkansas River watershed when two-day downpours, like this one in the 1940s, stack more water in the streets than flows to the prairie river. The "saucer" of central Sapulpa may be less prone to tornadoes, but when Rock Creek and the Pole Cat get out of their banks, area residents may need a boat to get down the street, as shown in this photograph not far from Chief Sapulpa's burial site.

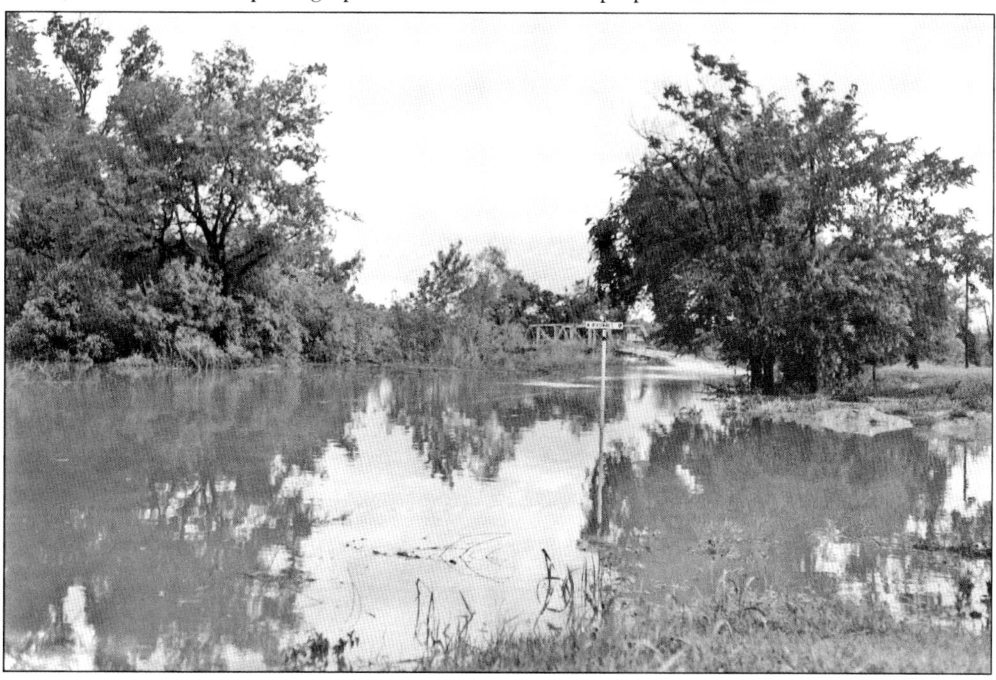

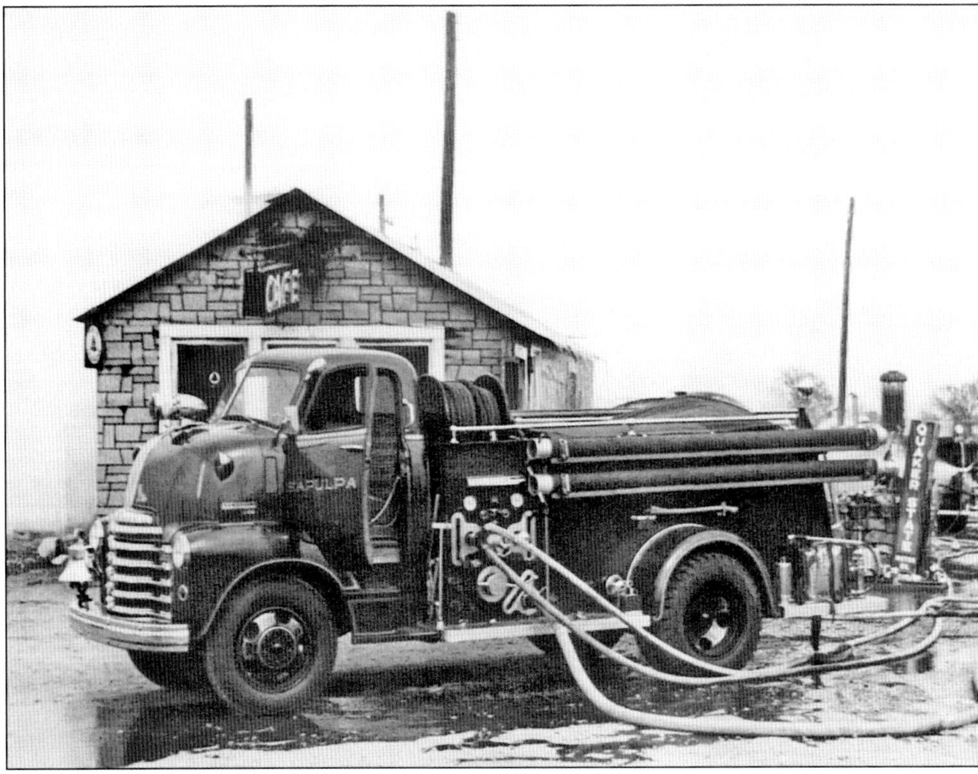

Lightning Strike? Not all mishaps are caused by natural disasters. This could have been caused by lightning or an electrical issue, but more than likely, when firefighters were called to restaurant/filling station fires like this one in 1950s, ignited oil, such as cooking or petroleum, was suspect. At any rate, then-modern equipment and firefighter expertise saved some of the property.

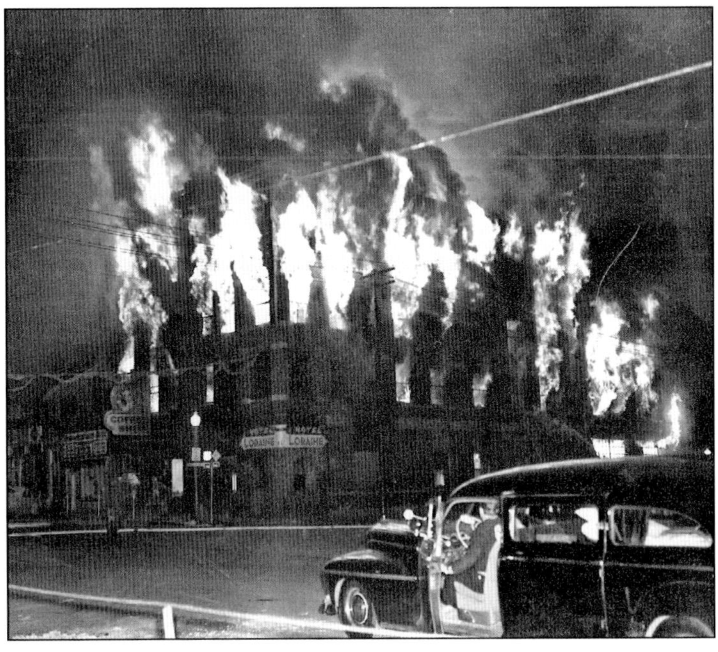

Destroyed by Fire. The Berry Building was at first an office building, with the Sapulpa State Bank occupying the first floor. It later became the Sapulpa Hotel and, in 1939, the Lorraine. It was destroyed in the worst fire in Sapulpa's history at the time. It burned to the ground on December 2, 1949. Two lost their lives. The nightclub at the hotel, like other clubs during the days of bootlegging and organized crime, was suspect of gambling and other illegal activities.

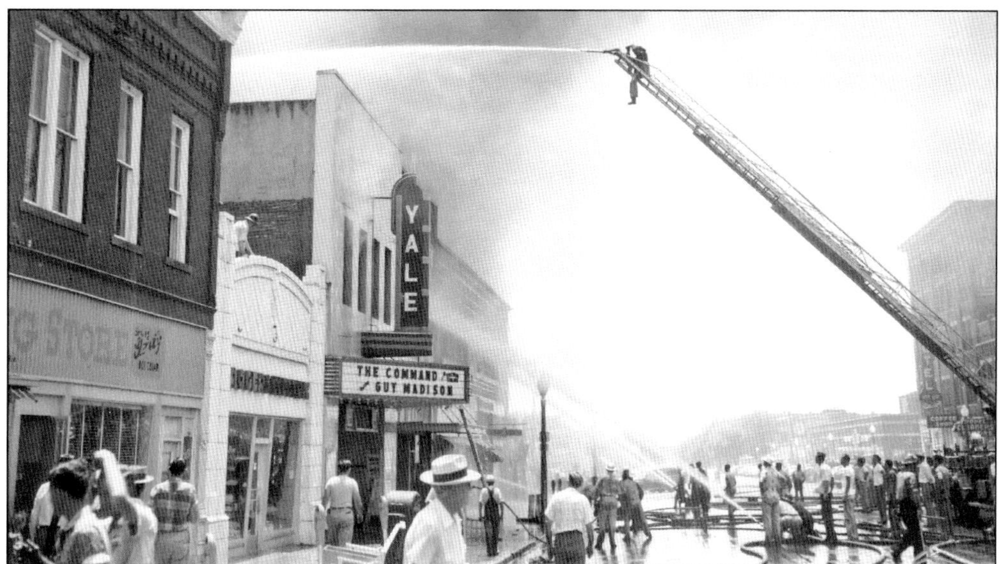

The Last Picture Show. A fire on July 27, 1954, in downtown Sapulpa gutted and caused the closure of one of Sapulpa's last old-time movie theaters. The Yale, which began in 1911, moved to 7 South Main Street in 1914. The building was saved and still stands today, but the theater curtains never opened again. Other theaters included the Criterion, the State, and of course, the Tee Pee Drive-In. Before talkies, there was the Empress, the Lucille Opera House, and the Air Dome, an outdoor theater.

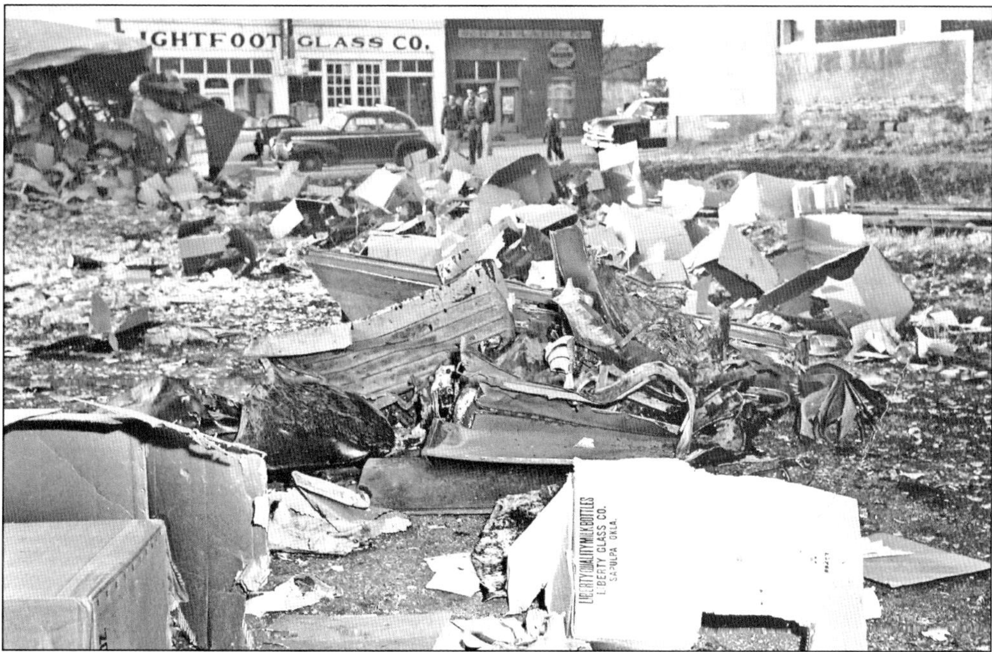

Hard to Stop a Train. Very little could be salvaged after this when a truck carrying a shipment of bottles from Liberty Glass pulled across the railroad tracks on East Dewey Avenue and got hit by a train in the early 1950s. Vern Lightfoot's plate-glass company is noted in the background, as is the 1949–1950 Ford police car in the upper right. Then as now, most of the raw materials arrive at the glass plant by train, and the finished product is shipped by truck.

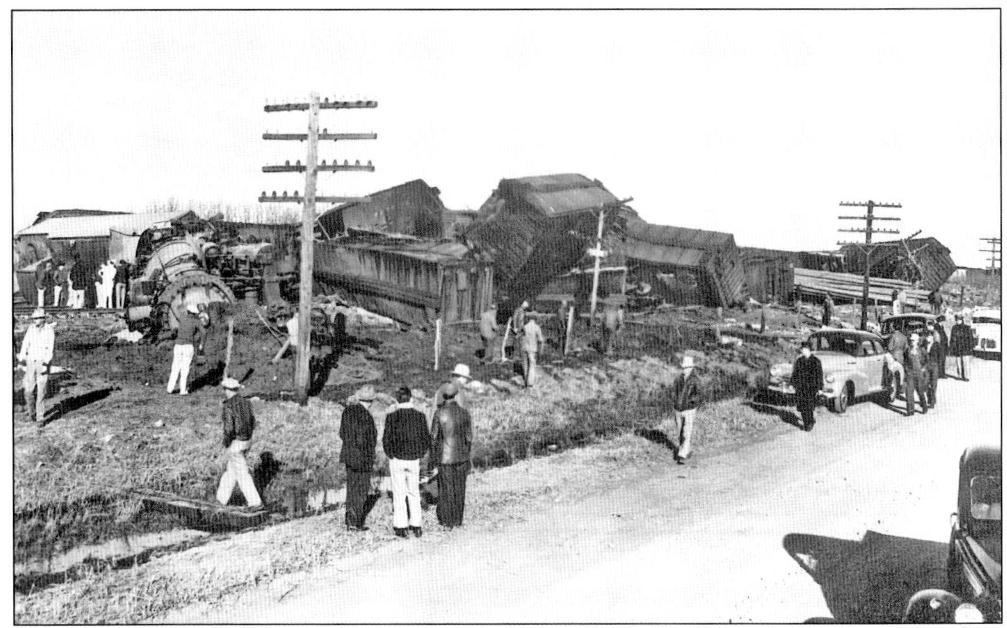

THERE WERE TRAIN WRECKS. From the beginning, Sapulpa has been a railroad town, and that means rail accidents like this 1940s derailment that attracted a lot of passersby. But the worst train wreck in local Frisco history is the head-on crash in September 1917 that killed 28 and injured more than 50, many of them very seriously. Many of the passengers were boosters of the Sapulpa football team scheduled to play at Bristow. No. 407 collided with an empty troop train returning from Fort Sill at the Kellyville bridge. Descriptive accounts of the scene were horrific.

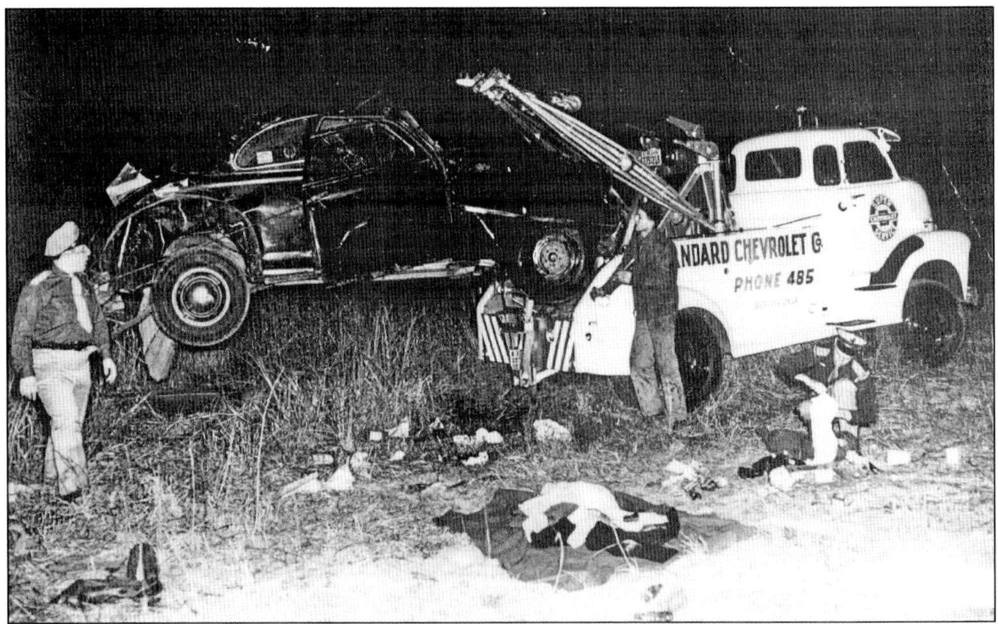

WRECK ON THE HIGHWAY. Even after the coming of the Turner Turnpike through Sapulpa in the 1950s, with wider lanes and less curves than Route 66, there were auto accidents, including rollovers like this one. Sapulpa police officer Logan Gantz (left) and Oklahoma highway patrolman Bill Green work the accident scene. Pete Belk is the wrecker operator.

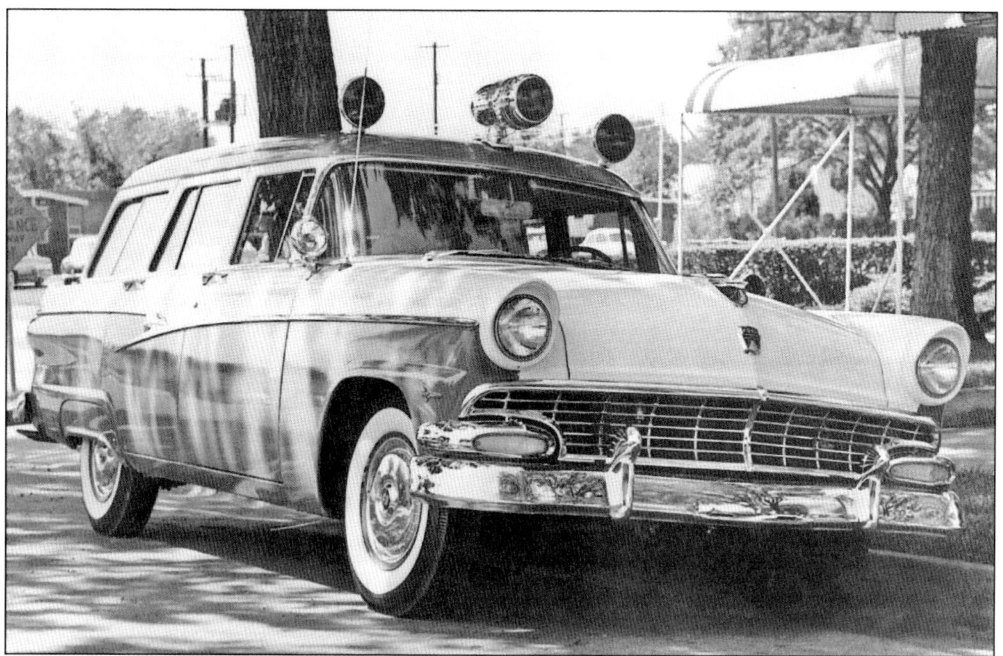

Ambulance Ready to Roll. Before Emergency Medical Services (EMS) with trained paramedics, ambulances like this new 1956 Ford, owned by Owen Funeral Home, were dispatched to medical emergencies by ambulance services, oftentimes operated by local mortuaries. The idea was to transport a patient to a medical facility as safe and fast as possible.

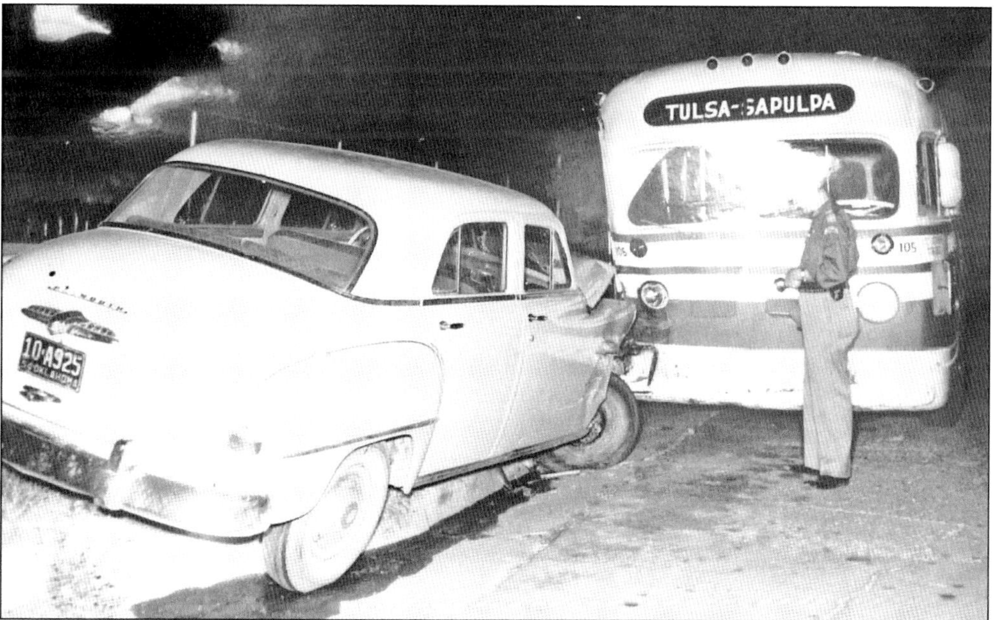

Plymouth, Bus Meet. Back when the electric trolley operated on rails on the streets of Sapulpa through the 1920s, automobiles learned to negotiate. City buses would later try to fill the railed trolley void, but some motorists in the 1950s still seemed confused about how to get around a rubber-tired bus. This one nearly met it head-on. Such wrecks got front-page play in the *Sapulpa Daily Herald*.

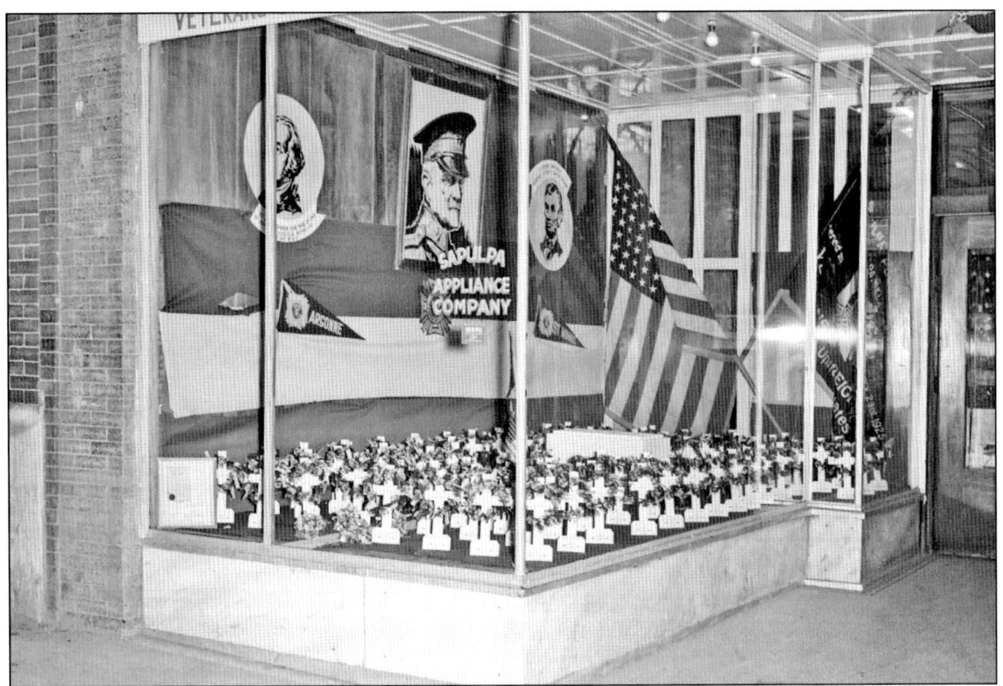

Fighting for Freedom. Only 20 years after its founding, Sapulpa was sending young men off to war. World War I originated in Europe and lasted from July 1914 to November 1918. Window displays in downtown Sapulpa reminded people that the boys needed prayers and encouragement. Some did not return.

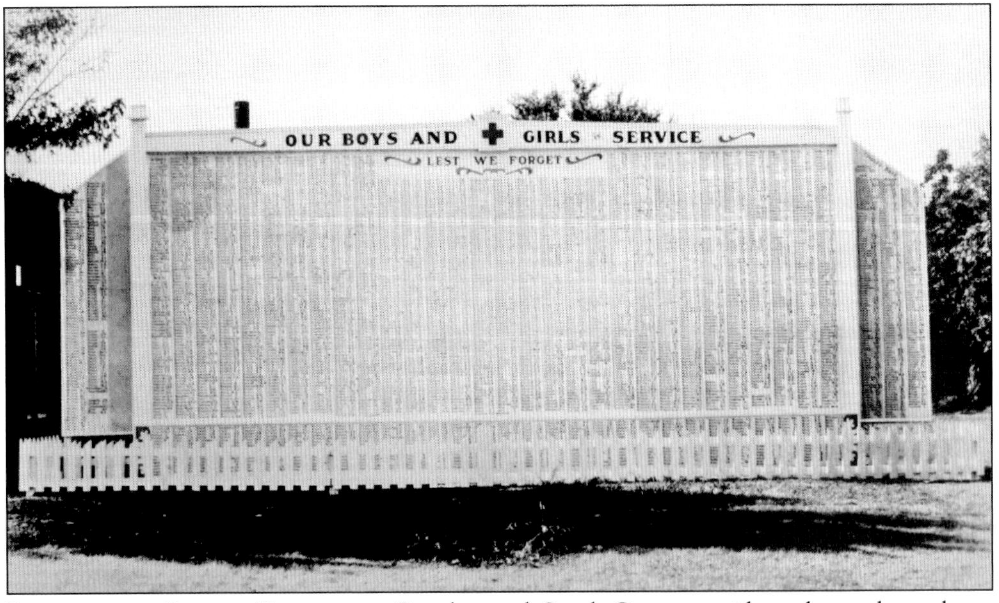

Remembering Service Personnel. Sapulpa and Creek County residents have always been careful to remember those who served their country during wartime. This honor wall of names was displayed near the corner of Mission Street and Dewey Avenue behind a white picket fence and included names through World War II. The (all wars) memorials now are at Green Hill's Veterans Memorial Garden and South Heights Cemetery.

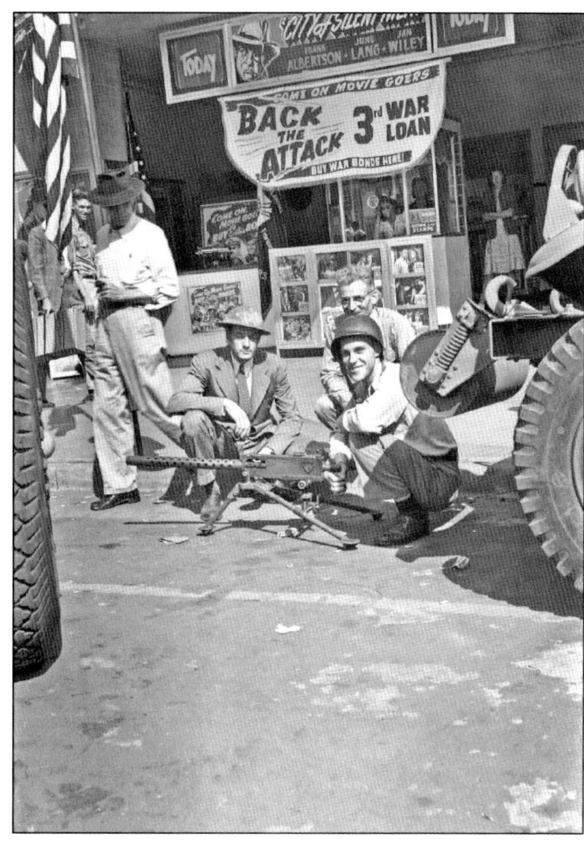

Money for the War Effort. Frank Albertson and June Lang were starring in *City of Silent Men* at a Sapulpa Theater in 1943 when men out front displayed weaponry and made an appeal for moviegoers to "Back the Attack" by buying war bonds in President Roosevelt's Third War Loan Drive. From its movie theaters and department stores to its factories and railroads, Sapulpa backed the country's efforts in World War II in the 1940s. The Tulsa Sapulpa Union Railway freight box motor No. 203 carried the sign "Buy War Bonds."

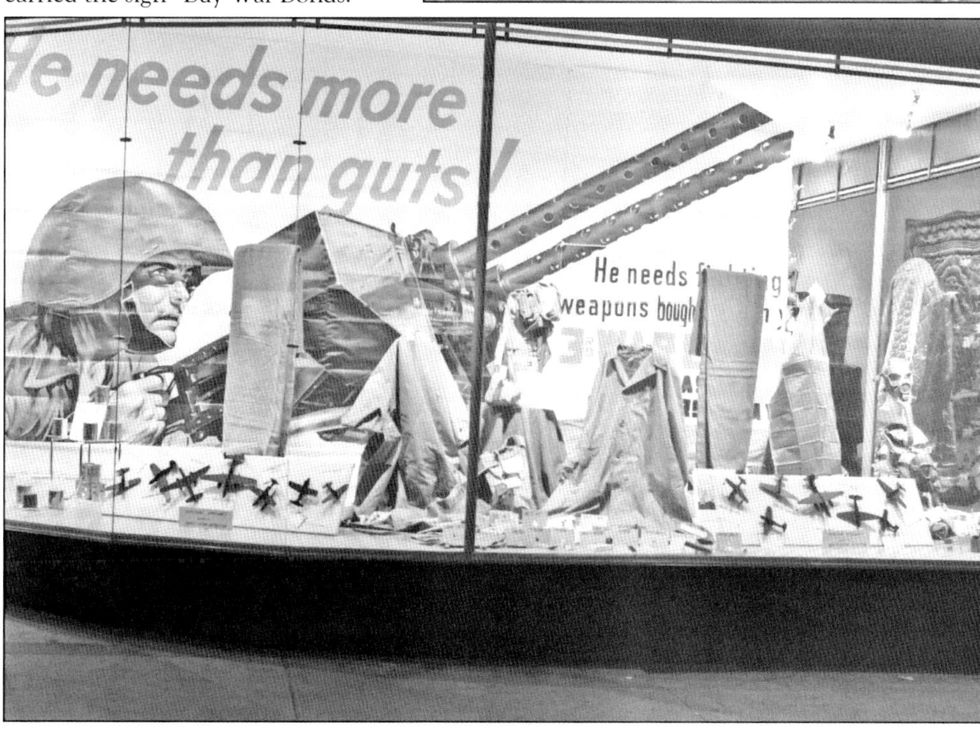

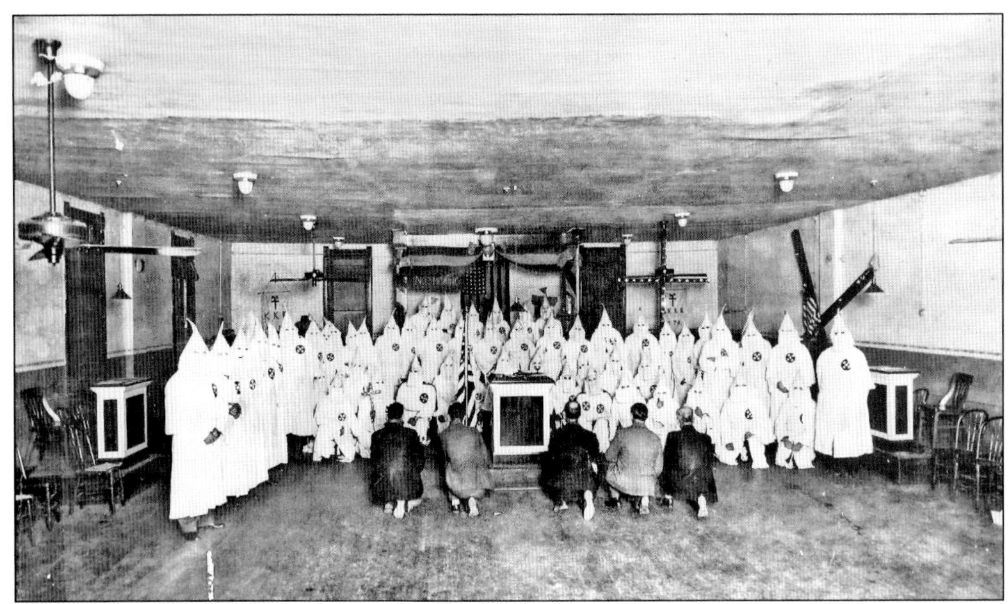

Days of Racial Tensions. This "overcoming adversity" section concludes with these 1920s photographs of Ku Klux Klan activity in Sapulpa. They were taken around the time of the infamous race riots in nearby Tulsa as tensions grew between blacks and whites across Oklahoma. The image above shows about 50 robed KKK members taking part in some sort of function at the Sapulpa IOOF Lodge, probably before the Tulsa exchange. The parade image is dated June 2, 1922, a year after the riot. Hundreds lined Dewey Avenue in downtown Sapulpa. The Klan regularly burned crosses on the hill overlooking Sapulpa until Oklahoma's governor sent the National Guard to halt the practice.

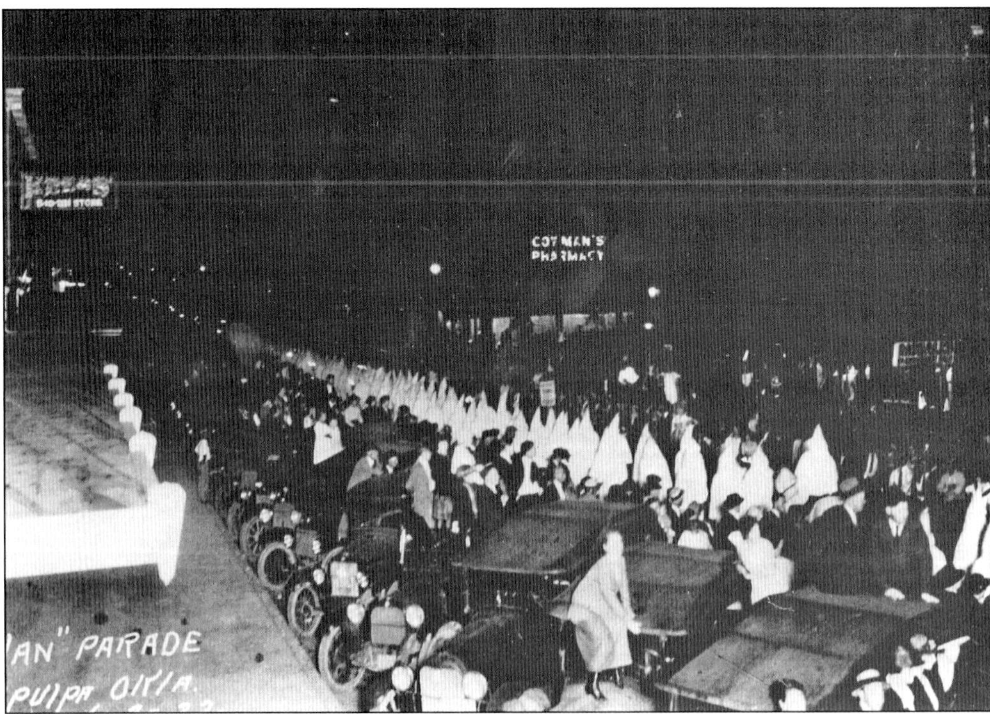

Nine

Our Past
Historic Tributes, Notable Icons, and Nostalgic Notions

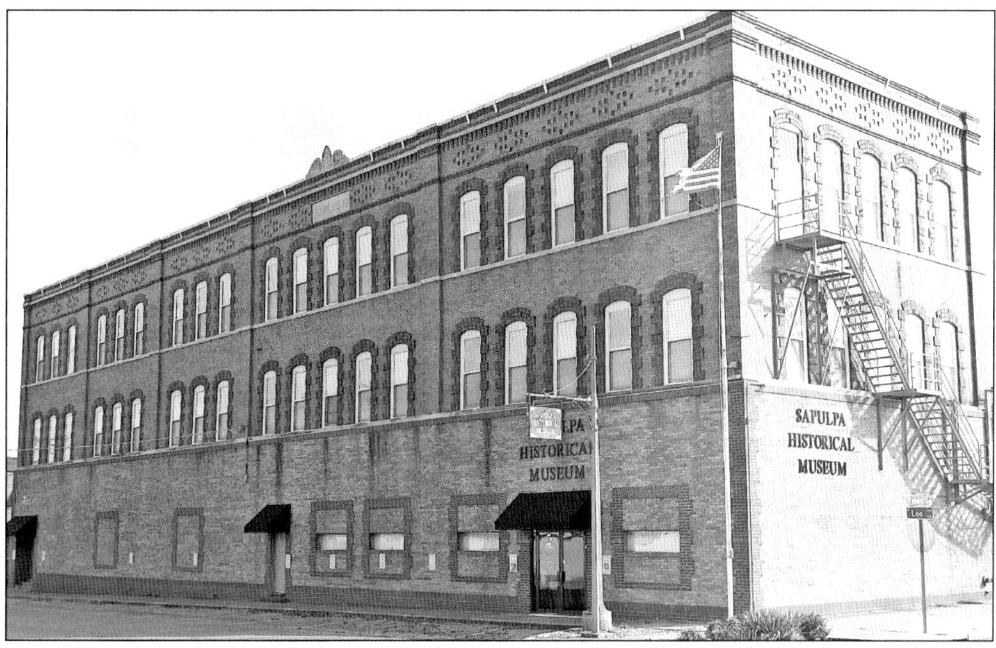

All Kinds of Displays. There are three floors of exhibits at the Sapulpa Historic Museum in the old Wills Building (built around 1915) at Lee Avenue and Water Street. There are Indian, train, and oilfield artifacts. There are thousands of photographs and documents and wonderful theme rooms with displays featuring a hundred years of local and area history. Staff and volunteers have created a small village to showcase some of Sapulpa's early businesses. Included are an early-day blacksmith shop, a sheriff's office, the John F. Egan General Merchandise Store, Rock Creek Indian Methodist Church, Euchee Mission Boarding School, and a diorama of the Frisco Railroad shops that were located here in the early 1900s. Other displays include Creek and Euchee Native American collections, an early territorial courthouse display, and a military room, as well as exhibits dedicated to prominent Sapulpans. A full tour of the museum takes approximately one hour. Trained docents guide the tour and answer questions.

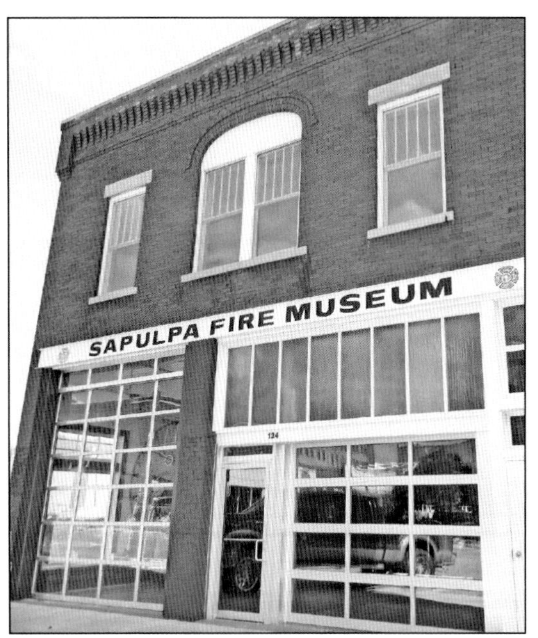

Fire Department History. The Sapulpa Fire Museum, just east of the main Sapulpa Historical Museum on East Lee Avenue, houses the century-long history of the Sapulpa Fire Department. Featured is a 1939 Ford fire truck, a preserved 1949 American LaFrance truck, and turn-of-the-century horse-drawn carts, ladder trucks, and other artifacts, including an 8-by-10-foot mural of the original firehouse.

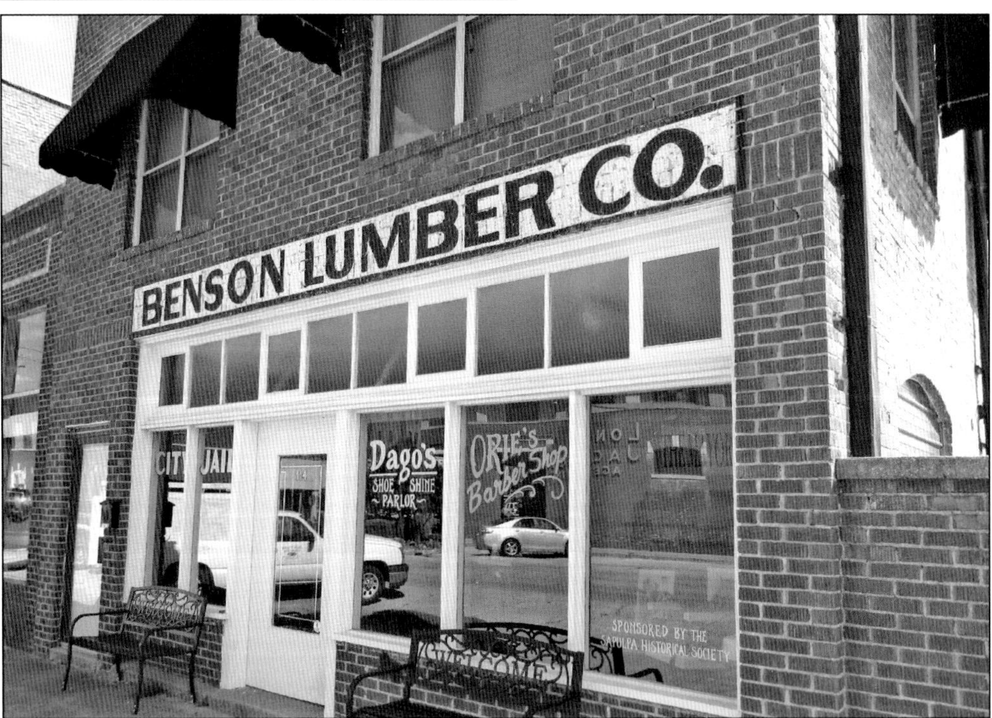

Signs of Days Gone By. Just next-door to the Sapulpa Fire Museum in the former Benson Lumber building are window signs that point to yesteryear, when barbershops and shoe-shine parlors were a regular routine for Sapulpa men. The original Dago's was on Main Street, and Orie's was on Dewey Avenue. Above is how Benson's appeared 50 years ago. Visitors also will want to take in the old Waite Phillips Filling Station on the southwest corner of Lee Avenue and Water Street. Operated by the museum, it has been restored to its 1923 opening era. The old station is a popular photograph shooting place for classic-car enthusiasts.

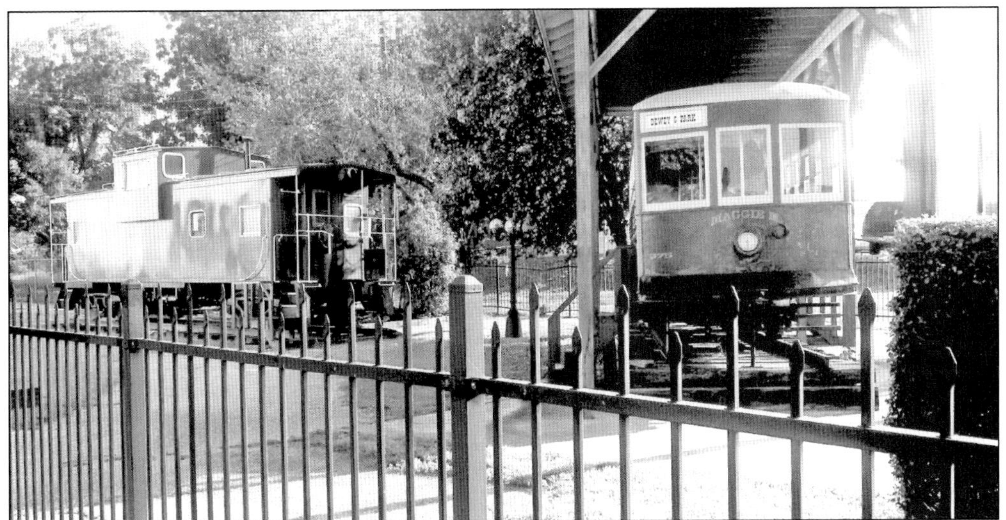

Trolley and Rail Museum. The last-known surviving trolley car to operate between Tulsa and Sapulpa was chosen for Sapulpa's centennial project in 1998 to be restored in memory of the town's electric streetcar system. The "Maggie M" is on display at the Jim Hubbard Memorial Park, along with a 1960s-era caboose purchased by TSU from the Burlington Northern Railway in 1988. The display is under the auspices of Sapulpa Historical Museum.

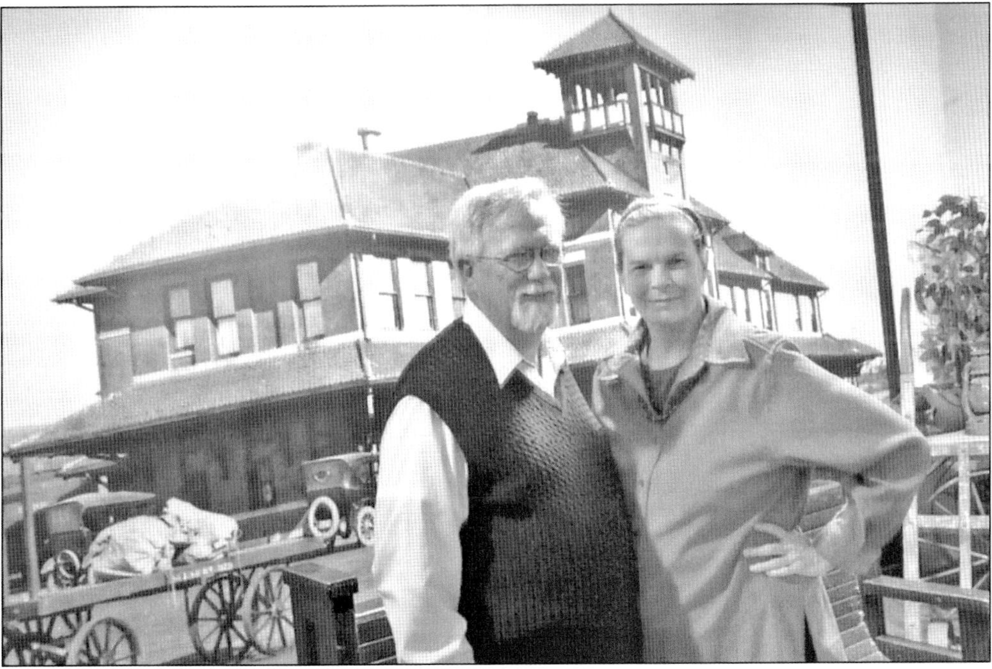

Waiting for a Train or a Tour? Sapulpa Historical Museum director Mike Jeffries and his wife, Christy, pose in front of a gigantic mural of the Sapulpa Train Depot displayed on the ground floor of the museum at 100 East Lee Avenue. The three-floor building was the Lee Hotel in the early 1900s. The professor who founded Beeson's Business College and occupied part of Dewey College in 1909 moved it here in 1918. The YWCA acquired the building in September 1921 and sold it to the Sapulpa Historical Society in 1980s. The museum is open to the public from 10:00 a.m. to 3:00 p.m. Tuesday through Saturday.